Investing in the Antiques Market

Anne Gilbert

Publishers · GROSSET & DUNLAP · New York
A FILMWAYS COMPANY

To David K. Hardin,
who contributed the most important part—encouragement

Also by Anne Gilbert

Antique Hunting: A Guide for Freaks and Fanciers (1975)
Collecting the New Antiques (1977)
How to Be an Antiques Detective (1978)

Photo of The Smithys, an antiques shop at South
Egremont, Massachusetts, by Mort Engel.

Copyright©1980 by Anne Gilbert
All rights reserved
Published simultaneously in Canada
Library of Congress catalog card number: 80-68250
ISBN 0-448-16552-X
First printing 1980
Printed in the United States of America

Contents

Acknowledgments

Allen Baker, Butterfield & Butterfield Auction Galleries, Michael and Francie Cowan, Chase Gilmore Galleries, Chicago Art Institute, Du Mouchelle Auction Galleries, Sotheby Parke Bernet, Joan and Bud Towne, Karen and Dick Commer (Cartoonerville), Dennis Todaro, Edward Jensen, Arthur H. Rubloff, Exchange National Bank of Chicago, John Evans of Grand Central Art Galleries, Judy and Alan Goffman, Walt Reed

Introduction

Like the weather, the antiques marketplace changes daily—one year's favorite can be next year's dud. And yet, in 1979 over eight million Americans invested their money in a wide range of antiques, collectibles, limited-edition items, and what they hope are the antiques of the future.

Accessibility is probably the prime reason that more Americans are turning to their collections as money-making devices in this time of soaring inflation. While the average person might not readily understand the jargon of Wall Street or how to interpret a stock market page, he can easily read the latest price guide changes or auction figures showing price upswings of such diverse objects as folk art and Russian enamels. It is an area in which the average antiques aficionado can feel important and confident. And why not? He often knows much more about his investments than many so-called experts. Who knows better than the collector that he paid too much last year for a certain limited-edition print that lost money? It doesn't take a college education with a business major to fathom the sometimes murky depths of what is happening in the antiques and collectibles market.

All a prospective investor has to do is to spend an afternoon selling at the local flea market or eavesdropping at any of the many antique shows. At the flea market, there is always a chance to make a profit, even of 100 percent, on a Sunday afternoon. It may seem like small potatoes to think of clearing from $50 to $100 every Sunday at the local flea market, yet thousands of Americans wheel and deal, turning junk into profit, or, if you prefer, into short-term investments. Senior citizens especially have found both junking and flea marketeering one way to add to their dwindling incomes. Old post cards, junk jewelry, and secondhand clothes may not be exactly your idea of an important investment, but multiply that $100 per Sunday by six months. Not bad, with only booth space fees and a little gasoline put out! A $25 initial investment in merchandise can net four or five times that amount. Looks like a profit to me. Where would a $25 investment on the stock market get you in six months? Sure, it isn't a definite $100 every Sunday, but, isn't there always that chance of doing even better the following week?

On the upper reaches of antiques investing, the stakes may be higher, but basically it's the same ball game. So important are antiques becoming as investment sources that in 1979 the *Wall Street Journal* devoted its Connoisseur's Corner to trends in the antiques and art market. In 1979, for the first time, an exhibition devoted strictly to investments opened booths to antiques and dealers. To give a hefty nudge to this new concept of buying not just for beauty, love, and status of an object, representatives of some of the most influential antiques dealers and auction houses told an eager public in stage whispers, "Antiques are your best hedge against inflation." The theory was that if enough people passed along these words, they'd eventually become fact.

But are collectibles and antiques your best investment? Can you sell your antique silver or art at a profit as quickly as a share of AT&T? Can you find a ready buyer for your collection of limited-edition plates and bells that you have been putting your money into for the past several years? Can you get a loan at the bank using your collection as security?

A collector can easily get squirrely while storing away antique nuts for the future. Clearly some type of investment planning is needed, just as it is in the real across-the-board investment world. How often have you read that a world-famous collection has cornered the auction market price and the former, dazed owner has taken off for a newly purchased castle in Ireland? Don't overlook that the owner was probably already a millionaire who could afford to spend thousands on his collecting habit in the first place. The fact that he was well known added to the publicity value of an already priceless collection.

What if it had been your collection? Do you think the fancy auction house would've bothered to let the world know in advance that it was auctioning off the contents of the Mary Smith estate? Chances are, they wouldn't have even handled your estate. Prestige plays a big part in who sells what in the antiques and art business, and the old saying that "it takes money to make money" is never more true.

Important paintings like this Eastman Johnson oil, "George Washington Crossing the Delaware," make the auction world go round. It was referred to by Sotheby Parke Bernet as "the most important American painting to be auctioned in recent times." It brought a record price of $370,000.

Sotheby Parke Bernet

Beginning investors in Victoriana would do well to visit museums and restored homes to view examples of the period. Pictured is part of the period living room (c. 1863) of the H. H. Bennett House, showing a Waterford crystal chandelier, a marble-topped table, and a chair designed by John Belter. The chandelier and the Belter chair have always had high prices. Currently, they outstrip the table and the French rococo mirror by several thousand dollars.

CREDIT: H. H. Bennett House, Wisconsin Dells, Wisc.

However, not everyone has to have their collections sold by Christie's or Sotheby Parke Bernet—for that matter, by any auction house at all. Unlike in the stock market, you don't necessarily need a broker to buy and sell your art, antiques, and limited editions. Liken the broker to an antiques dealer or an auction house: when they sell your items, they take a commission. When you eliminate the middleman and do it yourself, you save those commission dollars. But the do-it-yourself method isn't as simple as it sounds, and you may find yourself having to decide whether it is worth the extra time it may take to unload fifty shares of Depression glass.

The biggest hurdle for the average antiques investor is the selling. Contacting and finding someone who wants to invest in what you have to sell may take months or years. Nevertheless, be assured, there is someone somewhere who will eventually invest in your antiques or collectibles.

The first step in becoming an investor is to know as much as possible about the objects in which you plan to invest. For example, would you buy fifty shares of American Ticky Tacky without looking into what the company has done financially in the past several years? You could put the whole thing in the hands of a recommended stock broker. After all, not only does he have experience but he's been keeping track of the Ticky Tacky stock for years, while you don't have the time nor the inclination to follow market reports that closely. You can use the same approach with the antiques market. Hire a dealer or a scout to do your buying, presuming you can afford his retainer fee of either a percentage of the investment or a flat thousand or so a month, plus travel expenses. That's what corporations and the millionaire collector-investors do. But think of the fun they miss.

For the average collector-investor (you), the enjoyment comes from learning all you can about the rise and fall of such things as Hummel figurines, English furniture, and snuff bottles. It's truly not all that difficult. It is very important to make sure that the object you purchase is what it seems to be and not a fake or a reproduction. If it is a reproduction, it is important to be sure that it is recognized as the finest of its type and

Once only a few specialized collectors and museums appreciated the value of rare examples of embroidery, needlepoint, and other types of stitchery. These nineteenth-century embroidered starters or half-boots are museum pieces representing exquisite handwork. The field of needlework is one of the few that is relatively wide open for beginning collectors. Many fine examples from as late as the Art Deco period are worthy of collecting with an eye to future appreciation.

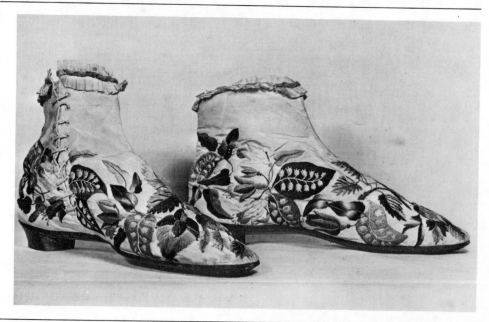

that it is being sought after by collectors—such as the American Colonial furniture reproduced and made by Wallace Nutting in the early twentieth century.

There is nothing like learning from the mistakes of others. This book introduces you to a variety of collectors who have purchased antiques and collectibles as important investments. Currently, some of them are winners, but that's today! As one dedicated investor-collector shrugged and said, "Win a little, lose a little," but how many of us can afford such a casual goodbye kiss to our hard-earned money?

Just what and how should you invest? If I knew the answer, I wouldn't have to spend my time writing books. However, if, after reading this book, you are still serious about investing in antiques and collectibles, you will realize that this is a decision only you can make. Study the active antiques marketplace. Take a look at what is happening around the country at some of the top auction houses, such as Butterfield & Butterfield, Du Mouchelle, and Sotheby Parke Bernet. Learn how to analyze what is happening in certain areas of collecting and how local or world conditions influence collecting.

To get to the true meaning of what is going on, you will have to be able to sift through the mountains of publicity put out by the auction houses. In other words, just because an auction house tells the world that there is a sudden interest by American buyers in preserved East Indian toadstools from the eighteenth century, it isn't necessarily so. In this instance, a careful reading of the auction's recent sales records reveals that only two purchases were made by Americans. The rest were bought by East Indian dealers and assorted Arab oil magnates. To the eye of the jaundiced antiques buyer, the brouhaha was clearly an attempt by the auction house to create a market and then manipulate it. How could such a thing happen? Very easily, especially if for two decades there has been little interest in buying the toadstools and suddenly an auction house finds that it has acres of toadstools to dispose of. Of course, toadstools seem a ridiculous example. Much more realistic are fifteen-foot-high Egyptian stone carvings or a collection of 400 antique paper clips. As you will shortly see, anything

Until the last few years, silver from the Arts and Crafts period could be obtained for a fraction of the cost of Art Nouveau and Art Deco pieces. Robert Jarvie, one of America's finest twentieth-century silversmiths, designed this punch bowl in 1910. Anything with Jarvie's hallmark can only go up in value. A small Jarvie pitcher, bought two years ago for $2, would now cost at least $150.

Cliff Dwellers Club of Chicago

The international buyer's idea of what makes a good investment is often quite different from that of the average American collector. This large painted enamel plaque and other massive Victorian artifacts sell well in Japan and Kuwait. An Arabian buyer purchased the plaque at a P. B. Eighty-four auction for $12,000.

Today's flea market bargain can be tomorrow's gild-edged investment. All you have to do is wait, say collectors of such recent items as this Japanese Noh mask in bottle form (c. 1961). Japanese objects, from lacquer boxes to novelties, keep going up in price. Who knows what this bottle will be worth in another twenty years?

CREDIT: New York Flea Market

and everything goes in the antiques market. Don't ask yourself why Arab sheiks are buying massive Victorian statuary or movie stars are buying old photographs. Obviously, people have their own ideas of what represents an important antiques investment. Maybe they just like the stuff. Something has at least piqued their interest enough to open their wallets. That something is what should concern anyone who wants to make money in the antiques market.

For starters, I have noted what has happened to some of the most important antiques and collectibles over a seven-year period. For instance, the market value of

Long-neglected examples of Arts and Crafts furniture are coming of age as potential investments. Prices have been rising slowly for pieces designed by George Elmslie, Frank Lloyd Wright, Gustav Stickley, and George W. Maher, who designed this chair in 1908. Arts and Crafts pieces can be recognized by their rectilinear form and the use of splats, as well as the high backs on the chairs. Most reasonably priced are the pieces by Gustav Stickley, extremely simple in design and constructed mostly of oak, with trim of iron and copper.

Japanese art and decorative objects has risen more than that of similar Chinese pieces. American paintings, folk art, and collectibles have shown the greatest increase in overall sales. Non-antiques, such as Art Nouveau and Art Deco, that weren't even noted seven years ago are now selling on a par (in price and volume) with some old master paintings. There aren't that many of the authentic old master paintings around any longer, and when they do come on the market, prices seem to be in the hundreds of thousands of dollars. The average investor would be stopped cold merely by the preauction estimates, whereas an investor who looks instead to the Art Deco, Art Nouveau market will observe a steadily growing upward sales trend.

These two categories, Art Deco and Art Nouveau, would seem a good place for those investment dollars. But take this a step further: What type of Art Deco or Art Nouveau objects? There are thousands of originals still around, and in hundreds of categories. Many pieces, especially in the Art Deco field, were commonplace even in their own time and maturity hasn't made them any better made or less ugly. Obviously, not every sample from a collectible period should be considered investment worthy. To be selective, the would-be investor should become well acquainted with the finest examples of each period and learn the names of their creators. Some of the names that are already well-intrenched as blue-chip investments are Gallé and Tiffany in glass and other fields; Buggati in furniture; and Chapirus in sculpture. Among less familiar names are silversmiths Jarvie from Chicago and Denmark's Georg Jenson, who created pieces from 1913 through the Art Deco period. Jensen was one of the first craftsmen to revive the silversmith's art during the mass production of the Deco period. As always, the one-of-a-kind quality piece will have a higher value than one that was mass produced.

So far so good for the average middle-class collector. Before you shriek and say, "What middle-class American these days can afford to put out money on an iffy antique?" hear me out. The way to make money is to buy the antique with a current value of $1,000 or more for half that price—or less. Be it Art Nouveau or Art Deco, this bargain buying adds a bit of challenge to the antiques game. It is also the line of demarcation separating it from other forms of investing, which is probably why collecting appeals to so many penny-counting people. Never mind what the dealers and hoity-toity auction houses put out in their publicity blurbs; it is still quite possible for you to find rare antiques and collectibles on your own—without paying dealer markup or auction percentages. If you are less concerned with *where* you do your buying and more interested in *what* you can discover, chances are you will make money.

When you get ready to sell your valuable Philadelphia lowboy, it won't matter where you got it but what it is and how much you paid for it. Of course, if the piece has "provenance" or documentation showing that it was in the Roosevelt family for 200 years, it will find more buyers and be worth more money. But if you aren't expecting to make the absolute top dollar on your one hundred-dollar investment, why worry? If you just double your initial investment, you're ahead, and if you can sell that one hundred-dollar lowboy for $12,000, you've really done well.

The idea of putting money into a collection has sparked a new approach to the antiques business. One midwestern dealer advertised the investment potential of his antiques and pointed out in one ad the desirability of buying Tiffany table lamps that had once sold in the 1910 catalog for $32 and were now valued at $700. He neglected to point out that from the years 1910 to 1950, you probably could have purchased that lamp for $5. Tiffany is a prime example of the fluctuation in value that can take place. If you had purchased that same lamp for $5 in 1955 and watched the interest in

One of the most popular antiques is the music box. This nineteenth-century example would probably cost well over $1,000. Like any antique, it should be in working condition to get top dollar. Mass-produced metal-disc music boxes from the turn of the century go for over $800. They originally cost around $50. Large floor models, for years forgotten and neglected by collectors, currently sell for $4,000 or more.

Collectors refer to these lithographed tin windup toys as industrial comic art. For full value they must be in mint condition. They represent one of the fastest growing collecting fields. Prices range from over $150 to whatever another collector will pay. The original box and any paper instructions will add to the value.

CREDIT: Dennis Todaro Collection

A weather vane collection can be worth thousands of dollars if the items are rare, such as angels or mythological or biblical figures. A collector may pay as much as $5,000 for a rarity, or as little as $150 for the white metal vane pictured. Old store containers in lithographed tin have been seriously collected for about five years.

There is great interest today in everything Russian. These Russian bronzes found buyers in a midwestern auction at prices ranging from $800 to $3,000. Before the famed Geraldine Rockefeller Dodge bronze auction, they would have sold for a fraction of those bids. It often takes an important auction and a famous name to revive a low market. Such was the case with bronzes before 1975. Prices have been setting records ever since.

Tiffany grow, you would have known that you had a pretty sure "growth stock." My big objection to the Tiffany dealer's ad was the headline: An investment that can't fail." Rule number one for the investor is to pay no attention to such tempting strategy. Who's to say that a giant Tiffany collection won't suddenly come to the market and saturate it, at least temporarily lowering prices? Temporarily could be for a decade. Or a rash of very good reproductions could frighten buyers away. There is already much fakery in Tiffany. Even an antique investment is never a sure thing.

Can you afford to take a chance on one of the growth investment antiques or collectibles? Who would have believed that such things as handblown glass German Christmas ornaments, original cartoons and magazines illustrations of the 1920s and lithographed tin toys would be considered good investments? Apparently somebody did. Faster than you can say "Katzenjammer Kids," prices for these items jumped, within the last three years, into the hundreds, sometimes thousands, of dollars. Before that, they found little interest at either auctions or flea markets. What caused the change? The answer may be found in the publicity given to a single collector in the form of museum shows, newspaper coverage, and TV appearances. As in the stock market, there is nothing like the media hype to stimulate the interest of the buying public. If you had paid attention to those early signs, you might have purchased fine folk art or pre–World War II Hummel figurines still reasonably priced. Now it's too late, in my opinion, for investing in folk art and the best early Hummels.

Like clothing and furniture, antiques and collectibles have their "in-fashion" moment. Fortunate is the investor who pays attention to fads and unloads these trendy objects before the public wearies of collecting them. Also wise is the investor who is wary of the false market created by dealers and other collectors.

This collection of Victorian glass objects and porcelain combines such rarities as Amberina and early-American pressed-glass patterns with K.P.M. porcelain and 1920s pewter. The market for cut-glass pieces, other than those signed by such names as Kawkes and Libby, is currently down. It is still possible to buy mint-condition cut-glass bowls of the Brilliant period for $35 to $50.

CREDIT: Collection of Sara Barnard

A study of catalogs and ads from Sotheby Parke Bernet might show an item that had sold for several thousand dollars last year coming back to the auction block. This time, its pre-estimate may be twice that of last year, meaning that the items were probably bought by a dealer or a collector strictly for investment. Seeking to cash in on current public interest in the object, he placed it back on the market a year later. Chances are good that it will find ready buyers at double the price. Should you buy it? No! It's already too late for you to make a quick killing on this item.

An example of this kind of selling was the May 1979 P.B. Eighty-four (Parke-Bernet on 84th Street in New York City) auction of toys, dolls, and mechanical banks at which several of the toys were the same ones that had been sold there the year before. What probably happened was that a dealer had bought in bulk at the earlier auction and held the items for a year hoping the prices would go up. When they did, it was time to cash in. That method is a little hard for the average collector to afford, but you can take advantage of a similar situation. Keep your nose to the auction books, and when you read that a large collection of items that you collect is coming to the block, ship your things to auction. It's a known fact that large collections in a single category always attract their collectors and ensure plenty of overbidding.

What if you don't want to sell but would rather use your collection as collateral for a business or personal loan from a bank? That will work only if you have additional collateral such as stocks, a car or a house, or a coin collection—unless the bank is known for advancing loans for intangibles such as art and antiques. To receive a loan of this kind, you will need a current appraisal of the objects to be used as collateral.

This book can only touch on a few of the hundreds of objects that recently have been attracting buyers as investors. Among them recently made American Indian objects, Walt Disney memorabilia, limited-edition pieces, political cartoons, and original magazine illustrations. These areas bear watching; some have already found a serious contingent of buyers and traders.

At the moment, it seems that the price an item will fetch for buyers as well as sellers is limited only by what the market will bear. John Marion, President of the Sotheby Parke Bernet auction galleries, told me "These days you can sell a good antique out of a phone booth." I don't doubt that he could. He's on top of the world market and knows what constitutes a salable item. But what about you? As tempting antique deals continue to be dangled under the noses of millions of inflation-weary Americans, you would be wise to remember there is always a tomorrow. Realize that to do well in this business requires almost a full-time commitment to keeping track of the immediate changes that occur in the antiques marketplace. If you don't keep in touch with what's happening, then forget about being an investor and buy for pleasure. And what's wrong with buying antiques just for the fun of it?

1.
What Is the Antiques Market?

Is antiques investing a Walter Mitty dream of the average American collector or the reality of only rich collectors and corporations?

For a shocking opener, around 70 percent of the antiques market is reproductions and outright fakes. Another portion of the market consists of the special classifications that aren't actually considered antiques—such as Art Nouveau (1870–1914) and Art Deco (1914–1930). Still another portion includes collectibles. These objects may be old (nineteenth century) or new, and they may even include toys made in the nineteenth and twentieth centuries as well as Elvis Presley souvenirs, political Americana, and hundreds of paper, wood, pottery, and china items *circa* all the way to 1950! It may soon include items from the 1960s. And yet another category is comprised of limited-edition plates, prints, and whiskey bottles as well. There are also collectors of porcelain figurines originally created by the German nun, Sister Berta Hummel, in the 1920s. Keep in mind that collector-investors are not only serious about but dedicated to the objects they have spent their money on. Nevertheless not all collectors buy strictly for investment. In fact, they may get a bit miffed if you suggest that they are looking at their netsukes and quilts as financial investments.

Who are the so-called investors and what are they putting their money into? Some answers may be found in the study conducted by the research company Erdos & Morgan for *Barron's* financial newspaper. The study pointed out that in the twelve months through June 1976, half of Barron's 1,200,000 readership spent approximately $187 million on investments in antiques or artwork. Of their 225,000 subscribers, 31 percent spent a total of $90 million on the same categories. Granted, these readers weren't collectors of limited-edition prints and plates or of Occupied Japan items. Rather, they were investing their money in already established antiques and art. For them, there was no huge gamble.

Another study from Salomon Brothers Investment Company covered nine years, through June 1977, and reported that among the top profit potentials were *Chinese ceramics*. Price increases during this time showed a gain of 23.7 percent. Other invest-

Fifteen years ago, there wasn't much of a market for western art. A few names such as Frederic Remington always found serious buyers, but prices were low. Renewed interest in anything and everything western has carried Remington's works out of the average collector's range. This 1903 oil on canvas, "His First Lesson," hangs in the Amon Carter Museum in Fort Worth.

CREDIT: *Amon Carter Museum, Fort Worth, Texas*

Since the Bicentennial, interest in eighteenth- and early nineteenth-century American-made furniture and decorative arts has put this desk into the high five-figure category. Made by Goddard-Townsend in the eighteenth century, it has more than doubled in value since 1970.

CREDIT: *Sotheby Parke Bernet*

ments studied were: gold, with a gain of 16 percent; paintings by old masters, a 13 percent gain; oil properties, a 12.5 percent gain; conventional bonds, a 6.4 percent gain; and publicly held stocks, with only a 2.6 percent gain.

In that same time span, 1976–1977, the "Gray Letter," a weekly report issued by Gray Boone, editor of *Antiques Monthly*, showed that the American antiques market had become a five billion-dollar industry. Twenty percent of the growth was due, of course, to a new interest in *Americana* brought on by the Bicentennial. With the resulting increase in collecting Antique Americana during those two years, wouldn't you expect buying to taper off by 1979? No way! The constant upward spiral since the Bicentennial proved that while buyers may have been initially sold on Americana and antiques in the spirit of 1976, they have stayed on to become serious investors.

Actually, Americana was beginning to find serious investors as far back as 1970 and 1971. At that time, John Marion was head auctioneer and executive vice-president of Sotheby Parke Bernet (S.P.B.). After a spectacular auction season, he stated, "The quality, the prices paid, and the diversity of American art on the open market this year at Sotheby Parke Bernet was nothing short of a phenomenon." The astounding part was that so many dollars were invested in American art and antiques in a year of recession. He also noted, "There seems to have been a very deep-rooted change in the sensibility of the public towards 200 years or more of American culture."

As public auctions are generally considered the barometer for trends in collecting and changes in art and decorative arts fashions, a trend toward buying American antiques had begun in earnest not only among Americans but collectors from around the world. *Western Americana* moved out of the West to form collections in the East. Two major collectors, Joseph Hirshhorn and Dr. Armand Hammer, began buying heavily into American paintings. Would that have been the time to buy Remingtons and other western art?

> **Tip:** Wise investors wait for a signal that the big monied collectors are showing interest in a specific area of new collecting. If you like it and can live with it even if you don't make money on it—buy it!

During that same period, important museums such as the Metropolitan Museum of Art in New York held exhibitions of Americana, and an ever-growing number of art books on the *American decorative arts and painting* were published. Even at this time, record prices were established at auctions for anything and everything of eighteenth and early nineteenth century Americana. World auction records scored at that time by Sotheby Parke Bernet included bids for Remington's "The Wounded Bunkie" bronze, Thomas Eakins' "Cowboys in the Badlands," and a Newport highboy by John Goddard, which brought $102,000. All were much higher than their preauction estimate.

A record sale of an object usually sets off a stampede among dealers and newly interested collectors who sniff a winner in the making. Around the time of that record-breaking auction, a brief mention was made in the September 1971 S.P.B. bulletin of "a highly unusual sale of American Indian artifacts." An alert investor would have realized that another potential antiques investment was emerging and known that there would still be several years for collectors of *American Indian artifacts* to buy inexpensively. I won't even tell you what such artifacts would be priced at today, if indeed any were available.

There are many other similar examples. The same standard Windsor chair that sold for $100 in the late 1960s was $400 by the 1970s, and a pine cupboard that had found buyers in 1967 at $300 rose to $1,200. These days a comparable American pine cupboard could cost $2,500 or more. In a department breakdown of sales totals at Sotheby Park Bernet and Los Angeles in 1968–1969, American paintings brought in $1,526,930. In 1971 they brought in $2,991,700. Just one year later, in 1972, they brought $7,985,320.

Another change in the buying area has taken place since the 1960s. These days, 69 percent of the lots are purchased at auction by private collectors rather than dealers.

Author and collector Dr. Richard Rush was one of the first to call attention in print to antiques as investments. Even today, some twelve years after its publication, his book "Antiques as an Investment" is worth reading. In it he printed the results of a questionnaire mailed to 385 dealers bids in 1966. The majority of dealers queried felt that Victorian and primitive American antiques were going out of fashion. Little did

Ten years ago everything in this photograph would have been considered almost junk. Today, the Victorian bed would have buyers fighting over it at auction for at least $900.

CREDIT: H. H. Bennett House, Wisconsin.

they know that in April 1979 there would be a record-breaking sale of *American folk art* held at Sotheby Parke Bernet. It grossed $1,340,450, double the presale estimate. Primitive paintings got top prices as did carved figures and weather vanes. Well, that just goes to prove that even dealers can be wrong.

Another interesting comparison between today's antiques market and that of 1968 is evident in Dr. Rush's comment, "The process of refining one's collecting by getting rid of the poorer antiques and adding better ones is not a very common procedure for most antique owners." Well, times have certainly changed. Go to any meeting of a collectors' club and all they talk about is upgrading. Only the best will do when they can afford to buy or trade up.

Twelve years ago, collectors and dealers seemed to be in agreement that the best places to find the finest antiques were in New York, Boston, Philadelphia, and Washington, D.C. I trust that by now we have learned that good antiques are found just about anywhere. So much the better if the buyer finds his Shaker chair in an out-of-the-way shop in Pittsburgh where nobody is in the least bit fascinated by Shaker: the

The Shaker chair that can't be given away in one part of the country may command hundreds of dollars elsewhere. This example, early nineteenth-century, found no buyers even for $100 in the Chicago area. It should be sold on the East Coast, where buyers are more knowledgeable about Shaker furniture and prices are higher. Traces of the original red paint and the original splint seat add to its value in New York or Pennsylvania.

price will be low. At one time, I could hardly give away a fine Shaker rocker to dealers or antique collectors in Chicago, even though the chair was authenticated early nineteenth-century New Hampshire and worth at the very least $500 retail. There simply were not enough knowledgeable or interested Shaker collectors to buy it, even for much less than retail price. Several said they didn't want it because it wasn't signed. Little did they know that the early Shaker pieces aren't likely to be signed as self-promotion was frowned upon by the Shakers.

This brings up an all-important problem to collectors who want to sell: the rarer the piece, the harder it is to sell, because the average antique collectors or dealers, unless they have become specialists in the object you are trying to sell, will pass it up. Lack of general knowledge on the part of others is your biggest stumbling block. It is easier to sell a commonly made, mass-produced item than a one-of-a-kind rarity, even at less-than-wholesale price. Finding the proper buyer is often a time-consuming effort, but don't panic and give it away. Patience is all important if you intend to be a successful seller.

Perhaps the biggest change in the antiques marketplace is who's in it. In the late 1960s, Dr. Rush observed, "Homeowners and housewives often become occasional dealers. While they can hardly be classed even as part-time dealers, they do buy and sell antiques for a profit." Tell that to the nationwide groups of "ladies who only do shows" or to the housewives who have formed cooperative antiques shops in their spare time. Many of these housewives began their careers by holding *conducted house sales*.

When I first began writing about the changing antiques market some fourteen years ago, only three "conducted house sale" groups were to be found in the classified section of my north suburban Chicago paper. Now as many as twenty house sales are listed for that same area every week. Quite a few of these women earn over $10,000 a year on this part-time basis. Among these estate sale dealers are Maggie Warden, Fay Spiro, and Shirley Mann. This trio does a brisk business holding conducted house sales, appraising antiques, and exhibiting at antiques shows. Probably one of the keys to their success is that each has a speciality. Mrs. Spiro is knowledgeable in art, paper items, and jewelry; Mrs. Mann specializes in antique glass and Art Nouveau; and Mrs. Warden calls herself an expert in junk. "That's where the money is, honey," she says. "People spend more on junk than they do on the good stuff. It's human nature not to be able to resist a bargain. You may think it's junk, but to someone else it's an antiques investment." She is referring to such currently salable but not quite respectable items as china figurines made in occupied Japan, old magazine covers, and junk jewelry from the 1940s.

Other part-time dealers earn tidy sums as *flea market "pickers"* who stand in line, rain or shine, in hopes of buying antiques and collectibles cheaply enough to resell to dealers at a profit. Many of these "pickers" live in upper middle-class condominiums and suburban homes. As one successful picker in her fifties tells it, "In the old days when you were my age, you sat around playing bridge or mahjong and eating chocolates. Nowadays women like the challenge of finding some new and interesting items to sell at a profit. We meet new friends. The same people are in line every week. We share experiences, and at the same time we're learning about the antiques business. We have something to talk about at the dinner table that even our husbands find interesting." She and others interviewed said their husbands often joined them on weekends as pickers. One man, about to retire, looks for old cameras and photo equipment. During the past two years, he has built up a specialty following among dealers. "It sent me on a Florida vacation last year," he told me.

Back in the 1920s, the experts felt the supply of antiques would dwindle and the

Extreme and exotic even for the Art Nouveau period (1895–1902), the work of Carlo Bugatti costs thousands of dollars. This mirror combines Moorish designs with vellum, pewter, hammered copper, and ebonized beech. It is doubtful that the average antiques investor will even have a chance to see Bugatti's work firsthand. It rarely comes to market. When it does, museums and millionaires vie for it.

market would soon be over. However, by the 1930s, Depression blues caused a decline in demand for antiques, leaving plenty of antiques for those who could afford them during those lean years. If you had the money, this was clearly the time to buy cheap.

Now, as then, the most important influence determining how many antiques reach the market is the big *estate sale*. Be it a castle, mansion, or Victorian house, there is nothing like the complete sale of its contents to pep up the antiques market. A perfect example was the giant housecleaning of Mentmore Towers in England, media hyped as the world's largest estate sale in May 1977. There were more than three thousand lots of furniture, works of art, porcelain, silver, paintings, prints, and drawings. During the three-day auction, $10,926,785 was spent by bidders, some of whom had been flown in on chartered jets. Rare pieces of signed eighteenth-century furniture appeared on the market for the first time in decades, some for the first time ever. Marie Antoinette's writing desk was bid in at $86,700, and a Louis XV desk was bid to $495,000. As you can see, this wasn't your everyday auction. Nor were these your everyday auction-goers. As television cameras panned across the heavily jeweled *haute couture* crowd, the one thing that stood out was their total boredom. To many, this was merely a social appearance. If the mood struck them, perhaps they would just put in a bid on a little $50,000 bauble—without enthusiasm, of course. Probably the cheapest things at the auction were the brass and wood coat hangers bid in at $30.60 each.

Taking a realistic look at the event, beyond its status symbolism, it did establish new sales records. But was it a realistic influence on the general antiques market? It was, afterall, a limited market not involving the great masses of the general collecting public. In fact, Mr. and Mrs. Average probably weren't even aware of the Mentmore auction. The antiques market isn't just one, but several. Sales like Mentmore are reminiscent of the antiques market of the "good old days," when only the upper strata of the buying public, posh antique dealers, and museum curators attended. Nonetheless, you and I should know what even rare and expensive antiques are going for, just in case one turns up in the local shop. By the way, is being rare the most important factor for an investor to consider? Only if it is a fine specimen in its category and currently sought after by other collectors.

Another important factor is whether the antique is really what it is supposed to be and not a *fake* or a *reproduction.* Most people are more impressed with a fake Chippendale or Queen Anne lowboy from a millionaire's estate than the real thing discovered at a neighborhood house sale. Pay no attention to the people who pooh-pooh the idea of discovering fine and rare antiques at any place but the fancy shops, auctions, and mansions. It happens everyday.

A horrible truism is that it is much easier to sell these fakes than the real thing. The human mind simply isn't prepared to find or even look for an American country Hepplewhite chest-of-drawers for $200 or a silver beaker (c. 1758 American) for $7. Yet both of these items were found at these prices in small antiques shops. If these same items had been priced at $4,000 for the chest and $2,000 for the beaker, there would have been a stampede of well-heeled collectors fighting over them.

Americans also seem to have a penchant for buying things in sets. Not long ago, while I was doing a radio phone-in talk show, a caller asked where she could find a dining-room set of matched Chippendale pieces. She went on to say she had shopped around in several antique shops but all she could find were reproductions, and not necessarily matching ones. She almost fainted when I asked her if she had $15,000 or more for an American Chippendale chair, even if one were available. Somehow I couldn't get through to her that it was unlikely that she would find a matched set of anything Chippendale. Americans are also preoccupied with signed pieces. Little do they realize that anyone can sign a piece, from glass to silver and furniture. Trying to explain that more faked pieces have signatures than do the real thing is a near impossibility. Somewhere along the line, we feel more secure with somebody's name on an item. Even better is a matched set with a fancy (often illegible) signature on each piece.

This then is also part of the antiques market too, where reproductions and fakes are often passed from buyer to buyer. To aid bidders Sotheby Parke Bernet has a term glossary in the front of every auction brochure. Other auction houses let the bidder rise or fall on his own interpretation. The S.P.B. glossary goes something like this:

Glossary for Decorations
(including Glass, Metal work, Lighting Devices, Pottery and other related decorations. Please consult specific glossaries where they are given.)
.1. **Pair of Chippendale Brass Candlesticks,** mid-eighteenth century. This

heading with the date included, signifies that the pair of candlesticks are, in our opinion, of the period indicated with no major alterations, repairs or restorations. This designation does not, however, specify the country of origin of the pair of candlesticks.

.2. Pair of Chippendale brass candlesticks This heading, without the inclusion of the date, indicates that while the candlesticks have a degree of age, they are not necessarily of the period suggested by their style, and does not guarantee their date or place of manufacture.

.3. Pair of Chippendale style brass candlesticks The inclusion of the word "style" in the heading indicates that in our opinion the pair of candlesticks are modern reproductions.

Other antiques market barometers are the items that show up at *quality antiques shows* such as the one at Lake Forest Academy in Illinois and the Park Avenue Antiques Show in New York. Generally, the trends start in the East. For instance, at the summer 1979 University of Pennsylvania Hospital Antiques Show, a quality event,

Two years ago, these American earthenware pieces were found for a total of $24 in two midwestern antique shops. The hand-painted eagle and designs are in the Pennsylvania Dutch style. The vase or jar would probably sell today for at least $300 at auction, the cup for $100 or more.

there was a growing interest in large furniture as well as country furniture and painted pieces. Another popular seller was American earthenware, along with needlework items and woven coverlets.

It may not be quality, but it surely is quantity at the annual World's Largest Antiques Show in Arlington Heights, Illinois. Twice a year, thousands of collectors trudge through acres of antiques booths in search of the ultimate treasure. Along with them are some of the finer antiques dealers who know there is bound to be a sleeper or two. At the spring 1979 Antiques Show, one dealer was putting all his money into any folk art carving he could get his hands on. Even though many were $500 or more, the price didn't stop him, for he had done his homework and followed the trends in the East, where folk art was going at record prices. To make a profit he must double the price of his purchase. Therefore, a buyer must feel pretty strongly about the future of folk art carvings to spend $1,000 for one. Now if the buyer had read the same price changes in folk art the dealer had and had beaten him to the carvings, he would have realized a nice profit from the purchase. If a collector buys the folk art carvings from a dealer who bought them at the show from another dealer, all the purchaser can do is hold on to them for a year or two, and hope that prices once again go up.

Tip: The antiques market doesn't always bring a quick profit. Often it's more similar to a lay-away plan.

A collector interested in Americana might trace its gradual rise in popularity from the early 1970s to 1973. By 1976 collectors from Chicago, Milwaukee, and the Cleveland suburbs thought nothing of phoning and mailing in bids to major auction houses around the country. By the sixth annual American Heritage auction, held in 1976 by Sotheby Parke Bernet, they were among the most eager bidders and buyers of eighteenth- and early nineteenth-century American furniture.

While *folk art* has spread in popularity from its original museum acquisitions and eastern collectors, it is just now gaining serious collectors in the Midwest. The Bicentennial celebration created the realization that Pennsylvania Dutch carvings, naive paintings, and needlework were important antiques. As prices at eastern auctions suddenly jumped in early 1979, a wide segment of the collecting population saw folk art as yet another antique, decorative art form to invest in. Probably the 1974 S.P.B. Garbisch auction of folk art, where over 200 American frakturs, embroidered pictures, and other folk art pieces from the collection of Edgar and Bernice Garbisch found new homes, marked the beginning of prices rising. Estimated prices ranged from $250 to $3,500—quite a modest set of estimates compared to the April 1979 S.P.B. folk art auction, which grossed $1,340,450 or double the presale estimate. Carved figures, weather vanes, and naive paintings also got top prices. Sixty-nine percent of the lots were purchased by private collectors. A wooden bust of Capt. M. Starbuck (Nantucket 1838) sold for $30,000, a new record for any folk carving, and a Revolutionary War whirligig sold for $5,000. Now you know why that Midwest dealer didn't mind spending $500 at the antiques show for a single American folk art carving.

Another phenomenon is antique dealers buying back pieces from old customers and selling them for double or more the price. Dealers keep track of expensive pieces they have sold their customers in the past. They also keep track of who buys the choice pieces at an auction. The day when a customer comes in with a "money-is-no-object" request, the dealer picks up the phone. In dulcet tones, he offers to buy back that Queen Anne lowboy for what the customer paid for it last year, with a few dollars thrown in. Now if the customer hasn't kept up with the market, he may think this is

This Tiffany lily lamp sold at a 1978 Sotheby Parke Bernet auction for a record $20,000. So many different items came from the Tiffany studios that there are probably many waiting to come to market. Furniture, hand-blocked wallpapers, rugs, and even hand-tooled leather wall coverings were made under the Tiffany name.

CREDIT: Sotheby Parke Bernet

a great opportunity to cash in on his antique investment. Perhaps it is. After all, he doesn't have a customer with the cash waiting in the wings.

According to Harold Sack, president of Israel Sack, Inc., New York, founded in 1905 by his father, "Our source for antiques now is buying directly from the people who own them. As prices have risen dramatically in past years, more pieces never before on the market have been sold. Many items that people had inherited have been turning up. Today there are hundreds of small but choice collections coming up to market rather than the giant collections. When the market gets flooded with a giant collection, prices drop." This hasn't happened lately, because collectors still shudder remembering what happened to the snuff bottle market several years ago when the Hugh Moss collection flooded the market.

Not all important items coming to the antiques market are antique. Clever collectors who began buying up the best examples of pieces from the *Art Nouveau* period have been richly rewarded. During the past five years, Art Nouveau prices have increased 100 percent. Other collectors smugly remember an auction in 1946 when glass and lamps from the Louis Tiffany estate sold for as little as $50 a piece. What may have gone a long way to change the public's disinterest was a museum exhibit featuring Art Nouveau pieces.

Tracing the investment growth of just one such piece of Art Nouveau will give you an idea of the investment growth cycles that can be attained. The piece, a huge, four-and-one-half-foot high Tiffany lamp, was sold last year at a Christie's auction for $70,000. Known as the Gould lamp, it was a far-out design when it was made, *circa* 1914. Try to picture this lamp, topped with a golden ball and held up by three iridescent peacocks. When it was first sold to a private collector, Richard Barnett, in 1946, the price was an unbelievable $225. In 1968 it came to market and was sold to another collector for $25,000. As you can see, it wasn't exactly an overnight investment winner.

When the collections of the Louis C. Tiffany Foundation were sold in 1946 at Parke-Bernet Galleries in New York, over 200 pieces of Favrile glass, including cabinet pieces and tableware, were sold at prices ranging from $25 to $145 for individual pieces. According to author Gertrude Speenburgh in *The Arts of The Tiffanys*, "These pieces represented choice and outstanding examples such as an artist and manufacturer would choose to adorn his own home." Compare even that top price of $145 for a bowl in 1946 with a 1979 auction price in the Midwest of $900 for a Favrile bowl. A market that was down and almost out has rallied to new heights, showing no sign of retreating in the near future.

During an April 1979 sale at Sotheby Parke Bernet of Art Nouveau and Art Deco pieces, interest had increased enough to send pieces over previous records and estimates. A rare, glass mold-blown elephant vase by Emile Gallé with an estimate price of from $15,000 to $20,000 was sold to a private California collector for $26,000. A similar Gallé vase had sold at another auction six days prior for $19,000. Sharp-eyed collectors would have also noted the rising prices for René Lalique's work at this same S.P.B. auction. A Lalique pendant with a preauction estimate of from $18,000 to $25,000 was sold to a New York dealer for $41,000. In turn, he will at least double that price for the retail trade.

Art Deco jewelry also began to show a real price rise at 1979 auctions. A diamond and emerald bracelet in Deco design sold for $6,000. Evidence of Deco catching on with serious, monied private collectors came with an article in the March 1979 issue of *Antiques World* magazine. Dr. Annella Brown, long a serious collector of eighteenth-century French furniture, decided to simplify her lifestyle after moving into a new apartment that had an Art Deco interior appearance. From then on, she began looking for a few Deco pieces. Most interesting is the fact that she eventually found great similarities between her French decorative art pieces and Art Deco.

Another clue that a new investment area in antiques is about to open is when important antiques magazines such as *Antiques* begin printing articles about later period pieces. This is a signal to alert collectors that these categories are about to be considered for serious investing. About six years ago, stories began to appear about craftsmen who had worked during the Art Deco period. This was followed by stories on the Art Deco influence in architecture and architectural decorations. Probably the next clue was the appearance of dealer ads featuring Art Deco pieces. By that time, it was already late in the game for beginning collectors, at least for those on the East Coast. Prices were on the rise, and the top names in Deco design would shortly become as well known as those in accepted antiques categories. By 1979 full color ads of items by such craftsmen of the Deco period as René Lalique were appearing in dealer ads not only from the New York area but from Miami, Florida. At the same time, the London-based Phillips auction gallery advertised a forthcoming auction of a Lalique collection in its New York branch. Clearly, there would soon be a shortage of good Art Deco objects. The question now is: "Where does the market go from here?"

Presently, the market seems to be going in several directions. A few years ago, only a handful of adults were seriously collecting *toys*. At least not many had come out of the closet at that time. Before the 1970s, toys simply weren't seriously considered an investment. They were more of a conversation piece, the exception being dolls. Early

This Humpty Dumpty hasn't taken a fall as an important antiques investment. Made around 1890 by the famous toy designer Schoenhut, it was originally enjoyed by children. These days, you can't afford to let the kids near it, not when a single clown figure has a price tag of $50. The market is a diversified one where a single toy can cost $10,000.

Even five years ago, most of these items would have never made it to a good auction gallery. Now they are highly desirable antiques. The turn-of-the-century bicycle sold recently for around $200. The handmade stave cradle, the doll, and the Victorian child's chest have a particularly good investment future.

Few collectors dreamed that when Mickey Mouse celebrated his 50th birthday, an important new area of investing and collecting would open up. Buyers of this new birthday watch have seen it go up in price in just a year. One collector bought several dozen anticipating a future boom.

CREDIT: *Dennis Todaro Collection*

nineteenth-century dolls with maker's names like Jumeau and Heaubach were, and still are, selling in the high hundreds, sometimes thousands, of dollars. However, a major toy auction held by Sotheby Parke Bernet in 1975 marked the entry of toys into the antique investment category. This was the collection of Mr. and Mrs. Archibald Stiles, and there were 620 lots that sold for the grand sum of $86,000.

One New York collector paid a new record price of $5,750 for a Hubley cast iron, four-seat toy vehicle. The last lot of that auction was a large, American hand-carved carrousel horse with jeweled eyes and mane. Before this, there were relatively few serious carrousel animal collectors. Now there are even collectors' clubs. At that same auction, a twenty-four-inch Jumeau doll with the original wardrobe fetched $15,000. When it was all over, you can bet that people who had never considered toys as a money-making investment quickly changed their minds.

Sometimes items that haven't even been classified as collectible appear at auctions and create a new market. Such was the case in 1972, when the first *Disneyana* auction was held in Los Angeles. A framed cel from a variety of cartoon strips might have been purchased then for as little as $25. By the time additional items came to the auction block several years later in 1978, there were collectors eagerly waiting. At that time, a framed cel from *Sleeping Beauty* brought $475.

On the heels of the Disneyana items came *original comic strip art*. Newly appreciated as a collectible art form, an original *Peanuts* cartoon sold for $475. A 1922 *Krazy Kat* original comic strip brought $750. Comic art had come of age as an investment possibility.

Some early collectors have not only enjoyed and profited from their cartoon collections but have made a successful part-time business from it. Successful collectors like to cite the rising prices for the original art of Hal Foster, creator of the syndicated Sunday page *Prince Valiant*. In the 1960s, his originals were offered to collectors for a token charitable contribution of $25 each. Today, those same original pages go for from $600 to over $3,500.

In 1974, John Marion of Sotheby Parke Bernet noted, "In the light of present uncertainties in all parts of the economy, people will now have the opportunity to buy good quality works of art, frequently at very reasonable prices. All kinds of good things will be coming on the market, and the competition for these items will probably be less than it's been for several years."

At that time (1974), heavy Japanese and European buying against the dollar, devalued since 1972, had been driving up art prices. By 1974 the current international economic situations kept many foreign buyers at home, and as a result some of the over-inflated prices returned to their preinflation levels. However, in that same year, the highest price ever, $207,500, was paid at a S.P.B. auction for five American Chippendale hairy-paw side chairs.

Even with money tight at that time, younger buyers purchased antiques for their homes instead of the higher priced retail furnishings. Middle-class Americans had finally realized that they could enjoy their antiques furnishings while they appreciated in value. Young career couples began buying long-forgotten, heavy pieces of turn-of-the-century *golden oak furniture*. Sometimes they even found it in alleys and garage sales. Not only was it possible to furnish an entire room for under $200 with golden oak discards but also with what had once been considered sun-room or porch furniture: *wicker*. Without knowing it, these young bargain hunters had stumbled upon what is currently one of the hot-ticket near-antique items, golden oak and wicker. They didn't buy it as an investment. But, they're probably glad to know that a Montgomery Ward golden oak table from the 1920s can bring several hundred dollars. An earlier Grand Rapids version could cost as much as $800 for the round pedestal style. Would the Mentmore crowd or the New York S.P.B. Americana auction-goers understand that such things are now investments? I doubt it. At least not now! But let a few years go by; many of the golden oak pieces will have disappeared from the marketplace. One sage old-time furniture collector nodded in agreement. "Look what happened to Victorian. Who would have ever expected to see it at an S.P.B. auction alongside Chippendale?"

The antiques market consists also of thousands of highly specialized collectors. A good example are the *mechanical bank* collectors. Even though there have been serious bank collectors for several decades, it wasn't until 1974 that Sotheby Parke Bernet held an auction devoted strictly to them. The rarest, and considered most valuable bank in the sale, was the Initiating Bank. It is a billy goat with large horns, a big toad, and a boy holding a tray. When a coin is placed on the tray and a button is pushed, the goat butts the boy, knocking him toward the toad. The coin slides off the tray into the toad's mouth. That complicated bit of whimsey had a preauction estimate of $4,000 to $5,000. Another important bank that made its appearance at this auction was The Dentist. The figure of a dentist is pointing a large instrument toward a patient's wide-open mouth. When a coin is placed in the dentist's pocket and a button is pressed, it activates the patient to kick the dentist. This in turn hurls the coin out of his pocket and into a slot behind him.

The rarity of these intricate banks often relates to how complicated their mechanisms are. Some had so many parts that they simply didn't survive. Another rarity are the banks that were least popular with children when they were produced.

Currently there are thousands of mechanical bank collectors in America and there is a Mechanical Bank Association. When the banks were originally produced after the Civil War, they cost as little as $2. Today, they just keep going up. One of the main problems for collectors in this field, as others, is reproductions.

> **Tip:**   Early reproductions when well made are being collected. Only time will tell how their value will rise.

Another large segment of the antiques market has always been interested in *Oriental art*. Collecting Oriental *objets d'art* can be traced as far back as the fourteenth century when Marco Polo introduced Oriental artifacts to Europeans. The resulting trade created a market that still exists for fine Chinese porcelains. Pieces of eighteenth-century Chinese porcelain exported in great quantity to Europe and America are among todays top antiques investments. Former President Nixon's trip to China certainly opened up the American as well as the European market for collectors. Prior to his visit, the 1971 archeological discoveries in China had been sent on exhibit to London and to give the collecting public a first-hand view of the beauties of Chinese artifacts. From time to time, superb collections have come to the market and have been divided up among dealers, museums, and collectors. All of these things have added grist to the antiques mill. Directly traceable to the Nixon trip was a S.P.B. auction of Chinese art in 1974. The first major sale of Chinese art, that season topped the one million-dollar mark and set a record for a single Chinese sale. A newsletter report of the January-February 1974 season sales indicated, "The volume of Oriental sales at Sotheby Parke Bernet has more than doubled from the 1968–69 season to 1973."

At the writing of this book, the results of President Carter's trip, as stimulus to the sale of Chinese antiques, has yet to be studied. One thing is certain, it will once again put Chinese artifacts into focus. Another generation of new collectors is waiting in the wings. What they will find is anybody's guess. Certainly there are plenty of brand-new pieces that will be passed off as antique. For those who take the time to study, unusual and inexpensive Chinese objects are still to be found. If marks can be believed, several fifteenth- and sixteenth-century Chinese porcelains were sold at reasonable prices at a Midwestern auction in 1978. An early Ming brush jar with Wan Li chop-marks (1573–1619) was a bargain at $625. That same piece might have gone for several times more in a New York or San Francisco gallery.

Many modest collectors are turning to Oriental lacquer boxes. The field is still wide open to find painted *lacquerware* from not only China and Japan but Korea. Many of the painted lacquer boxes still available were made for the 1876 Philadelphia Centennial. A set of picnic boxes in Chinese lacquerware that once sold for a mere $25 to $50, was recently sold at auction for several hundred dollars. One of the problems with lacquer is chipping. It is often as expensive to repair a lacquer piece as it is to buy another in good condition.

Oriental art is currently very popular. Even though most of the pieces that are sold at auction are not antiques, nobody seems to mind. As long as this kind of carefree buying attitude exists, go ahead and buy. The fact that the pieces aren't Ming, T'ang, or Ching hasn't hurt their prices. This carved coral Kwan Yin figure found a buyer for $2,000, though it is less than six inches high and not carved out of jade.

CREDIT: *Gilmore Gallery, Chicago*

Probably the most amazing growth cycle is to be found in the *limited-edition market*. Plates, spoons, bells, and bottles along with prints and sculptures are offered to a seemingly bottomless pit of collectors. Many collectors will deny they are buying for investment. Well, it seems collecting and investing meld into each other, and it is hard to tell where one stops and the other begins. Despite the tendency to look down one's nose at antiques investment, who among us isn't interested in the value of a purchase? If people don't think of their collections as investments, then why are the writers of price guides on top of the antique and collectibles book sale lists? What else could explain the letters devoted strictly to how much things are going up and down in value? Apparently many people think it's important to know what their objects are worth.

If there weren't a frenzy of buying and selling of limited-edition plates, there wouldn't be a need for a Bradford Exchange. This plate brokerage puts the seller in

Japanese lacquer is going up in price. It is considered superior to that from China or Korea. Nineteenth- and early twentieth-century examples are getting harder to find. Just a year ago, you could buy a fine nineteenth-century box for around $20. Now it sells at $100 or more. Boxes range from elaborate tea containers and picnic boxes to small delicate glove boxes. Pictured are a signed nineteenth-century box and a turn-of-the-century bowl.

A plate is like money in the bank when it's the original of this 1969 first Mother's Day jubilee plate issued by Bing & Grondahl. The original cost around $9 at issue; today it's sold for $500 or more. This is only the first of future issues planned at five-year intervals; 1984 will be the next. The plate is of fine hard paste porcelain, hand-decorated in characteristic B & G blue.

touch with dealers who charge the seller 20 percent of the sale price. Waiting breathlessly for the next collector plate to be issued are 3.9 million known plate collectors. According to Emil S. Polk, president of the Collector Platemakers Guild, "Most seem to be in the thirty-five-plus age group and are predominately female (74 percent). Over 90 percent have combined family incomes of $10,000 to $50,000 a year. It is largely a middle-class field of interest." Hard to believe, but until 1950 there were only three people in the United States actively engaged in plate importing. By 1965, plate collecting had become a mass-market hobby. It was due to the making, for the first time, of a limited-edition crystal plate by the revered French glass firm of Lalique. *"Les Deux Oiseaux"* (The Two Birds) was offered at $25. Its value rose within several years to $1,700.

The first Yule plates made by Bing & Grondahl in 1895 were the early beginnings of what is now a worldwide market. Until the last twenty years, they were collected mostly by Scandinavians and Americans of Scandinavian descent. Gradually manufacturers from other countries and the United States began creating plates in limited quantity as an art form. One of the biggest successes, as far as investors are concerned, was the "Heavenly Angel" plate issued in 1971 by W. Goebel Company. The original cost was $25. Evaluations as of May 1979 place it at nearly $1,000. Not until the late 1960s did United States platemakers become strongly involved in collector plates. Famous names such as Gorham, Pickard, Lenox, and Reed & Barton are considered quality names, an important consideration for collectors, even more so after the influx of shoddy plates that began to get in on the action a couple of years ago.

Not only do investors worry about the quality and the name of the maker, but the names of artists. The name of Norman Rockwell is apparently money in the bank in the plate-collecting field. Most are reproductions of his most popular *Saturday Evening Post* and *Look* magazine cover paintings.

According to Arch W. Patterson, founder and head of the Rockwell Society and a sponsor of the 1979 National Plate Collectors Fair, "It's a bull market." After Rockwell's death, prices began to zoom upward. The Bradford Exchange's Bradex (the plate collector's version of the stock market) scored a fifteen-point gain during the four weeks after Rockwell's death. It was the second-highest advance ever registered by the Bradex. For the moment at least, the Rockwell plates are blue chip.

Beginning in the nineteenth century, corporate patrons of the arts included names like Vanderbilt, Astor, Freer, and Carnegie. They bought fine arts and objects of virtu, then donated them to namesake museums. Now, it's not the individuals but the corporations themselves who purchase millions of dollars of antiques and artifacts. They have been rightly named the "new Medicis of the market." Sometimes their collections reflect their business image. The Campbell Museum, for instance, has priceless collections of rare soup tureens. Others, like the J. C. Penney Company do tie-in sponsorships of traveling museum exhibits that may coincide with the founding anniversary. Such was the case with the 1978 major art exhibition "American Art, The Turn of The Century." It showed works dating from 1890 to 1910. The company was founded in 1902.

Banks and smaller businesses use antiques and art as combination investments and image makers. The items they purchase aren't necessarily of the antique variety. One ad agency has bought heavily into *country store items* with which they decorate everything from the boardroom to the executive washrooms. Another agency is wall to wall American Indian artifacts. At least a dozen years ago, the Exchange National Bank of Chicago began buying up *photographs* by such noted photographers as Ansel Adams and Alfred Stieglitz. These were added to important pioneers in the field like Mathew Brady. Since that time, the collection has quadrupled in value.

A permanent collection of both old and contemporary photography is what the Exchange National Bank of Chicago, Illinois, has put its money into. Pictured with an example of the over 2,000 prints in the collection is Philip M. Lewin, president. The collection represents the work of over 170 photographers, pioneers and modern masters alike. It was begun at a time when photography wasn't taken seriously as an investment except by a few avant-garde collectors. Now, however, photography increases yearly in value.

The August 1978 issue of *Money* magazine noted, "Photography by Ansel Adams, probably the most revered of modern photographers, has zoomed in value. 'Moonrise Hernandez,' a photograph that sold for about $200 a decade ago, brought $1,550 at an auction last October. The photograph was sold again in May for $2,500, breaking price records for works of living photographers."

In order to keep such collections viable, there must be a constant upgrading. This is what periodically puts choice items back on the market. When major museums do the same thing, it is called "deaccessioning." Wise investors will take advantage of such opportunities. The selling off by a museum or a bank doesn't detract from the worth of the items. It may be that the museum has run out of space for a particular category, or that it is changing its decorating scheme.

A wealth of new jobs for curators and consultant buyers has been created by the entry of corporations and banks into the collecting field. What neat jobs they have, traveling the world, often on retainers plus commission, in their search for corporate treasures! These glorified "pickers" aren't competition to the average antique collector. They belong in a different sphere, along with the Mentmore crowd.

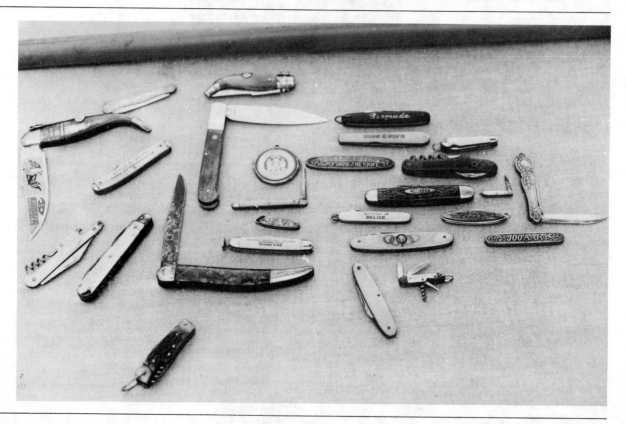

Is a collection of pocket knives an investment? You're looking at only part of a collection that's valued at over $2,000. It belongs to a teenager. By beginning with a relatively untapped market, he has built up a collectibles investment with a very good future. Current values range from a couple of dollars to several hundred for rarities.

Probably on the very bottom rung of the antiques and collectibles market are the kids, usually from age twelve to eighteen. Yet, they influence trends and investments and often create new markets. Consider that collections of *beer cans, pocket knives, Star Trek items,* and *movie memorabilia* got their start with the bubble gum set, as these were the only things they could afford. As usually happens, the adults then took over and prices began to go up. Lucky were the kids who held on to their first-edition comics and early Star Trek items. Often unknowingly, they have acquired some of the important investments in the collecting world.

Yet another market, still developing, is that of *celebrity items.* Wild adulation sent prices skyrocketing for the late Elvis Presley's old gym shoes. An entire artificially produced collectors' market was instantly created upon his death and found ready investors in anything and everything "Elvis." One example are the dolls in his likeness that sold twenty years ago for $5. In recent years waiting buyers were willing to pay as much as $1,500. At the moment, this seems like the most speculative market of all. As the years pass, will the celebrity items drop with a thud? Apparently lots of fans don't think so as they hoard their Elvis items. The best you can do is compare similar celebrity items and what happened to their price after the star died. Even then, this is no guarantee of a similar price rise or fall. Wait and see is all that I can say. Consider the California auction of Judy Garland's memorabilia. Generally the outcome was a disappointment to the sellers.

The celebrity marketplace spills over into other categories, most notably collector's plates. A super success was the "Over the Rainbow" issue put out by the Knowles, American China Company, honoring the film *The Wizard of Oz.* A series of seven different scenes from the film were issued over several years beginning in 1977. At that time, the issue price was $19 per plate. By the spring of 1979, it was noted in the Bradford Exchange current quotations at a high of $30. It was at that time still available for $28.

Perhaps you are wondering why the big investors attend auctions mostly in New York or London, or why so many of the most important pieces seem to end up there. John L. Marion, president and chairman of the board of directors of Sotheby Parke Bernet, Inc., offered one good reason: "There are few places that can offer the broad international opportunities found in New York. We auction off items in one-and-a-half-minute lots. Five million dollars passes under the gavel in those one and a half minutes."

It seems to me that a New York auction house is a nice place to sell, but there is no place like home for buying cheap. This explains why several collectors buy all over the map, but when it comes time to sell, they hop off to New York or London and hand carry a few baubles.

If facts and figures are to be believed, the market is anything that somebody wants to buy and sell and just about anybody who is involved in it. It cuts a wide swath that covers everyone from just plain folks to the Rockefellers.

Finally, it includes those who buy thousand-dollar antiques from a mail-order catalog like Horchow's of Dallas. According to the catalog, each item is "unique and only a limited number are available." I should hope only a very limited number, especially of the antique Himalayan wooden clothing chests offered for the sum of $1,750 each.

2.
Assembling Your Investment Portfolio

Approach the antiques investment marketplace just as you would the stock market, in which decisions are made by studying which bonds will yield the best investment. Are you setting your course for instant profit or long-term stable investments? Do you want to gamble on long shots with potential? And who will be making the ultimate purchases and decisions? Some antiques investors, at least those on the grand scale, seek counsel from top-flight auction gallery specialists. Others will get chummy with owners of antiques galleries who specialize in what they covet. (You'll note I say "galleries" not shops. When you're in the thousand-dollar-plus buying category, "shop" doesn't seem quite fitting.) Then there are mavericks who feel they have studied the antiques market enough to do the selecting, buying, and selling without advice from any so-called experts.

First things first. Let's assume you already have several collections of objects, some antiques, some collectibles and some limited-edition collectors' plates. Making a further division, your antiques fall into two separate financial groups. One group consists of pressed glass, Victorian art prints, and late Victorian furniture. The other group includes some eighteenth-century American furnishings and decorative objects like pewter and textiles (quilts, coverlets). You may want to further separate these groups into *artists*, *style*, and *condition*. When this has been done, attach any papers that will *authenticate* the individually made items and write a *detailed description*. One example might be:

New Jersey Rockingham-glazed hunting pitcher, 19th century. Molded on one side are two hounds chasing a stag, and on the other, two mounted hunters. Covered in a streaky-brown glaze. Unmarked. Height, 10 inches. Bought from collection of Archibald Corporation at Slippery Auction Gallery, 1976, for $450.

If possible, at this stage decide which pieces will be in your permanent collection. Those magnificent ancestral oils, for instance, may have become like part of your

With prices for Art Nouveau and Art Deco jewlery soaring, collectors include related pieces in their collections. This brass belt buckle of the Art Nouveau period has been turned into a brooch. Carved rose quartz, malachite, and amethyst are the unusual semiprecious stones that put it in the investment category. Found originally in the junk jewelry box at a church rummage sale for $35, it has a current value of around $400.

A few years ago, you could have bought this oil painting by Norman Rockwell for a few thousand dollars. Today, if you were lucky enough to have a chance to bid on it, the price would be somewhere between $50,000 and $70,000. This would still be a blue-chip investment. The owner could display the painting in important art shows and in catalogs.

family. Or perhaps you are planning to leave your collection of Bennington pottery to your nephew—anything that might be earmarked for a museum gift, or a collection you plan to use as a permanent collection or traveling exhibit. A further step includes taking a good *color slide or Polaroid picture* of every object that is going to be appraised.

Once you have done all the leg work with your existing collections, you are ready for a *professional appraiser*. Much of this preappraisal work will also save time and money that would have gone to the appraiser. Any items you are thinking of selling in the immediate future should be put into a separate file. Of course they should also be appraised, but, if possible, contact Sotheby Parke Bernet for a *preauction estimate*. If they know you are serious, they will go over the descriptive letter you send and the detailed color slide. Their answer isn't the absolute final word. Neither their experts nor anybody else is infallible when it comes to identifying and pricing antiques and art. But every opinion is helpful when assembling a portfolio for future sales. Sotheby Parke Bernet has no charge other than postage. This is additionally helpful when an item similar to the one they pre-estimated comes to auction.

By the time the appraiser has arrived, you should have gathered together any cancelled checks or bills of sale for further evidence of price, date of purchase, and previous owners. This is part of what is known as *establishing provenance*." Even if it was only your Uncle Al who collected those Mettlach steins, that information is still a form of provenance. I don't have to tell you how important it is to have some kind of provenance when it comes time to sell. All you have to do is read the dealer ads. "Fine Georgian silver teapot from the estate of the late Hermione Giltedge." Now, neither you nor I have ever heard of Ms. Giltedge. But it does sound very impressive, and it's that bit of provenance that will up the ante on the teapot. This line of provenance is like a chain letter that builds up, owner by owner, until the final possessor has a long list of impressive former owners of the teapot. Eventually, there will be nobody left to remember the Hermione Giltedge who found the teapot in a Salvation Army store where she worked as a part-time cleaning lady. Consider, on the other hand, that your lace tablecloth was supposed to have belonged to Mary Todd Lincoln. Without that dated letter, handed down in your family, it could be just any old tablecloth.

> **Tip:** Carefully hold onto any family letters that could later help identify family antiques. They can be extremely important to future owners.

There are times when a letter of provenance means nothing or is in fact misleading. Such might be the case when, for instance, you bought a Coromandel screen at a local antique shop for $900. Supposedly it was made a couple of hundred years ago in China, not yesterday in Taiwan. The dealer insisted it was worth far more than the price tag. She had "papers." The papers were a single typed sheet of paper listing an antique shop in Shanghai that declared it an authentic Coromandel screen 200 years old. The shop owner's names were signed in Chinese. Now common sense should have told you that if this were actually an antique screen, it would have been priced at several thousand dollars. Anybody can print a provenance letter. And does.

There is still another category of hoked-up provenance that you should be aware of —rip-off, mail-order antiques investment clubs. A group of people nobody except their own mothers knows suddenly sets themselves up as experts and sends out a mailing. Lucky you can buy one of their original King Tiddle artifacts straight from the pyramids. Only one to a customer. Guaranteed authentic fifth century B.C. And who has authenticated these marvels? Why Gabriel Gauche, of course, "Expert in Egyptology"! There is even a picture of Gabriel, with a beard, of course. Doubtless it will serve him well when disgruntled investors try to find him and file suit for misrepresentation and fraud. Strangely enough, people do keep this kind of bogus business going. Just use common sense before you bite. There wouldn't be enough King Tiddle or Tut objects to service a mail-order mailing list, not unless they had a mass production setup in the pyramids.

Now that you are ready for your appraisal, you are about to encounter the most difficult problem in assembling your portfolio: *finding a reputable appraiser.* Sorry, it isn't just a simple matter of flipping through the pages of the phone book under Appraiser. That can cost you dearly in more ways than one. Before another naive moment in your life passes, realize that there is nothing like the art and antiques appraising business to attract crooks. Horror stories are endless. The appraisers who are very, very good and reputable will have plenty of fine references to show you. By all means, check those references. Also be sure that the references aren't the appraiser's cousins or best friends who are in cahoots.

Call your local art museum curator who deals in the type of object you collect. He can, and usually will, have some names of appraisers for you. Another approach is to look up the local chapter of the American Society of Appraisers and ask for a specialist in your type of collecting. Members are very strict about ethics and before they are accepted must take a very tough written examination.

Above all, beware the appraiser who offers to buy your things and save you his fee or an auction gallery percentage. Even though you may desperately want to get rid of something the appraiser tells you is worth only a few dollars, don't act hastily. This is one of the oldest cons in the antiques game. The crooked appraiser tells the victim, "That Victorian cracker jar isn't very good and I'll take it off your hands for $15." What the appraiser doesn't tell you is that the Victorian cracker jar was made by the Mount Washington Glass Works and has Crown Milano-enameled flowers. As such, it is worth over $300. It is what disreputable appraisers don't say that can make the difference.

It's amazing the approaches that are used to do in the victims. One appraiser has been getting away with such chicanery for years. His favorite approach is the widow who timidly asks if her silver tea set is worth anything. It's been in the family for years. Somehow he can't properly identify the fact that it is Georgian, even with a fine hallmark right under his nose, and offers to take it to his office where he can examine it carefully. In return, she gets a scribbled note with an unrecognizable signature on it. Months pass, and the widow waits. Finally she calls to inquire about the tea service. "What tea set?" the appraiser asks. When she reminds him that she has a slip that he signed, he asks, "Does it say I removed a tea set from your home?" As you have already guessed, the paper merely states that "Sam Scoundrel, appraiser, received $200 for examing the contents of Mrs. X's home." Oh yes, the lady also paid him before he left. Believe it or not, the laws being what they are today, the widow never gets back her tea set. She has no witnesses, nor anything to indicate that she ever even owned a silver tea service. It is now her word against his.

Another problem might arise if the appraiser is part of a theft ring. He gains entry to the home, notes the value of various antiques and their placement, and several months later while the owner is out, his pals pay a visit. In one Midwestern suburb Friday night was the usual night for antique and jewelry thefts, as that is when upper middle-class suburbia dines out.

Whom can you trust? Well, try your banker, lawyer, or people who deal with trusts and estate sales, for they have to ferret out the most knowledgeable and honest appraisers for estate appraisals. Another advantage in hiring appraisers recommended in this way is the constant flow of items that come under their noses. They have to keep up with current market prices, which is the second most important qualification for an appraiser you want and need: a working and up-to-date knowledge of current market prices.

You have finally found your appraiser. Don't expect the fee to be cheap. Respect his knowledge as much as you do the stock broker who knows exactly what just crossed the board. The *appraiser's rate* for services can either be a percentage of the total worth of your portfolio or from $60 to $75 an hour, including the final typewritten appraisal and his time spent on research. Or he may charge a flat fee of $200 plus an hourly fee for research time and collating the material. Fees vary across the country.

If you have already put your portfolio in order, he may seem to be retracing steps. Not really. He may be able to add the valued provenance to the same objects, for he may have a photo in his files of a similar object and its origin.

Final figures will give not only the *current market price* but also an evaluation for insurance purposes. There is a *replacement price* when the listing is for insurance, which will be higher than the price for selling as insurance prices take into consideration your need to pay a shop price if you have to replace a piece. This price will be based on current prices in your area as well as on a national price, unless, of course, you have a rare piece that has an established international price. Replacement price will begin with a recent auction price plus another 10 or 20 percent for auction house fees. It may also take into consideration what a similar piece is now priced at in a local antique gallery.

For average items such as Victorian decorative arts, golden oak furniture, and Carnival glass, an appraiser will check figures for your surrounding area. His estimate is based on what they have sold for in your home town of Apple Core, Maine, not what they sell for across the country. The end result will be a medium price between the highs elsewhere and your local highs. For instance, a primitive painting of a certain size has sold locally for $200. It will be matched against a similar auction item sold where these items get top value, in the East. Perhaps figures will be taken from Garth's Auction Barn in Pennsylvania or a folk art auction at Sotheby Parke Bernet in New York. In the East, that same primitive may have gone for four times more. The appraiser justifiably puts a middle value on the piece of $600. However, if in his judgment the piece is an unusual rarity, he may assume that you would eventually plan to take it east to get the top price. In this case, he may make an appraisal of $900. By now you can see that this appraising business is a bit complicated. All the more reason to hire the best appraiser money can buy. He is part of your investment. His fee is also tax deductible.

When the appraiser has finished his job, you should have a folder with descriptions and prices. To this you can add a duplicate color photo of the object. All of this, of course, serves a dual purpose. With thievery on the rise, you'll want to be doubly sure your investment can be identified.

Your appraisal must be kept current to be of any use. Frankly, with today's wild fluctuations, the wise investor keeps his own notations alongside the appraiser's. It's a good idea to have a reappraisal every three years. The next time around, it will merely be a matter of up-dating and adding any new items. The appraiser will, in the meantime, have furnished you with two copies, one for yourself and one for your insurance agent.

Where did this idea of an antiques investment portfolio begin? In 1974 a combination of rise in the value of metals and inflation caused many financial experts to look

While others are investing in Spode and Limoges, some collect children's dishes decorated with comic characters. Though these items were made by the hundreds in the 1920s and 1930s, they are relatively rare today. Those that remain continue to go up in price. As part of a collection of industrial comic art, they are a potentially good investment.

CREDIT: Dennis Todaro Collection

afield. Perhaps unknowingly, they played into the delighted hands of the major auction houses and antiques dealers, for suddenly they were recommending that the public buy metals in the form of works of art and utilitarian objects as investment hedges. Hundreds of people who never before thought of collecting anything except bills discovered a new pot of silver: *Franklin Mint objects,* and *English and American eighteenth- and nineteenth-century silver.*

Heading the parade, Sotheby Parke Bernet offered a sale of English and Continental silver, and "utilitarian objects such as coffee pots, candlesticks, etc." Their entire October 1974 News Bulletin played up "newly emerging fields ideal for beginning collectors, attractive hedges against inflation." The seed was planted. However, it grew very slowly and didn't actually begin blossoming until after the 1976 Bicentennial. When it did, it far surpassed the bounds of the typical monied S.P.B. buyer. It stretched to the young blue-collar couple who believed that at $25 for a limited-edition plate or art print, they couldn't lose. Art galleries specializing in limited-edition prints by Norman Rockwell, Leroy Neiman, and Chagall sprang up across the country. An investment in collector's plates that began in 1960 just for fun became a collector-investor boom of over two million people by 1976.

By this time, the *Market Bradex* was established by the *Bradford Exchange* as the plate collectors' trading market. It had survived its own "crash of 1972" and still made many investors profits. That crash can be likened to what happens in the antiques world when, for example, a flood of reproductions of early Staffordshire figurines or fake folk art hits the market. In the case of the collectors plates, more and more plate makers pushed into the lucrative limited-editions market, many hoping to ride on the coattails of the Franklin Mint silver plate successes. As a result, many inferior products were purchased by dealers and collectors and the market became overstocked. Many who had put all their dollars in one type of plate lost heavily as first silver, then all the other new plate issues shattered. As the 1978 *Bradford Book of Collector Plates* tells it, "Thousands of plates were melted back into silver. Established makers cut back production dramatically, and the bedroom dealers faded from the scene." As in the antiques market, one spectacular item brought the plate market back up. It was a first plate, "Colette and Child," painted by artist Edna Hibel, issued by Royal Doulton in 1974. The plate market in America was on its way to bigger and better things, and along with it came the redevelopment of a lagging European market.

For investors in the plate field, the name Hummel is just as important as it is to specialized Hummel collectors. In a sense, one feeds the other. In 1977 the collector demand for back issues of the entire *Goebel Hummel annual series* led to the growth of another new market. It all began with a story that appeared in the September 1976 newsletter of the National Association of Limited-Edition Dealers stating that 60,000 of the 1972 plates had been destroyed to increase collectability. Rumors of the scarcity of 1972 and 1973 caused fast and furious bidding for those left on the market. As a result, the "entire series rose an average of 98 percent by year's end" according to the Bradford Book. "The '71 issue in the series went from $580 to $996; the '72, from $38 to $109. The '76 was up from $50 to $72." Hummel fever mounted even higher as a book and price guide, *Hummel Art*, by John F. Hotchkiss hit the bookstores.

Clearly a big misapprehension about both the limited-edition plate market and the Hummel art market was forever eradicated. It was not just little old ladies, housewives, and blue collar workers who thought this was a serious market for investment. The snob attitude toward this area of collecting had been replaced by a monied coterie of buyers from the professions and a group of young marrieds. The latter hadn't felt at home in the stock market. "At least," one young couple explained, "now we could visually enjoy our investment. And it wasn't hard to understand why it was going up or down financially."

Perhaps you like plates but only antiques. Let's assume that you want something that seems to have a long-established market value, perhaps *dark blue Staffordshire*, English pottery made for the American market. Thousands of these pieces were originally shipped to America from England in the 1820s. Then, as now, they were popular because these transfer prints reflected views of American life and famous scenes. If you had begun buying in the 1940s, you probably would have paid around $10 a plate. These days, $150 to $175 a plate is commonplace among collectors, sometimes slightly more or less depending on where and from whom you buy. In a book on the subject, *Historical Staffordshire* by David and Linda Arman, they point out that in the last four years alone prices have risen from 10 percent to 50 percent. Will they

It takes a large home or a museum to accommodate a Georgian breakfront of this size. As a result, prices are lower than ten years ago. Notice the pristine condition of the piece. About fifteen years ago, this would have found high bids at an American auction. Today it will do better in Europe.

continue to do so, or will they face a downturn like the contemporary limited-edition plates once did? A lot depends on the rarity of the piece, a flooding of the market by the sale of a large collection, or an influx of reproductions. As one dealer in Hubbard Woods, Illinois, noted, "I have a collector who will pay almost anything within reason for an unusual piece of Staffordshire blue. A recent purchase was $450 for a mint condition sauceboat in a scarce pattern."

Consider Staffordshire blue pottery, then, as an established investment in the pottery field, but realize that as a beginning investor, you face the problem of prior investors as well as already high-established market prices. There are several possibilities. One is using only one or two good pieces of Staffordshire as decorative accents to other collections of Americana from the same period. Another is simply to buy the more common plates that sell for $25 to $30 and hope they will eventually appreciate. A third is to buy them low and sell the entire collection to buy one rare piece.

Whatever you do regarding investments, nothing is more important than knowing that you have purchased only authentic items. There is such fakery in the finer pieces, from pottery to porcelain and furniture, that even Sotheby Parke Bernet acknowledged the problem with a countermeasure: In September 1973, they stated, "All property sold at our New York auctions will be guaranteed to be authentic, that is, not counterfeit." By doing so, they became the first of the world's major art auction houses to offer this *guarantee of authenticity* and protection to purchasers. Sounds great! Isn't this just what every antique and art investor dreams of—the absolutely, positively authentic antique? The idea, of course, was to give buyers more confidence and less worry about buying a fake or a reproduction that had been represented as the genuine article. According to the S.P.B. announcement, if a painting were offered at

Fine eighteenth-century Wedgwood pieces hold their value, going up every year. Twelve thousand dollars for a rare vase would find buyers. Nineteenth-century pieces are less valuable. These two stoneware urns similar to eighteenth-century black jasper dip, would be a buy for under $1,000

auction as the work of Vermeer and was later proven to be a Van Meegeren forgery, under its guarantee the buyer would rescind the sale and recover his purchase price. There's only one little problem as I see it. What if you and your team of experts lock horns with the S.P.B. team? Frankly, I would save the price of lawyers and merely put the piece back on the auction block for some other dolt.

This guarantee was the beginning of the admission by not only Sotheby Parke Bernet but other auction houses and antiques dealers that there was a whole new world of collectors coming to market; they were from the middle class. Young people in their twenties and thirties wearing their imported blue denim "threads" were rubbing shoulders with the jeweled and jet-set bidders. Unlike many of their predecessors, they were interested not only in having the most expensive antiques and collectibles but also in seriously studying and gathering objects of historical or aesthetic appeal, even if it meant skimping on some other facet of their lifestyles.

The entry of this new group of collectors also marked the beginning of *printed presale estimages* of each item included in the S.P.B. auction catalogs. Many other big auction houses shortly followed suit. Obviously, the new young bidders had something else in mind than just decorating their split-levels and high-rise apartments. Though they had not said so openly, many were building what could be considered their first antiques investment portfolios.

Since then, the S.P.B. catalogs have expanded their detailed information sections. They quickly realized that their catalogs were as collectible as the items they offered, espcially for the beginning collector. An example of their helpful descriptions that assist collectors in separating the wheat from the chaff is to be found in a catalog devoted to English furniture. A chest-of-drawers is listed in the beginning of the catalog as follows:

> "George II Chest of Drawers, mid-18th century." This is the way Sotheby Parke Bernet guarantees that the chest was made in England in the mid-eighteenth century and isn't a nineteenth- or twentieth-century reproduction. What puzzles me a bit is this followup statement:

> "The benefits of the new guarantee of authenticity are available only to the original purchaser at the auction and not to subsequent owner."

Hm! "Caveat Emptor" strikes again!

One year later in 1974, John Marion had become president of Sotheby Parke Bernet and was making the most of the participation of this younger, average-income auction crowd. He enticed them with: "Most art objects sold at auction in our galleries today bring less than $1,000, which defies the propaganda that art has become so expensive it can be bought only by the very rich." Under Marion's encouragement, Sotheby Parke Bernet began its highly successful "Heirloom Discovery Week." The average American was being made excitingly aware of the potential value of taken-for-granted family possessions. "It will go far to emphasize the democratic reality of Sotheby Parke Bernet and offset its plushy image of exclusivity," said Marion. Yes, you and your Uncle Oliver may find yourself bidding against the likes of Jackie O. and Dustin Hoffman. But not for long. Ah, but where else indeed is there such an arena of working democracy as the auction gallery? There are the gladiators and the lions to be sure.

If you read the *trade publications*, as any serious stock market investor reads the

Drug jars were used to decorate early drug store windows and were often filled with colored liquids. The heavy footed base of this example is characteristic of Pittsburgh as well as the New England glass factory. Mold-blown and engraved, it was recently sold in a shop for the ridiculous price of $30. A fine investment, it has a current value of around $250.

Wall Street Journal and *Money* magazine, you would have noted a 1978 interview with Christopher Weston, chairman of Phillips, that offered an alternative to the way new investors might spend their money: "Investments in normal terms should be measured by things which give pecuniary returns. New collectors should invest a certain proportion of funds elsewhere so that cash is available when necessary. Decide on how much money you have to invest." He also noted that specializing in the best possible quality in every recognizable category of antiques is important. "The best growth area in the art market is in the field of antiques valued at between $750 and $3,000 to $5,000.

"The spread of wealth is a very important factor to remember when considering the art market," Weston observed.

Taking a tip from Weston, let's assume you want to invest a certain amount each month in a relatively new area of collecting such as *American nineteenth- and early twentieth-century textiles*. This field could include quilts, coverlets, hooked rugs, laces, and various forms of needlework for starters. While collectors began considering American quilts as worthy of investment as far back as the year before the Bicentennial, the pace moved slowly. The earliest collectors were alerted to a new investment when a 1971 exhibition at the Whitney Museum in New York showed quilts hung as paintings and works of art. Prior to this, they were simply considered textiles, utilitarian objects once made by somebody's grandmother. News media, especially the trades, picked up the Whitney exhibition, and the public began to open its eyes.

At this time, there was also a renewed interest in folk art and Americana, and once quilts and coverlets were considered a form of graphic art, prices began to rise. Shops began to use them as specialty items. The finest examples today can garner from $3,000, but the majority can be bought for from $50 up at both estate and shop sales. Anything with an American flag, eagles, or a signature always fetches a higher price. Floral quilts are usually more popular than geometrics, unless they are more visually exciting. To consider them of investment quality, ask yourself how long they will continue to show up at the market. Will the collectors continue to buy? A positive sign has been a revival of the craft by the Berea, Kentucky craftspeople. Even the best examples of these brand-new quilts are bought for over $100, preserved as investments, or hung as art.

Condition is the most important price consideration. Think of investing in quilts as you would investing in primitive paintings. A fine primitive could cost anywhere from nine hundred dollars to several thousand, but a quilt that would be equal to the painting might still cost only from $300 to $3,000.

Even the quilt field isn't safe from fakery. Old quilt tops are rebacked and quilted, then sold as old. To the novice who doesn't recognize fine, old stitchery, a new quilt in an old pattern may appear authentic.

Types of quilts vary according to region. *Amish quilts* reflect the bright colors found in Pennsylvania German quilts, and they used large clocks of color that resulted in a somewhat abstract look. They didn't use the patterned materials found in most American quilts. Common Amish designs were variants of the checkerboard grid called "Sunshine and Shadow." They also used a design formed from one or more borders enclosing a large field of color. Rather than cotton, they used wool.

Totally distinctive are *Hawaiian quilts* from the nineteenth century. The outlines of the appliqué are followed out in a concentric pattern, each line of stitching one-half to three-quarters of an inch from the next. The designs are based on naturalistic foliage motifs or Hawaiian historical symbols.

Still realistically priced but going up steadily are *hooked rugs* and *needlework* from the Art Nouveau and Art Deco period. Interesting figural hooked rugs dating from the mid-nineteenth century to the 1930s can still be found at private sales for $20 and up. These are the same quality hooked rugs that are bid at up to several hundred dollars at Sotheby Parke Bernet or P.B. Eighty-four. They also get high prices elsewhere in the East, such as at Garth's Auction Barn. Even though hooked rugs seem commonplace and in good supply, nothing lasts forever in the antiques market. They might be a good starting point for a beginning collector in search of a growth market.

Now, just because I have been quoting the likes of Sotheby Parke Bernet and Phillips doesn't mean you can only find good investment-quality antiques in shops and at auctions. To the contrary. Some of the finest collections have been culled from such diverse sources as flea markets and private house and garage sales. One very successful collector of Americana has built up an antiques investment portfolio worth over $250,000. He and his wife began haunting flea markets and private sales in the late 1940s. However, some of his most valuable pieces of eighteenth-century American furniture and the decorative arts have been discovered in the last two years. "One of my secrets of success," he observed, "is that I'm not picky about where I buy, but what I buy. Why should I pay $150,000 for an American Chippendale highboy at a fancy auction, when I can lay my hands on one from a private seller for $8,000?" This collector-investor has gone through all of the previously outlined steps right down to getting a good appraiser and keeping up-dated appraisal sheets.

"I subscribe to the catalogs from Garth's and Sotheby Parke Bernet," he said. "Sometimes I even put in bids by mail." One successful mail-order bid netted him some rare Indian peace medals for about half of what he had expected to pay. "Guess I was just lucky. There either weren't any interested bidders, or the bidders just didn't know what they were passing up."

This collector's portfolio is the perfect example of a diversified combination of items relating to a single period. His goal has been to furnish house and portfolio with everything that was part of the upper-class American home up to the beginning of the nineteenth century, as it includes early newspapers printed by Benjamin Franklin, export china and copper pots and pans. This has allowed him a wider range for his investment dollars and has narrowed the competition somewhat. It could be an especially important consideration to the collector who is faced with a specialized auction of only American pewter, brass, and copper. While the majority of bids at this auction may be for copper, driving those prices up, a lesser amount may be bid on pewter or brass. As a result, he can add to his collection but won't be forced to overbid.

In the field of textiles, the *Oriental rug market* is one example of a stupendous recovery. Much of this growth can be attributed to the expansion of the rug market to include the tribal rugs and bag faces and to display them as art. Another influence on prices was the enforcement of child labor laws in Iran. This sharply curtailed the expansion of the new rug market. Investors wisely observed that what had once been an endless supply of Oriental rugs was about to be sharply diminished. Logic would say prices for existing rugs would continue to go up as demand outstripped supply. There is an even greater demand in Europe for Oriental rugs, and even retail rug dealers keep coming to the United States to buy. This keeps prices rising. In 1974 an article in the *Wall Street Journal* referred to the "Wild Bull Market in Orientals." It was the result of a survey taken between 1968 and 1973. A graph showed old silk Kashan carpets up 500 percent, and Nain carpets up 750 percent. Even more noteworthy, during the survey the Dow Jones Industrial Average decreased 0.8 percent and South African gold shares increased 187 percent. Most Oriental rugs, even recently made ones, are now appreciating at a rate of between 10 percent and 12 percent every year.

This mid-nineteenth-century Daghestan prayer rug is considered an important investment. The value lies in the overall design, age, and condition. Because of the shortage of good nineteenth-century rugs, even those from the 1920s have jumped in price. It pays the beginning collector to find a dependable dealer, since valuable Oriental rugs are difficult to recognize and often lack signatures.

Shown in the nineteenth-century French gold leaf rococo mirror reflection is a Waterford crystal chandelier. Other Victorian pieces shown are two what-not shelves and a pair of girandoles (garnitures). Most important is the Waterford chandelier worth several thousand dollars.

CREDIT: H. H. Bennett House, Wisconsin

If it's any help, one dealer named the four types of Oriental carpets he predicts will increase the most in value in the future. He chose them because in his opinion they are the best being made today and because the changing social structures of the countries where they are made will most likely ensure their future scarcity. They are Nain, Kum, Isfahan, and silk Kashan. With this in mind, a beginning buyer might include some new Orientals in his portfolio as growth items.

Whatever you do, don't think you'll find a bargain in advertised Orientals sold by traveling dealers. Ignore the tempting ads. These characters are here today and quickly gone tomorrow, and you will be left with a tacky rug that has been souped up with a chemical wash or cleverly repaired.

It is still possible to discover good buys in old Orientals at estate sales and church rummage sales. Before you try your luck, study the finest examples available in shops and at any museum exhibits.

During the 1920s, hundreds of Oriental rugs were exported from Central Asia and the Caucasus, and many are still around waiting to be discovered. Some may have slightly thin surfaces. These unrestored rugs are expensive to put into investment shape. However, consider purchasing them cheaply now and having them restored when you can afford it. Their value can only rise when well restored and in the meantime you can enjoy their beauty.

According to at least one successful antiques investor, "Furniture is the best investment you can make." Her specialty is Victorian. While others were running around grabbing up newly popular golden oak and wicker, she carted home *Victorian furniture*. She found a beautiful mid-Victorian balloon-back side chair at a garage sale for $15. "All it needed was polishing and dusting. I saw one like it in New York City for $150," she said. A more recent coup was an entire parlor set consisting of a settee, armchair, and side chair, all upholstered and with medallion backs. For the set, she parted with $800. She is well aware that had she bought it in a shop, the price would have been almost three times as much. She plans to enjoy living with her investment until she needs the cash. By following the buying trends in major cities, she knows that from St. Louis to New York, Victorian is getting more expensive and scarce.

Going back about fifteen years, I recall trying to sell a mid-Victorian sideboard in Renaissance style. Not only did the dealers laugh in my face, but I had only one serious offer for $75. These days, I wouldn't part with it for $3,000. I know better.

Many of the Victorian pieces you come across will probably be in need of re-upholstering. If the price is low, grab them. You can always take a high school extension course in reupholstery and do it yourself.

Only recently has Victorian furniture hit the big-time auction circuit. As is to be expected, the pieces up for bid were scarce examples of laminated rosewood by John Henry Belter. Made in the 1850s, a single chair could fetch at least $2,000, and even a chair by one of Belter's imitators could be over $1,000. By contrast, auction houses like Du Mouchelle's in Detroit have been doing a big business in Victorian furniture for several years.

Many otherwise astute investors are overlooking furniture made from 1815 to 1830, which is priced way under Victorian. In fact, the *American Empire pieces* are just beginning to come to market. Ask yourself why a generation that will spend $4,000 for a ten-foot-high Victorian headboard won't part with even $200 for a magnificent c. 1830 mahogany bookcase or desk? At this very moment, I know of an owner who refuses to accept the highest offers for several pieces of Empire. After two years of advertising these pieces, the highest offer was $200 for a superb solid mahogany chest with brass lion head drawer pulls and animal feet. The other piece, mahogany veneered, has original drawer pulls and glass. She reasons that if she can just hold out another year, she will profit $2,000 or more. I think she's wise. Tell you why.

Recently, some of the top trade magazines such as *Antiques* have done stories on fine Empire furniture. Several years ago, the 1829 Empire furniture made by Anthony G. Querville was featured in that publication. This is usually the signal that a new market is on the rise, but not so with Empire. Only recently has there been any noticeable change in the market. In one of the price guides, a secretary bookcase of the type owned by "the little old lady" has an evaluation of over $1,200. That means that at some auction in some part of the country, a collector or dealer was willing to pay $1,200 for a piece that a few years ago would have brought around $200. This, then, would seem the time to choose the best examples of the period—before prices go up. Choice would be any pieces attributed to Querville, a Philadelphia cabinet-maker. Apply the same rules to Empire that you would to investing in other types of furniture: only the best examples.

One of the biggest drawbacks for many buyers of Empire is missing veneer. How to repair it and still come out ahead? You'll either have to do repairs yourself or find a cabinetmaker or furniture restorer who can do a creditable job. Remember, an investment must be in top shape in order to realize a profit for the seller. Not all pieces of Empire are bulky and oversized. Worthy of second thoughts are game tables with carved pedestal bases and breakfast tables.

If you would like to collect furniture but do not have the room for large pieces, consider these interesting alternatives: *children's furniture* or *miniatures*. The subject of miniatures is discussed more fully in Chapter 3. Several areas of miniature collecting, old and new, as well as special categories of silver, glass, or wood, can form an important investment portfolio. A single miniature copy of a historical full-size Chippendale highboy can cost as much as $900 brand new. As in all areas of investing, the price is dependent on the quality of workmanship and the name of the maker. In

One of the biggest markets involves the smallest items—miniatures. At one time, miniature rooms and furnishings were the hobby of royalty and the wealthy. The large Queen Anne chair pictured is a large miniature. The two smaller chairs are second size. The third size would fit in a doll house.

CREDIT: Mary Jane Graham Collection

the case of a newly made Chippendale lowboy, certain master craftsmen (and women) are already recognized as such, and prices are almost certain to double in the future for their work. For instance, a single piece of miniature silver made by master craftsman Eugene Kupjack can cost several hundred dollars. He is known for the Thorne Rooms, part of a permanent display in the Art Institute of Chicago, which he designed and made pieces for in the 1930s and 1940s. For at least a decade, monied collectors have had Kupjack create and furnish a miniature that duplicates a favorite room in their home, even though his price ranged from $10,000 up.

Worthy of mention on the subject of miniatures is professional western artist Sandi Gipe. Her detailed oils of western scenes are done on cigarette paper. Prices range from $50 up and would fit into the portfolios of both western art and miniatures.

As you are by now aware, many collections and categories overlap. This can be a benefit to investors. If the market goes down in one category overlap, there is still good money riding on the others. Let's say that for some unimaginable reason, the market on western art takes a fall. Perhaps there are too many Remington prints coming to market or the public fancy suddenly falls for military prints. The investor in western art may do one of two things. He may assume the fall is only temporary and decide to buy good examples at the current low price. In fact, he may use this opportunity to upgrade his portfolio by selling off some currently high-priced paintings in another category. Or, if he is a collector of anything and everything western, he may put up furnishings or decorative arts that are enjoying high prices and buyer interest. He has learned how to ride the waves. Above all, he knows that the quickest way to wreck his investment program is to sell in panic. It could also stampede others into panic selling and his own particular market category could collapse.

The field of Oriental art is broad and has attracted both big and little investors for decades. Where once only Chinese art and artifacts were considered worthy of big money, now Japanese and Korean works are also drawing buyers. Many see the medium-priced *Japanese pottery and lacquerware* and *Korean pottery* as good long-term investments, and a portfolio might be broadened to contain not only the finer examples of Chinese porcelain and pottery but Japanese Satsuma, Kutani, and Arita. One collector who started picking up Japanese porcelain that dated from the early twentieth century has found it slowly growing in price. She reasons that although it is relatively inexpensive now, as it becomes harder to find, the price will accelerate. Another collector began buying Nippon porcelain years ago for nickels and dimes. This porcelain was made in Japan after 1891 to 1921 and is marked "Nippon." After 1921, it was marked "Japan." Now, finely hand-painted pieces can cost anywhere from $50 for a cigarette box to several hundred dollars for a vase. The secret of buying these "futures" is to buy cheap.

One drawback both beginners and seasoned collectors face when buying Oriental porcelains, especially Chinese, is rampant fakery and reproductions. Another is being able to know if a piece is Chinese or Japanese. Canton blue-and-white Chinese porcelain has been reproduced, copied, and even adapted by Japanese and European factories since it was first made during the Ming Dynasty (1400 to 1600). Those who have been collecting blue-and-white, as it is known, for years say it helps if you read a bit of the philosophy of both Japanese and Chinese cultures, for their philosphies are reflected in their designs. The Chinese figures seem serene in contrast to the ferocious, active figures shown in Japanese art. Chinese subjects usually have themes from nature and are quite subtle. Observe the popular Chinese Kwan-Yin white porcelain figures with their placid expressions. A sharp contrast is offered by the Japanese figures that appear realistically as men, not deities. A close study of bottle shapes will also help differentiate between Chinese and Japanese ceramics. The Japanese bottle will have a long neck and the body may be melon-shaped.

If you take the time to study what's happening in the export business and make side trips to special Oriental exhibits, you may be able to take a chance and invest in Oriental *objets d'art*. If possible, visit a giftware show or at least a gift shop specializing in Oriental porcelain and pottery. This way, you'll know what the new stuff looks like. Pay no attention to booth after booth overflowing with purportedly old blue-and-white porcelain at the fancy antiques shows. Instead, compare it with the pieces you have seen in the gift shops, where at least, a plate is only $30, not $130.

There are two other really important areas that serious collectors should include in their permanent portfolios: *glass* and *silver*. Both categories have endless spinoffs. Rather than discussing the most expensive and rare pieces, let's see what's around that the average collector can afford. That means you the housewife, you the school teacher, and you the senior citizen who go antique hunting on weekends and would like to feel a little more secure.

How little you spend and how well you can do depends on what's around and how well you've done your research. Being a millionaire doesn't necessarily mean you'll have the finest authentic antiques. Usually, it means you'll spend more and have more reproductions in your collection. Unless you conscientiously study the characteristics of the objects you are buying, you can lose your profits.

One of the best current investments in glass is *art glass,* made from 1876 through the 1920s. The one-of-a-kind examples can cost thousands; they can also be found for under $100. In this category, you may find a magnificent vase signed "Gallé" or a lampshade signed with an 'X' for Quezal. A signed Gallé vase may find buyers from $500 to $50,000, depending on the artistry of the vase. A Quezal glass shade (made from 1901 to 1920) may find a buyer at $95. Now you say, "Swell, but how can I afford to buy these great investments? You're talking big money to a poor teacher like

Under the heading of Victorian art glass are portraits of individuals and classic Grecian profiles executed in sulphide. It was an art of ancient Rome, revived in England in the 1870s. Today's prices range from $40 to $75. The vase in dark green with gilt trim appears to be English. At $35 in an antiques shop, it is a sleeper with good potential.

me." Legwork is how you and others will make money in antique investments. Nothing good in life is that easy to come by, especially valuable antiques. Make up your mind that you will go looking for nothing but art glass—not just any rotten design, but the big-money stuff. Poke around garages, dusty shops, and flea markets. Not every dealer or secondhand shop owner knows everything about everything, especially art glass. Only in the past few years have there been important museum exhibitions and books written on the subject. Bet on the inherent laziness of the average collector where research is concerned. Often choice items are passed up because the name isn't a familiar one. Would you, for instance, be familiar with the name G. Argy-Rousseau? Obviously somebody was. A pate de verre bowl (c. 1925) decorated and signed by Rousseau, sold for $600 at auction a few years ago.

About five years ago, Jerry Sloan, manager of the Chicago Bulls basketball team, became interested in art glass and *art pottery* before it became popular. He has since seen a Newcomb vase that he paid $12 for rise to over $400. Other signed pieces of Rockwood have tripled in value. When he decided that art glass would be a natural companion to the pottery made during the same period, nobody seemed to know much about art glass. "It was hard to identify some of the pieces when I first started," Sloan said. Finally, after numerous trips to museums and libraries, I found answers. Wavecrest and Nakara are some of the earliest pieces in my collection. Since very few of my American pieces have labels, you have to recognize them by shapes and decorating techniques." One such piece is a cracker jar without a label for which Sloan paid a few dollars. Since then, research has shown him it is a Wavecrest piece worth over $125.

Sloan had to do plenty of checking to find out that the Pairpoint Manufacturing Company made only plated silver holders for art glass baskets, holders, and cracker jars from 1880 to 1894. After that date, it bought out the Mount Washington Glass Company but continued to produce decorated glass. A specially decorated group of *opal glass* referred to in the Pairpoint catalog of 1894 as "Rich Colonial Decorations" was similar to pieces produced by the C.F. Monroe & Company during the same period. Sloan commented, "If you think that's confusing, some of the glass blanks used by the Monroe Company were from Pairpoint. Wavecrest was the name used by Pairpoint after 1898." Sloan admitted that in the beginning, he made some expensive mistakes. "Before I spent time studying. You can't build an important investment in antiques without doing lots of studying."

The sterling of art glass, aside from Tiffany, is *French-style cameo glass*. During the last two years, collectors have seen relatively small investments triple or quadruple in value. In a copy of "Art at Auction 1972–73" including international figures, a wheel-carved inlaid free-form glass vase (c. 1900) with the script "Emile Gallé", his initials, and the Croix de Lorraine enclosed within a shield was auctioned in London for $5,750. A *Webb* (English, c. 1880) *cameo glass* vase marked "Webb" was sold in London for $6,000. Contrast this to a December 1978 Christie's auction in New York. A Gallé triple-overlay table lamp twenty-five inches high took a bid for $42,000. By now, Gallé has gone beyond the collecting capabilities of the upper middle-class collector. Except for lucky discoveries in out-of-the way shops, as one dealer who paid $400 for a Gallé vase observed, "It's whatever the traffic will bear."

There are still good possibilities in *Lalique glass*. Signs that it will shortly be in the upper strata of collecting were evidenced at a September 1978 auction held at Christie's in New York. This was to date the largest collection of Lalique to come to auction. One of the top bids went to a scarab-decorated vase for $5,000. By November, Sotheby Parke Bernet had sold a seven-inch Lalique box for the unbelievable sum of $18,000. Will it last? Chances are, the $18,000 high will level off on similar pieces.

Fine examples of Art Nouveau and Art Deco glass definitely belong in a strong glass investment portfolio. Now is the time to speculate. You can't go very far wrong.

Strangely enough, *early American blown glass* never seems to command the excitement of art glass bidding. Perhaps it is because not much of it comes to market these days. The best pieces seem to be forever bound to museums and private collections. Even during the enthusiasm of the Bicentennial celebration, late eighteenth- and early nineteenth-century pieces could be bought at an S.P.B. auction for just hundreds of dollars. An exception was a bottle collection with several flasks that sold for over $1,000. Yet, early American blown glass as well as some pressed glass can be

Pressed glass, long the staple of antique shops, is still priced for investment. Pitchers, cake plates, and a variety of other clear-glass serving pieces can still be bought for $20 to $500 each. Pictured is the top of a pressed-glass cake plate of unknown origin. It has two designs used by the Boston & Sandwich Glass Co.—the chain and the star. However, it might be Canadian or American of an unlisted pattern.

considered a stable investment, like a share of AT&T. It may not zoom up in price, but it can always be sold for at least what you paid for it.

Often it will do better as a total collection of several hundred pieces than a few scattered commonplace items. Specializing in many types of glass from a single factory, such as Boston & Sandwich or New England Glass Company would be of more interest in the marketplace than one example from several different factories. For some reason, buyers are drawn to total collections of like objects. Perhaps they know subconsciously that other fellow collectors will be on hand. Heaven forbid the other collectors get something they don't.

For a while, anything in *American Brilliant cut glass* (early 1900s) found buyers. This was especially true in the Midwest, where purchasers scrambled to buy it. These days, only the finest signed examples by Libby, Hawkes, Dorflinger, or even 1920s pieces by Sinclaire are doing well. Expect to pay from $450 for a Hawkes cut-glass pitcher to $700 for a pair of Hawkes signed candlesticks in the Brunswick pattern.

The last six years has seen the growth of the *stained-glass market*. Before that, some of the most interesting turn-of-the-century examples could be found at salvage companies for around $50 or in shops for around $100. If you were lucky enough to have bought any designed by L. C. Tiffany, you no doubt have seen the value of your purchase increase to thousands of dollars. Still around, and interesting, are many stained-glass windows from English pubs, private homes, and businesses. They are still plentiful but priced high, from $250 to $1,000, depending on the size and subject. Many a smart investor has willingly paid $50 for fine examples in need of repair. These days, there are craftspeople turning out custom-designed stained-glass windows at every bend in the road. They also do repairs, and many even have a supply of old glass that can possibly match your pieces. If you feel like speculating, you might seek out the best of the new craftspeople and buy for the future. You can always use another stained-glass window in the house, can't you? Who knows, there may be another Tiffany among them. What we take for granted today may become scarce tomorrow.

So far I have been talking about one-of-a-kind pieces. There are also important glass rarities in massed-produced items. After all, *amberina peachblow* and *Carnival glass*, late nineteenth-century *pressed-glass* pieces that once were made by the thousands, are now getting scarcer with time. Some of the choice color patterns such as holly amber and purple slag are already priced over $1,000 for a butter dish or a cake stand, and there are still hundreds of patterns to choose from in the $25 to $50 range. The major problem is with reproductions. Like just about any popular antique, *pattern glass* has been heavily reproduced, and there are reproductions of the 1920s, 1950s, and the 1970s to reckon with. Still, a good glass portfolio should contain a couple of important pieces, perhaps a punch bowl set or a cake stand. What used to be a flea market special has become the highlight of most important antiques shows across the country.

Steuben glass, especially anything with a Frederick Carder signature, bears watching, as the market has been going up for quite a while. Yet, many investors on a beginning level are afraid to pay even $100 for a fine Steuben bowl. Their insecurity stems from a lack of confidence in their own knowledge even though it is still possible to purchase a choice piece for $50 at estate sales and in shops. Once again, signature-happy collectors are reluctant if they can't see a signature or a paper label. They would be wise to buy a copy of *The Glass of Frederick Carder* by Paul V. Gardner that contains the history, identification, and classification of all types of Steuben glass as well as detailed drawings of just about everything the factory made. Hence, a

Is it or isn't it Steuben? The loving-cup form and the deft application of the handles are typical. So is the color, Pomona green. The problem is that there is no signature or paper label. The collector paid $25 for it at an estate sale five years ago. If it is Steuben, it is worth well over $100. Authentication papers from a museum or a reputable appraiser would be necessary to establish its value.

candlestick is shown with colors and size. There is also a paperback price guide by glass authority John F. Hotchkiss that reprints many actual pages from original Steuben factory catalogs. The only way to be a successful investor in glass or anything else is to become an authority yourself.

Many collectors of Steuben were stimulated by the nationwide traveling exhibit organized by the Toledo Museum of Art to celebrate the seventy years of Steuben glass production in 1973. That was the clue that Steuben glass of all types was fast becoming an important investment. While the finest one-of-a-kind designer pieces cost hundreds and thousands of dollars, many of the mass-produced tableware catalog pieces were modestly priced. Thirty or so years ago, pressed- and cut-glass items came to the market as a generation of owners grew old. Now the generation of owners who married in the 1920s and 1930s is disposing of their glassware, and much of it will be the Steuben they received as wedding gifts. This is the time to get acquainted with its characteristics. With hundreds of items made by the company, it is still entirely possible to buy an entire set of tableware for less than something you'd buy in the hardware store today.

You could say that early collectors of *antique silver*, whether American or English (Georgian), have struck gold. While the gold and silver markets on the exchange have had wide ups and downs in the past few years, choice name silver keeps going up, regardless of scrap silver prices. The same holds for gold pieces.   There are several

Coin silver made in the early nineteenth-century by American silversmiths such as Samuel Kirk is one of the few underpriced antiques. A spoon such as this can be found in antiques shops for as little as $10. Tablespoons go for $15. Chances are good that they will soon be reappreciated and go up in value.

schools of thought on the importance of a name in antique silver. Just as the American collector is concerned with signatures on glass, furniture, and porcelain, so there must be a status name on silver. Names worth remembering, at least for the moment, are Hester Bateman, Paul de Lamerie, or Paul Storr for Georgian silver. In American, should you be lucky, you may find a piece of silver by Paul Revere, Myer Myers, or Simeon Soumain. Names like Philip Syng (c. 1769) and Julian Blanck (c. 1679) are nice to be familiar with.

An *American silver* tankard by Syng had a preauction estimate in a January 1979 S.P.B. catalog for $4,000 to $5,000. A rare caudle cup with attributions to Blanck had pre-estimates of $15,000 to $25,000. Nice if you are the seller. Even better if you had the pieces gathering tarnish for twenty years and decided to ship them off. Not all American antique silver is so high priced. At the same auction, you might have bid on nineteenth-century pieces in the $400 to $700 range. Assuming you may want to invest only $3,000 a year in American silver from the eighteenth or nineteenth century, you will be building a strong silver portfolio. From time to time, if the market is good for what you own, you might sell off and buy one spectacular piece from the sale of three. Or begin by collecting small but well-executed pieces by recognized fine eighteenth- and nineteenth-century silversmiths, for a collection of several hundred pieces can represent an important investment. This could be flatware or such items as nutmeg graters or salt dips.

The area of *Georgian silver* from the early eighteenth to mid-nineteenth century is considered a solid investment, some more secure than others. For instance, though Hester Bateman and Paul Storr are among the best-known Georgian silversmiths with the general collecting public they are not necessarily the best. In fact, one top dealer, Virginia Packer, who with her husband, Charles, owns a shop dealing only in Georgian silver, doesn't recommend Bateman.

"When a person wants to buy a Bateman piece it is a sign of insecurity," she said. "Hester ran a factory operation and took advantage of the Industrial Revolution to grind out lots of lightweight stuff to please a rising middle class. She didn't do any pieces for royalty." Instead Packer, tries to educate serious collector-customers about the fine workmanship of Ebenezer Coker, John Scofield, and Richard and David Hennells. Their work was consistently good. As might be expected, a set of four candlesticks by Coker, c. 1771, carries an $11,000 price tag. Packer suggested that investors should avoid the fad silversmiths and that beginners should build up a collection of good flatware. Also to be considered are fish slicers, sugar tongs, and wine funnels all of which are priced at under $200 each.

As in other areas of antiques, silver by famous makers has been faked by such trickery as the placement of a hallmark from a spoon on a higher-priced item. Extensive repairs cleverly camouflaged lower the value. Hallmarks should be clear, and the design should be not only good but of the period. Because silversmiths turned out incredible quantities of silver during the reign of George III, there is still quite a bit around, but not all of it is investment quality.

Many collectors are buying the best examples of *Victorian silver* and *silver plate* for future speculation. With elegant pieces from the early Victorian period still priced under $100, why not dabble in this market? Silver-plate items are roughly one-third the price of solid silver, and there are many silver spinoffs in the Victorian market: silver deposit, silver overlay, silver lustre, and silver resist.

Another neglected area for investment is *coin-silver pieces*; and one of the most famous makers was Samuel Kirk. Coin-silver serving spoons dating from the early nineteenth century can be purchased in shops for $50.

These are only a few of the many opportunities that exist in both established and potential categories, but before you spend one nickel on any item, make sure you know its financial history. How did it do ten years ago? Was it even considered worth collecting then? What has made its price go up: an artificially created market with fanfare and publicity, shortage of the item, or an important discovery in this category? All of these facts should be considered before you assemble your portfolio.

3.
What Others Are Investing In: Why

When it comes to using the term "investment," many collectors pass it off. "We collect only for pleasure," many have said. Yet, when you pin them down, "investment" is no longer a dirty word. Despite their protestations, it becomes obvious that money making is a consideration that determines what they buy, how often they buy, and when they sell. In the first place, a collector must know what the prices are for like objects. Nobody but a fool would sell or buy without having some kind of idea as to the current market value of his collection. It doesn't matter whether people dabble in collectibles on a nickel-and-dime level or in rare enamels and porcelains for the thousands of dollars. Each collector you will meet on the following pages keeps a close eye on market developments.

One of the most fascinating aspects of collecting, aside from monetary and pleasurable benefits is its direct relation to the individual involved. A person who might not otherwise be financially or socially able to move out of his dominant lifestyle becomes an important individual as a collector. Celebrities and millionaires may include him in their collecting world, especially in the field of *miniatures collecting*. For many years, collecting miniatures, from eighteenth-century English silver to twentieth-century complete miniature rooms, was a hobby for only the wealthy. The change came when people learned how much fun it was to make the miniature pieces themselves. Suddenly the fireman discovered he could create a prize-winning model room alongside the wealthy suburban housewife's and achieve personal recognition outside his own group.

Many have interwoven collecting with their businesses. I am not speaking of the usual antiques dealers who rent shop space but the serious collectors who because of luck, knowledge, and smart buying become overstocked. Generally, they are already in some other line of business. The natural sequence is for them to open a related business based on their collections.

65

Mary Jane Graham, an interior decorator in a posh midwestern suburb, had collected miniatures for years. About seven years ago, she observed that there were many individual craftspeople who specialized in different types of miniatures. She put them all together in one of the most successful miniatures shops in the country: It's a Small World! She can enjoy the best of two small worlds by buying for herself and her business. In this case, you can ask, where does investing end and business and pleasure begin? Mary Jane Graham sees the important silver, textiles, and furniture miniatures being made today as good investments. To that end, she has collected over 500 of the finest miniatures craftspeople under one shop roof. As she pointed out, there are many mass-produced miniature items, "but the finest are certainly the antiques of tomorrow. Many of the pieces are signed, and most are one of a kind." Graham also observed that many of the detailed miniature rooms made by suburban housewives will also be in the heirloom class in another twenty-five years. "Especially those that are duplicates of the owner's own rooms or lifestyle. Just as paintings reflect our decorative arts past, so do these rooms. This is one investment you can make with your own hands."

Another area being considered by collectors is *Russian art and artifacts*. In 1979 it was stimulated by a traveling exhibition, "The Art of Russia, 1800–1850," sponsored by several midwestern universities. During the same year, there were other exhibits around the country displaying everything from Fabergé jewelry to ballet costumes. Possible reasons for the sudden influx of Russian shows could be attributed to the Arts and Artifacts Indemnity Act that was passed by Congress in 1975. It at least paved the way for exhibits from difficult countries by paying some of the insurance for valuable foreign exchange exhibitions. It has been mainly the last three years that have seen a wide variety of collectors buying Russiana. Everything from icons to enamelled spoons has found buyers and created an active new market. Apparently not only are recent emigrés putting up small items at auction but dealers are also doing a brisk business in some of the more expensive bric-a-brac. As soon as Russian cultural objects were liquidated, they found their way to an eager United States market.

In the 1971–72 department breakdown of S.P.B. sales, Russian items brought a sales total of $408,900. By 1976–77 the total was $856,040.

Nineteenth-century Russian porcelain has found a growing group of collectors putting in substantial bids. For many years, there were only a few notable antique galleries such as *A La Vieille Russie* in New York that specialized in the Russian decorative arts. Now shops are springing up in major cities across the country. Where there is a demand, there has to be a supply.

According to an article in the January 1979 issue of *Antiques World* magazine, "Collecting non-Russian antiques in the Soviet Union is difficult, because the domestic source is hardly ever renewed from abroad and what remained from pre-Revolutionary times has long since been redistributed. So, inevitably, the focus of the Soviet antiques market is on Russian antiques."

California is a good market for buying and selling Russian arts. Perhaps this is in part due to the large Russian colony in San Francisco. In 1977 one of the most important exhibits of Russian paintings sent from the Soviet Union was on display. Many were icons dating back to the fourteenth century. At that time, one dealer in Russian decorative arts, David Orgell of exclusive North Rodeo Drive in Beverly Hills, found few interested Americans. Most of his customers came from the Middle East. At that time, he stated that Fabergé and Russian items of virtu "haven't kept pace with such fashions as English silver, Victorian jewelry, and French porcelains." Nor did he think the Russian items could be put into an investment category. However, he also has a group of monied younger American collectors who collect pre-Revolutionary Russian items, especially bronzes. These are often by such sculptors as Lanceret or Woerffel. Orgell isn't your everyday antiques investor, not when he has such offerings as the Tricentennial Fabergé Easter Egg of 1913 priced at over $100,000. Now that's an investment.

In Russia, commission stores accept antiques from Russians for only a 7 percent commission of the sale price, which applies only if the piece is sold. This has forced Russians to find other ways to make money from their antiques. The ones that do find their way to the commission store are usually nineteenth century. It was at commission stores that Marjorie Merriweather Post began her collection of rare Russian antiques before anybody else was thinking about it.

Interesting to note, in Russia as in the United States, the burden of knowledge in sales transactions is upon the seller. If you don't know what you own and something about its value, you may dispose of a valuable antique. No wonder Fabergé eggs, rare glass, and icons found their way into the Post collection.

The lifestyle of the average Soviet citizen also determines his collecting habits. Most live in small and few rooms where there is little room for early nineteenth-century furniture and lots of bric-a-brac. Hence these items find their way to market, and many of the finest pieces are found these days in Paris and New York.

American collectors in the young professional group seem to be buying investments they also enjoy living with, which accounts for the increase in purchases of antique furniture. The budget-minded who bought golden oak when it was junk shop special have seen it become at least a momentary successful investment. As one collector related with glee, "I found a huge round golden oak table with paw feet just sitting in an alley here in Pittsburgh. When I brought it home, my wife thought I'd lost my marbles. Today, if I wanted to sell it, the price would be $2,000. That is *if*."

Today's young collectors often do better with their investments because of their eclectic tastes. They don't worry about mixing a funky wicker floor lamp with a pleated-silk and tasseled shade, with a couple of patchwork quilt wall hangings. This eclectic market does interesting things to the overall auction picture. "Whatever turns you on" seems to be the only gauge or limitation to the type of object.

Buying the so-called *nostalgia items* began with college students, who then branched out into collectibles of every variety. One young man who began buying original movie posters when they were almost giveaways recently sold them to pay for his last year of college.

One of the fastest growing areas for collectors is not even antiques: contemporary *American Indian decorative art*. When Joan and Bud Towne bought their first pieces of Indian jewelry seven years ago, it was because they fell in love with it, "not as an investment." Today their collection of over a thousand examples of both new and old American Indian artifacts and art is more than an important investment growing constantly in monetary value. It has grown into one of the recognized shops in the United States: The Squash Blossom in Highland Park, Illinois. They admit that part of their success both in collecting and business is their ability to recognize new talent.

"We opened our first shop six months after our visit to Albuquerque, New Mexico. At that time, we purchased just a small amount of jewelry and pottery," Joan said. "It is easier for collectors to buy now, because there are many fine books on the subject. *Art and Indian Individualists* by Guy and Doris Mothan and the quarterly *American Indian Art* magazine have been a terrific help in educating the public on who is selling and what is available."

In 1973 various collectors' trade publications noted that interest in American

Indian-made items was at an all-time high. This interest coincided with the controversy at Wounded Knee, South Dakota. Even that early, trade publications warned of fakes and foreign-made products that were being passed off as genuine Indian items. This isn't a problem for the Townes, who pride themselves not only on direct purchases from the craftsmen but also on a good personal relationship with them. When they decide to have a special showing of one or more artists, they stay at their large home and get to know each other as collector and craftsperson.

Probably one of the biggest events towards establishing prices in Indian objects were the McCormick auctions in Phoenix, Arizona, five years ago and the 1975 S.P.B. auction, also in Phoenix, of the C. G. Wallace collection. "It would be a good idea for collectors to become familiar with Wallace and his collections," advised the Townes. His collection included more than 2,500 items. Wallace lived and worked on the Zuni Reservation in northwestern New Mexico. He got a job in an Indian trading post and, several years later, bought the post in the village of Zuni. In their publicity blurb for the collection, Sotheby Parke Bernet quoted Wallace, "From the very beginning, I was interested in their artistic ability, their ways of worship, and how they combined religion and pleasure together in their daily lives." Wallace impressed upon the Indians that they should stay with tradition and do unique pieces. The individuality and authenticity were, he believed, what made Indian jewelry valuable.

By 1919 Wallace had become well acquainted with the five silversmiths in his village. Their work was primarily for their own people and some for the Navaho. Wallace marketed pieces even during the Depression. At the time of the auction, he estimated that since the 1920s, prices have soared ten to twelve times over the price for which he originally sold his pieces. "I didn't want their work to become too common," he said. The Townes note that Wallace made a statement collectors and the investors should seriously consider about silversmithing. "There are only a few keeping the quality way up. They're the ones making big money. There's such a demand for Indian jewelry that anything can be sold."

The Townes feel that in *Hopi jewelry* the most important name is Charles Lalome. "Indians are now deeply involved in fine art. While they aren't accepted as fine artists by the eastern seaboard art critics, they are eagerly purchased as such by European and Japanese investor-collectors. Many of our customers who plan to travel abroad buy Indian art as gifts."

When the Townes began collecting they had one room they called Indian. Now they have a house filled with Indian and southwestern art. "I like to think these are tomorrow's antiques," Bud Towne said. "As Indian tribes become more sophisticated, there are few of the crafts being done. There aren't that many naive pieces still around. Of course, Indian art will go up—that is, the best pieces, not the tourist art. That is what really damaged the image of Indian art crafts. People have a picture in their minds of getting souvenirs at the train depots. Europeans have more respect for American Indian art than we do. For instance, I recently sent a feathered headdress back with a manager of Gucci when he returned to Italy, and Doug Hyde and Kevin Redskin just did an exhibit at Pierre Cardin in Paris."

The Townes exhibit their private collections at museums around the country whenever possible. "It's been shown in the Nassau County Museum in Glen Cove, New York, and The Gerhard Miller Gallery in Door County, Wisconsin. This is bound to create more interest and more collectors who will buy." They feel that The Institute of American Indian Art, the first school for Indian artists in Santa Fe, has done much to correct public thinking on American Indian Art. "Most of the top Indian contemporary artists are graduates," the Townes pointed out. Allan Hauser, considered the dean of Indian sculptors, holds classes there.

Bud Towne has purchased many metal sculptures by American Indian sculptor Charles Pratt. Shown here is Pratt's "Ear of Corn". Another choice Pratt piece is a cast bronze chess set complete with cowboy and Indian chessmen. Its original cost was $2,000 several years ago. It has appreciated in value since then.

This small section of the Towne's family-room wall shows some of the diversity in American Indian art and artifacts. The large painting to the right is an oil by Kevin Red Star. The dolls are dancing figures by Pueblo craftswoman Lucy Lowden. Also considered an important artifact is the silver pot with the 14k gold bear on top. Next to it is a fetish bowl of black jet overlaid with shells.

Joan Towne considers contemporary Indian baskets as an important long-term investment. Baskets such as this may cost several hundred dollars today. Scarcity and quality of workmanship will be important factors in determining their price several years from now. Shown is a favorite doll basket made by the Papago tribe, one of four tribes still doing basketry. It and many other pieces in the Townes' collection were purchased last year at the Indian market in Santa Fe during a two-week ceremonial and exhibit event.

"We collect everything. That's part of our problem," laughed Joan. Their family entertainment room is wall-to-wall pottery, paintings, Kachina dolls, and sculpture. "We like pots and sculpture best. The *Pueblo pottery* is all handworked and a very tedious process. Currently the most expensive and interesting style of pottery are the *Cochiti story dolls*. They were originally created by Helen Cordero. Now their cost for the large dolls (over a foot high) is $2,000 or more." The Townes advise that other artists are doing similar pieces. "Beginning collectors shouldn't hesitate to buy on time and buy the finest you can. A small sculpture by Doug Hyde begins at around $275. A large piece, such as "Medicine Woman" carved from Colorado alabaster, can cost $2,250."

Another wall of their home is filled with shelves of *Pueblo pots* and *baskets*. "The real money is in the old baskets," Bud said. "We were lucky enough to buy an entire collection of old baskets about five years ago. Now they are priceless. Beginners should consider buying the Hopi coiled plaques (shallow baskets), because they aren't being done much anymore. Prices will really go up when the last basket is made. Now a small one costs around $100." As in all areas of collecting, there are names to be well remembered. The Townes have bought such artists in pottery as Joseph Lone Wolf and Tony Da, grandson of the revered potter Maria Da. "A Lone Wolf pot can cost as much as $20,000."

American Indian sculptor Doug Hyde is considered one of the masters in this field. Works such as this carved alabaster sculpture are considered important art investments by collectors of American Indian Art. Large sculptures may cost over $2,500. A beginning collector can find small, table size pieces for around $300.

The Townes have also found that keeping an eye on what artifacts aren't being made or are about not to be made can lead to good investments. They cite the *corn-husk masks* woven by the Iroquois, which used to be sold for $45. Now the Iroquois are more concerned with keeping the masks as important traditional ceremonial pieces, and as a result, the few that come to market will be probably triple in price before long. The Townes are also on the lookout for revivals of old Indian crafts such as *ink on buffalo hide paintings*. A new one by Paha Ska, chief of the Sioux, costs around $650.

As far as older items go, the Townes point to strong figures. "For the last two decades authentic Indian pottery has been increasing in value by about 20 percent per year. For acknowledged top potters, that figure is closer to 90 percent. Many collectors are willing to pay over $3,000 for a name potter. The finest sign and date their work on the bottom. Choice, of course, would be the polished black pottery first made in 1919 by Maria and Julian Martinez. They were among the early Pueblo craftsmen who gave a new push and image to a traditional craft.

"Look at what things went for at the Wallace auction just four years ago," they said. "That was only the beginning of this market." A set of six inlaid *Zuni figures* made in 1941 by Red Leakala was bid in at $7,000, and a set of sixteen *Navajo wooden dancing figures* made by Klitso Deadman in 1927 sold for $6,000.

A representative for the American Indian Arts Center in New York offered a caution: "Many articles sold in the Southwest are made in Hong Kong, Taiwan, and Japan, then falsely labeled as American Indian." He advised:

—Indian rugs are heavy, not lightweight.

—The best merchandise is individually made.

—Beware when there is more than one of an item as it will be machine made. Mass-produced silver items are lighter in weight than handmade items. There are no trademarks on individually made pieces.

—Avoid pieces with tags reading "Indian designed" or "Indian-type."

Dennis Todaro, another collector, is as convinced as the Townes that his collection of art and artifacts is an important investment. In fact, every room of his small one-bedroom apartment is filled to overflowing with *industrial comic art*. Included are toys, games, even soap shapes like Orphan Annie and popular cartoon characters. The bedroom has been given over to banks, posters, and other objects fashioned in the image of Charlie Chaplin, Mickey Mouse, and Superman.

He says it all began when he was a small boy and his mother bought him some do-it-yourself toy cartoon character kits. Since then, Todaro has logged 100,000 miles in search of the ultimate Mickey Mouse, or "just hunting things." The youthful grandfather of three has even discovered new items while on his job as a painting contractor. One discovery was a Mickey Mouse sound slide-film projector for $75. It is original and complete right down to its record player needle. "I wouldn't sell it today for $300," he says.

Winding up a rare tin Charlie Chaplin toy, he told me, "I'm just small potatoes in a rich man's sport. In this market you have to stay ahead to make any money." Staying ahead means buying up quantities of relatively new items such as space toys, and watching for special exhibits that will create interest in a new comic toy. "For instance, I figure the hottest items are new *space toys*. The Chicago Art Institute gift shop is having an exhibit called "Robo Kaiju" from Japan, a survey of American and Japanese science fiction toys. These are the blue-chip toys of tomorrow, and the time to buy is now, when you don't have to pay hundreds of dollars."

In this market, values are also influenced by other outside factors such as movies, TV specials on, for instance, Charlie Chaplin, and of course special events such as Mickey Mouse's 50th birthday.

Todaro admits to being a "big Mickey freak." When he and his wife combined a business and pleasure trip to California last year, they naturally stopped at the Disney studios. Todaro bought in quantity some anniversary reproductions of the original Ingersol Mickey wristwatch for $17.95. "Be sure you keep the original card and plastic case with Mickey's picture on it," he advised. "The minute a collectible like this is made, it starts going up in value. These watches are bound to keep rising as the years pass by."

According to Todaro, collectors in this field do most of their heavy buying from each other. You'd better believe there is some hot and hectic trading at the toy shows. "Before the show is when the best stuff changes hands," he said. "Collectors get together in motel rooms and it's every man for himself." Unlike other areas of collecting, this field has no specialized dealers.

"If you know how to repair the windups, you can come out way ahead. Condition is everything. To get the right price, windups have to work. They're some of the most expensive pieces when they work." Before I knew it, he had a tin Orphan Annie jumping rope while a Ham and Sam team played the piano and Charlie Chaplin in

Dennis Todaro likes to think of himself as a winner. And why not? To the far right is a prize-winning ribbon for best toy display at one of the local Chicago area toy shows. At current market values, you are looking at over $2,000 worth of industrial comic art.

On the left is a replica nodder of Lou Gehrig, baseball great. On the right is a less-than-flattering Winston Churchill. Staffordshire versions would cost from $75 to $100. These two have a current value of from $50 to $75.

Sometimes the box is just as important as the object. Having the original box for this tin Charlie Chaplin windup toy doubles the value. Dennis Todaro found the toy on the right in nonworking order. By repairing it, he has increased his investment and ensured its value. The Chaplin windup toy on the left is considered a rarity because it has the original clothing in good condition.

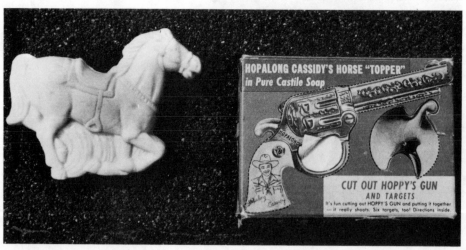

Would you believe that soap can be an investment? Well, at least a Hopalong Cassidy horse in the Todaro collection is going up in value. Even Todaro wouldn't say it was eventually going to be worth hundreds of dollars, but as part of his collection, it will continue to appreciate.

his little tramp outfit shuffled along. These three toys alone have a market value of over $1,000.

Todaro researches whenever possible. He learned that many of the top makers of *comic windup toys* were working in Germany prior to World War II. Hitler hated Mickey Mouse and all cartoon tin toys. He felt they corrupted the minds of little boys. So he closed all the Nifty Toy factories. Early closing during their period of manufacturing is what had made these toys so expensive. Also, they were partially hand-painted on tin. Barney Google's horse, Spark Plug, for instance, was made in that factory before it closed. Its current value is around $1,800. Todaro is still dickering over a rare tin Chaplin windup toy that has seven movements and a price of about $1,800. "I know of only two others. One is in a museum and the other is owned by Oona O'Neill Chaplin."

All told, Todaro figures he has seventy-five different categories including paper, tin, china, iron, and plaster. Speaking of plaster, he lugged out two fourteen-inch-high *plaster figurines* of Orphan Annie and Sandy. The likenesses weren't very realistic, but he said, "That doesn't matter. These carnival prizes were made in the 1930s in limited supply. Not many have survived, because they were considered cheap and they chipped easily. That's what makes them rare. They're worth $40 a piece today. I don't know of any others who are collecting them either."

In the paper category, Todaro has an *original cover art* for a Popeye Big Little Book worth more than $500 along with dozens of early first-edition comics and Big Little Books, posters, and original cartoon cels from Disney cartoons. There are also labeled boxes that may or may not contain toys. "Sometimes the box is as important as the contents. They are the first things tossed," he advised.

Todaro suggests that beginning collectors not pay too much attention to the price guides. "Generally, they aren't accurate. You can't keep up fast enough with the price changes." Like other collector-investors Todaro realizes his is a highly speculative field. "The bottom could fall out if there is a recession, unlike the established antiques market. Of course, the blue-chip toys such as "Popeye in the Spinach Cart" made of cast iron will always be marketable. The early toys, especially the ones made of iron, can be considered an established market." Todaro is fortunate to own an original with the King Features Syndicate stamp on it. The value as of January 1979 was $695. "When a new price record is established at auction for a specific type of toy, you can figure that it is also a blue-chip item. A Mickey Mouse *hurdy-gurdy toy* did just that at a London auction a few years ago. The new price was $3,600. Instantly every collector hopes to find one." Another blue-chip toy is a seven-inch-high Mickey Mouse, valued at around $9,000. So far, there are only two known in existence. One of Todaro's blue-chip discoveries turned out to be a twelve-inch-high battery-operated Popeye toy that blows bubbles out of his pipe, then eats a can of spinach. Todaro turned down an offer of $250 last year. "That's an investment that will keep appreciating," he said.

Much of the current mass appeal of toy collectibles, according to Todaro, is that they are the toys of the working class, made to appeal to a mass audience. Any serious collector must keep up with what's happening in the buying and trading market. But even more important, Todaro believes, is research. There are old toy catalogs yet to be discovered, and old toys waiting to set net price records. "Know who the foremost toy manufacturers were, the countries they worked in, and when. Probably tops in the tin toy field is Fernand Martene, followed by Louis Marx." He also advised collectors to go to as many toy shows as possible and exchange ideas with other collectors. If you need an appraisal, get it from a reputable collector. The market changes so rapidly that only an involved collector can stay on top of what's happening.

Allen Baker is a collector who believes, "It's always the middle-price collector who gets hurt. The finest pieces, whether antiques or collectibles, will always command a good price. But the so-so pieces, even though they go up, are more difficult to sell." Baker's collection contains the finest examples of Wedgwood, eighteenth-century furniture, and glass, and literally hundreds of other blue-chip pieces. "I buy as a collector. I hope that in the long run, I will come out ahead. But I can't say I buy strictly for investment. I have to like the object, or need it to enhance an existing collection or to begin a new one."

Baker, who began collecting only nine years ago, believes it's never too late to get into collecting. "If people waited to get started at the right historical time, they'd be dead. How well you do with your investing depends on your tracking down all good leads—auctions, sales, and word of collections going on sale." Baker recently cashed in on one of his collections, Japanese Inro, which are small medicine boxes worn centuries ago. He had been collecting them for seven years, and following the trends in American and European markets, he calculated this was a good time to sell. He realized approximately $15,000, "the down payment on a Florida condo," he said, smiling broadly.

Baker feels that the biggest auction houses are the best places to sell really choice items. They get the best, most expensive pieces as well as the most sophisticated, monied buyers. "You have to take your fine items to London and New York. Before you sell at auction, you must get an appointment with the auction specialist in the field you are going to sell. Dealers are charged only 6 percent by the auction house instead of the 10 percent. Many of the large auction houses like Sotheby Parke Bernet send out traveling representatives to major cities where they don't have galleries. That's a good opportunity to take items in for an appraisal and a preauction estimate."

Baker feels that the postwar baby boom is creating a new housing crunch. "That will in turn create a huge new market when this group has a high disposable income." He keeps complete records and card files of every item in his collection. Each contains the item, description, and insurance number. Also listed are any reference books where the objects have been photographed or found and any similar items that have gone at auction or have been exhibited at museum shows. "Take pictures by all means and attach them to the card," he advised.

Among his favorites is a *box collection* that includes vinaigrettes, nutmeg grinders, traveling wax seals, Russian silver, and a Dutch silver snuff box. Included are what he believes are fine examples of contemporary boxes. The miniatures are in a glass display curio table, and the larger boxes are scattered about his large apartment. One bargain he recalled was a Queen Anne wooden lace box that he bought for $60. Currently, it is worth over $200.

"I don't hesitate to buy a fine piece even if it needs restoration. Not long ago, I previewed some furniture at a Southeby Parke Bernet auction in New York that needed extensive restoration. After all, if it were really made before 1830, it isn't unreasonable to overlook the condition. Not so on a piece of eighteenth-century Wedgwood, art glass, or Chinese porcelain. A single chip lowers the price 10 percent."

As a collector of eighteenth- and early nineteenth-century *Wedgwood*, Baker observed that some of the current ripoffs are new pieces with the words "made in England" ground off, dating back the piece at least 100 years and upping the price. If you aren't knowledgeable as to feel and appearance, you might be taken in. After all, even an authentic Rosaline by Steuben is so expensive that it is now being reproduced.

Baker recalled when he first began collecting he tried to buy every piece of dark

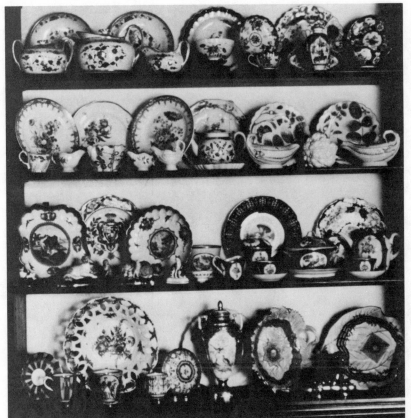

A sizable portion of Allen Baker's magnificent porcelain collection is housed in a massive dining room cabinet and includes Dr. Wall, Worcester, Sèvres, Chelsea, and Swansea. Baker advised that pieces must be in mint condition to be considered investment quality.

A curio table contains important investments in objects of virtu. Among these blue-chip antiques are paperweights, miniature portraits painted on porcelain, and some Russian enamel spoons as well as small relics of Egyptology.

CREDIT: Allen Baker Collection

When other collectors abandoned the snuff bottle market several years ago, Allen Baker saw it as an opportunity to buy some good pieces at depressed prices. Each bottle is listed in a card file which includes its insurance number, a photograph, and the names of any auctions where it may have been sold.

blue Wedgwood he could find. "That was before I realized it wasn't choice, and was Victorian. I put an ad in the paper and got rid of all of it for $1,500. Then I began going to England, where I could find better pieces, cheaper than in the United States."

Art Nouveau and Art Deco pieces mix happily with an English secretary-bookcase or miniature portraits from the eighteenth century. "I have found that Milwaukee, St. Louis, and Chicago are excellent areas to buy fantastic Art Nouveau and Art Deco cheaply. I began buying it several years ahead of everybody else when it really was inexpensive. For instance, I bought a bronze by Chiparus at a Chicago auction for $125. I didn't even know whether it was signed or what it was at the time, I just liked

Long before other collectors were even thinking about Art Deco objects, collector Allen Baker began buying them. He is pictured with a fine Chiparus bronze in the Art Deco style. Typical of the use of unusual materials and inlays during this period is the ivory cloche worn by the figurine. Baker paid only a fraction of its current price.

it. Today it's valued at $2,000." Baker thinks his most important investment is his large collection of reference books. "I couldn't do without them." For investors considering fine eighteenth-century or even Art Deco decorative art, he advised, "Look for things that have handwork that can no longer be duplicated."

Collectors Michael and Francie Cowen have learned that even in the over-populated field of Oriental antiques, there still can be a margin of profit for new collectors. When they began collecting seriously ten years ago, prices were still rising for Chinese antiques. In fact, at first glance Michael wasn't sure whether he could afford to get involved. The answer seemed to be collecting Japanese artifacts and Chinese glass such as *Peking glass*, for prices were quite low for both areas of collecting at that time. During Michael's eighteen months in the Far East as a Marine, he studied the various art forms and also acquired Japanese lacquerware. He is now considered one of the renowned experts in Japanese and modern art. "You'd be amazed how well a Picasso etching goes with a Japanese woodblock print."

The Cowens have their cake and eat it too. Michael has parlayed his love of fine art into a relatively new job classification: corporate art consultant. His home in a midwestern suburb is also his office. "The only problem," he confided, "is parting with an acquisition I have purchased for a client. We may live with it for a couple of days, then out it goes." Although he wouldn't let them be mentioned, his clients are among some of Chicago's most prestigious banks, corporations, and art dealers.

"As a private collector, my goal is to get the finest of what is not only affordable but available. The secret to collecting is, whatever you buy must be the best example of its type. Then you can use it for comparison." He recalled buying his first important piece, a signed Picasso etching, on time payments for $900. It's now worth around $8,500.

One corner of the family den is filled with an impressive collection of Peking glass. "Only recently has it been appreciated in the United States," Cowen noted. His pieces date to the eighteenth and nineteenth centuries. "There is a similarity between Peking glass and Gallé art glass. Both are a type of cameo glass, often with applied carved-glass designs such as leaves and flowers." Cowen also pointed out that Peking glass is one of many Oriental artifacts being reproduced. "The only way to keep from being ripped off," he advised, "is to really know what the early pieces look like. With prices ranging in the high hundreds of dollars, you can't afford not to know what the authentic pieces look like."

The Cowens have made many a discovery at local estate sales and auctions for a fraction of their value. He said one way to identify old Peking glass is by the depth of the cutting and the way the glass has been heated to resemble jade, amethyst, and hard stones.

Traveling to the New York auctions has plumped up the Cowens' collections. "If we see something we like, we'll eat a lot of hot dogs to pay for it. For example, we just bought a good abstract expressionist painting worth $9,000. We paid $2,000." They have found the best way to upgrade their collections is to periodically sell off. "We have been lucky advertising in New York papers or selling at auctions. Prices are highest in New York."

A few years ago, Michael joined the American Society of Appraisers. "This is one of the ways for people to find reputable and knowledgeable persons to appraise their collections. There are so many art ripoffs today, either you have to know what you are buying or hire somebody who does."

Like so many collectors who are doing well in the antiques market, the Cowens are reluctant to classify their collections as investments. "Only an investment in pleasure. It's not how much you spend but how well you spend it," they said.

You might say that collectors Karen and Dick Commer not only enjoy their art investment but have turned it into a profitable business venture as well. They ensure its constant spiral growth pattern in the collectibles art market by their steady public relations and promotion of Cartoonerville and its collection of *original* and *comic art*. Their growing business, now strictly mail order, is proof that plenty of other investors feel that the cartoon is a viable art form. One of their customer-collectors, a well-to-do St. Louis stockbroker, definitely collects original cartoon art for investment purposes. He feels it is a "chronicle of the times: a page out of history that graphically shows who we are and what we're all about."

The Commers may not have been the first to recognize the importance of this art form, but their gallery in Huntington, New York, has become one of the focal points for exhibits and special events in the United States. Museums and universities have been building collections during the past fifty years, now more private collectors are involved. Commer and his wife, Karen, note that Benjamin Franklin probably drew the first important political cartoon in the colonies, his "Don't tread on me" cartoon that helped the colonists mobilize in their struggle for freedom from British domi-

Cartoon collectors Karen and Dick Commer have cornered the market in the new area of cartoon collecting. Among their favorites is this caricature of them by award-winning magazine cartoonist Don Orehek. The Commers have turned their collection into a successful business that recently became direct mail to collectors.

A popular contemporary cartoonist, Brickman, would represent a good start for a collector, according to the Commers. His social satire makes him an investment at prices from $75 to $150. It wasn't too long ago that cartoonists sent originals to admirers who wrote asking for them. Today, those giveaways can be worth $2,000.

nation. Since the Commers began collecting seriously seven years ago, they have seen original comic art sometimes quadruple in price. Dick Commer was introduced to comic art as a boy. His father was a boyhood friend of Walt Disney in Kansas City. When he visited Disney in California, he was given several original, autographed Disney cartoons.

Collectors can specialize in any of several types of original cartoons. There is the *comic strip* (usually appears in the daily and Sunday newspaper comic section); the *cartoon panel* (the one-panel gag cartoon, such as the syndicated newspaper feature "They'll Do It Every Time" or the more sophisticated examples from magazines like *Playboy* and *The New Yorker*); the *political cartoon* (usually appears on the editorial page of a daily newspaper and on the pages of national news magazines); the *comic book page* (the actual artwork done for comic books, such as *Marvel Comics' Spiderman*); and the *animated cartoon cel* (such as a scene from a Walt Disney animated movie).

Like so many examples of early American art forms in their early stages, many original cartoons were thrown away after they were printed. One example was George Herriman's *Krazy Kat* cartoons. During Herriman's lifetime there was no collector's market. Today his cartoons are considered priceless, and originals find anxious collectors waiting to plunk down from $1,000 to $5,000.

A beginning collector might consider original cartoon art by today's contemporary artists as future investments. Currently, they are reasonably priced. Right now even the Commers admit that second-guessing tomorrow's most important contemporary artists would be just that—a guess. However, they think some of the best buys are in today's underpriced cartoons, and suggest a Sunday *Johnny Hazard* page by Frank Robbins or a page of comic book art by George Evans. "Evans," said Commer, "is considered by many of his peers to be the leading aviation-adventure illustrator in American cartoons today." Commer also noted that Morrie Brickman's satirical *The Small Society* cartoons, can be purchased for as low as $75. Others in the contemporary category are priced from $40 to $400.

Of course, if you want an already accepted investment, you can pay as much as $5,000. This could get you an illustration by Alex Raymond, creator of *Flash Gordon*. "He is the finest illustrator in the business, the Picasso of cartoonists," said Commer.

Some examples of prices as of January 1979 are: a Charles Schulz *Peanuts* daily begins at $210; a popular Al Capp *Li'l Abner* daily goes for $75 and up; and a Harold Gray *Little Orphan Annie* daily from 1949 sells for $300. If all the usual barometers applied to other areas of the antiques market hold true to the comic art field, *Little Orphan Annie* should go up steadily as long as the musical *Annie* is top box office. Whether or not it will then level off or even drop is the chance speculators will have to take. Obviously they can't go too far wrong.

When the Commers became the first distributors of comic art, there hadn't been any sufficient quantity to offer to the public. Collectors had to buy piecemeal at auctions or in shops. (I can recall buying three years ago a vintage John McCutcheon eight-panel original cartoon for $75 in an antiques shop. Its current value is around $800.) At the rate the Commers are going, they may have to change their standard salutation of "See you in the funny papers" to "We're laughing all the way to the bank."

"I'm a hobbyist, not an investor," Ed Jensen told me. "I don't sell any of my political collections." Presently he has some 5,000 political campaign buttons, posters, photographs, and cartoons. "It's the professional person who seems to be buying for investment. Doctors and lawyers turn up at the conventions and buy up thousands of items at a time."

Jensen began his *political memorabilia* collection thirteen years ago. His first purchase was a $4 McKinley-Teddy Roosevelt jugate pin (when both candidate portraits are on one pin). "I wanted to find out more about it, so I looked through the yellow pages and found a store specializing in political items," he recalled. "From them I learned about the American Political Items Collectors club. I've been a member ever since." About that McKinley-Roosevelt purchase, it is presently worth over $100.

Ed Jensen is pictured here with one of his favorite finds: a rare pillow depicting Theodore Roosevelt as a bear.

Jensen says that when you consider the thousands of different types of *campaign buttons* made over the years, they haven't really gone up that much. "During the 1976 campaign, there were Carter buttons that became rarities overnight. Such was the case with the special 'Carter and Howlett for Governor of Illinois' button. At that time, collectors were offering from $50 to $75 for this three-inch button. They knew it was going to be a future rarity. However, other types that go up during a convention can go down pretty fast. This happened with 'Tennesseeans for Carter' buttons. During the convention, the large size cost $30 to $35. Now the value is way down." He also mentioned the *Lincoln ferrotypes* that used to sell for around $60. They have doubled in price. "However," he noted, "an early McKinley button that cost $4 a year ago is now only $6. On the other hand, Eugene Debs buttons are presently going up fast."

One of the many collections of political buttons and Presidential campaign items that Ed Jensen has put behind protective glass frames. He has acquired many unusual items not only by trading but by diligent searching in shops and flea markets.

Jensen suggested some tips for finding investment items. "After a man becomes President, look for buttons showing the political offices he held before. For example, consider a "Truman for Senator" button. Ten years ago that button was worth $17 or so. At that time, I passed it up. Then I noticed, last year at our convention, they were selling for $145. I bought one. Now they have a price tag of $175." Another tip; third parties are rarer than the usual Democrat or Republican buttons, and it's their rarity that can make them important.

"If you are really lucky, you may find the most expensive political pin there is, a four-inch "John W. Davis for President." He was a Democrat who ran against Calvin Coolidge in 1924, but since he wasn't expected to have a ghost of a chance, not many buttons were put out. The rarity makes a single button worth $1,300 to a collector."

Although he disclaims being an investor, Jensen admitted to "buying a *Coolidge-Davis jugate*" from a collector because it is an unusual pin. There is a good possibility that it will go up quite a bit. He still regrets the one that got away, a large collection he could have had for only $25. One of the discoveries from that collection, and the only item he bought, was a Hoover-Curtis jugate. "I paid $15 for it. Today it is worth $500."

Like most collectors, Jensen doesn't limit himself to a single political category. He has a *Bryan pocket watch* he enjoys wearing. A favorite find is a *campaign poster* of Cox and Roosevelt that he bought for around $30. It is now valued at $150. Another is the Teddy Roosevelt pillow he found in a northern New York state antique shop. It cost $7. "When I showed it at last year's convention, one collector offered me $75 for it. No one seems to have ever seen one like it." Jensen does feel that flea markets still offer knowledgeable collectors the best opportunities for bargains. Most of the professional antiques shows are overly light on political items. "Doesn't mean you can't find a rarity." he advised.

Paper political items, such as this 1930s poster, were once thrown away. Who would have thought they would be an investment? Now they are not only rare but getting more costly every year.

CREDIT: *Ed Jensen Collection*

In 1975 the monthly S.P.B. newsletter described that year as "The Big Bronze Up," the year that huge prices were posted "by American sculptors whose bronze casts hitherto sold for prices not much more than the contemporary cost of the casting in a foundry." The lead-off event in *bronzes* was the offering of the collection of the late Geraldine Rockefeller Dodge. For investors, it was very important, because at the time bronzes by the important school of American sculptors of the late nineteenth and early twentieth centuries were underpriced.

One of the interested spectators at the auction was millionaire real estate developer Arthur Rubloff. As he recalled, "I really hadn't intended to bid until I saw that Indian." He was referring to a nine-foot, towering bronze figure of an Indian, entitled "The Passing of The Buffalo." It had been specially commissioned by Mrs. Dodge from Cyrus Dallin. Recognized as one of the greatest American bronze sculptors,

Arthur Rubloff bought this bronze sculpture, "The Sun Dial," by Charles H. Humphries, for quite a bit more than its $8,000 preauction estimate. Prices of bronzes continue to go up after a long period in the doldrums.

Collector Arthur Rubloff stands beside the magnificent Cyrus Edwin Dallin Indian bronze titled "The Passing of the Buffalo." The figure, over ten feet high, was sold at the Geraldine Rockefeller Dodge auction at Sotheby Parke Bernet for $100,000.

Dallin created it near the end of his career. Yet, its preauction estimate ranged from $15,000 to $20,000. It went for $150,000. "I had hoped to buy it for $10,000," Rubloff said. "But the bidding opened at $10,000. In less than three minutes, I was an under-bidder at $47,500. I even made the buyers an offer after that, but they wouldn't take it."

It is typical of Rubloff to speak matter-of-factly of past auction bids of $100,000 as if they were $10. He seems to recall every bid he has missed with regret. At the London sale of Guggenheim estate *paperweights*, he bought $100,000 worth of weights at a single crack. But he goofed; he didn't buy everything offered at the auction. "It would have saved me considerable time and money. I only had to spend more for them at a later day and spend time tracking them down." Paperweights, bronzes, and Oriental artifacts are among the collectibles that Rubloff invests in aside from real estate. As a developer, he was responsible for creating Chicago's "Magnificent Mile" on Michigan Avenue and Sandburg Village. He buys high, but you'd better believe he sells higher. Or in the case of his paperweight collections, he has "gifted the Chicago Art Institute with his $500,000 collection." Presently, he is "trying to collect all of the bronzes I can." Will he corner the bronze market? No doubt about it, if he really wants to. He keeps close watch on any auctions for bronzes and paperweights. In fact, in the desk drawer in his executive suite, he keeps every S.P.B. catalog on bronze auctions, presale estimates, and final prices.

It is important for investors to become Rubloff watchers. There really wasn't much action in paperweights and bronzes till he began scooping them up. Who knows what he will start collecting next? What is important is that such major purchases stimulate particular collecting areas and keep prices rising. A market for mass collecting of paperweights might be attributed to the first major exhibition in a decade or more at the Chicago Art Institute, which took place about six years ago. Rubloff and several other major collectors lent their collections for the exhibit. A wealth of media publicity generated public awareness not only in antique weights but also in fine contemporary examples. A secondary market was thus created for the average collector. Even the limited-edition market cashed in on it as many fine craftspeople turned their hand to paperweights. A collector of Rubloff's financial stature is certainly "influential in the antiques investment market." He also has a bit of advice for investors: "Spend lots of money and buy only the best."

4.
An Analysis of Some Recent Good Investments

In the antiques business, dealers are constantly asking, "What's new?" This isn't as strange as it sounds. How else will one dealer get ahead of the competition unless he has at least an inkling of what item will become popular next? It is the natural instinct not only of dealers but collectors to follow a leader. Collectors can learn what's new by reading the want ads in the trade journals. There are dealers who want old dog collars and dishes, leg irons, and Nazi items. Max Rosenthal is one lawyer who is trying to anticipate a trend and a profit. He bought heavily into relics of the People's Temple. Ugh! His purchases include the oak pulpit used by Rev. Jim Jones for $1,250 and several dozen copies of long-playing records made by the People's Temple choir for $2 each. There's a perfect answer to "What's new?" in the antiques business but not necessarily an investment. Or is it? Before you laugh too loudly at Rosenthal, you should know that one collector recently put out $3,500 for Adolf Hitler's gold-plated license plate.

Five years ago, collectors would have had a hard time finding any shops specializing in Art Deco objects from the 1920s and 1930s. Today there are dozens of shops in most major cities around the country specializing only in objects from this period. As one dealer said, "Some of the stuff may leave you cold. But believe me, there's somebody, somewhere waiting to buy all of it." In his shop you'll find everything from old magazines and department-store Deco objects to architectural fragments such as a glass plaque, frosted Lalique-style with the figure of a svelte female and her greyhound dog. It wears a price tag of over $500.

To get a fix on what's happening in a certain area of collecting, you have to go back and see what went before. Most fascinating are the opinions of experts. Note a couple of quotes on the future of Gallé and Daum Frères glass from the 1970–1971 edition of *Auction Antiques Annual:* "The two great glassmakers of Nancy, France, Daum Frères and Emile Gallé, continued to hold the attention of collectors. Pieces signed by them come up quite often at auction. Marked vases by Daum or Gallé usually bring $200 to $300, although fairly representative examples of their work brought less this season. This does not appear to be an advancing market." They also observed that vases and bowls of the 1920s signed "G. Argy-Rousseau" averaged $200 each this season." A 1979 auction record was set by a G. Argy-Rousseau piece of that description for $6,000.

So much for the experts. Collectors and dealers say nothing has given such a flip to the antiques market in the past few years as has Art Deco. Born at the Exposition Internationale des Arts Decoratifs et Industriels Modernes in Paris, 1925, it represented the union of art and industry—the age of mass-produced art. It was adopted by the avant-garde of Europe and was characterized by geometric forms and bold colors with splashes of white, silver, and gold. By the late 1930s, it had been expanded for mass appeal and had lost originality of craftsmanship. It was all but forgotten in the rush by collectors to get in on the Art Nouveau market (1876–1915).

As recently as three years ago, there were only small pockets of collectors of Art Deco for both the top-quality pieces and the kitsch. One early collector was John

Many pieces of European art glass are unrecognized because they lack a signature. This small pitcher with purple-and-green iridescence is of a type made in Austria in the late nineteenth century. A collector bought it in an anqiques shop for $30, identified it as a piece made by Loetz, and now owns a $125 investment.

Keefe, curator of the American Decorative Arts Department, Chicago Art Institute. He said, "I was forced out of collecting Art Nouveau when that market began rising out of sight some thirteen years ago." At that time, he began his collection of *Art Deco jewelry*. One early purchase, a vermeil silver and topaz bracelet, was discovered for $20. It is worth over $500 today. Keefe suggests that in the Art Deco market "in some instances, rhinestones can be as important as diamonds. It is the design that decides the value." Old names like Van Cleef & Arpels and Cartier used real gems adapted to the Deco look. On the other hand, Coco Chanel, Paul Brandt, and Schiaparelli used fake gems on their clips and bracelets. Keefe observed that some of these fine pieces still turn up at flea markets. "When the design is good, they end up in good shops for over a hundred dollars."

Another good jewelery item of the 1930s is the ivory bracelet. An S.P.B. sale in March 1979 of Art Deco decorative objects and jewelry showed a definite established market. An Art Deco diamond and emerald bracelet with an estimate of $5,500 to $6,500 was bid in at $6,000. Keep in mind that Art Deco has had a growing band of collectors during the past five years, so the pre-estimate based on recent past history came off close. On the other hand, there were surprises in the pre-estimate of $2,000 to $3,000 for an Art Deco jade and enamel desk clock. It was bid in at $5,000. Was it a fluke, a fight between a couple of serious bidders, or a newly developing interest in unsigned decorative objects? Only time will tell. But for the moment at least, this could be interpreted as a developing trend, and whether it was purchased by a private collector or a dealer would make a difference as well. If purchased by a dealer, it could be expected that he will either set it aside until an even more favorably established market has developed or sell it for from 40 to 50 percent more. "The bids shows that interest generated has exceeded all expectations," noted S.P.B. expert Barbara Deisroth.

There are still good buys to be made in sculpture from the Art Deco period, and there is also lots of junk. For instance, an *Art Deco pottery lamp* in the shape of a parrot found bidders at $150 in a Chicago auction. It was more "kitsch than collectible" observed the auction dealer. "It certainly didn't sell as fine art." The collectors are also warned that this was a time when pot metal was covered with a bronze finish. To this day, many unwary buyers may pay big prices mistaking pot metal for bronze. Prices have also been rising for *D. H. Chiparus figures* that combine ivory and precious metals and once sold in the big stores and jewelry shops. In 1973 examples were picked up in the United States for from $600 to $1,600. By 1977 the prices had risen to from $800 to $2,500. These days, they have doubled or more, depending on the quality of the piece. Similar price spirals have occurred with other famous names such as Bouraine, Paul Jouve, and Rembrandt Bugatti.

Some of the finest European examples of handmade *Art Deco furniture* design show up in Florida. European refugees brought their best pieces when they fled Europe for New York, and later, when they retired to Florida, the pieces came with them. Expect to find pieces combining ivory with old designs in wood grains. Names that are important are Ruhlmann, Le Corbusier, Dufrene, and Brandt. In the marketplace, you can pay $5,000 and up for a single chair by those designers.

The all-important clue that the Art Deco market was gaining new respectability and collectors was an exhibit held at the Minneapolis Institute of Arts in 1971 devoted to the *Art Deco decorative arts*. By 1973 there were enough serious collectors for an exhibit at the University of Chicago's Bergman Gallery. Joseph Fell, better known these days as a dealer in Oriental rugs, got into the Art Deco market as a result of the U. of C. show. He credits his early discoveries to research and knowledge, with a little bit of luck. "You must know more than the person you buy from," he said. Using this

Royal Dux porcelain company of Bohemia (Czechoslovakia) mass-produced hundreds of porcelain figurines like this dancing couple. Currently, this porcelain has more value as Art Deco than as Royal Dux. You'd have to pay several hundred dollars these days for this piece.

CREDIT: National Antiques Show, New York City

These pieces of pottery have been authenticated as Galena. They represent several thousand dollars in a newly developed market for pottery. About ten years ago, you could have bought them for a fraction of their present-day value.

CREDIT: *Philip Trier Collection*

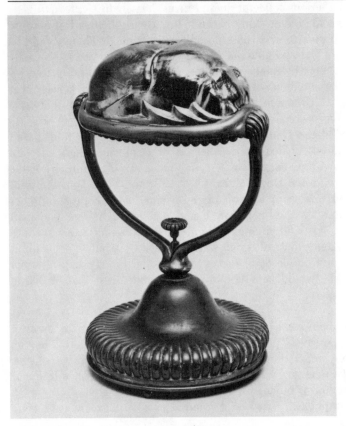

This Tiffany scarab lamp made between 1892 and 1902 combines bronze with iridescent blue-green glass.

CREDIT: *Private Collection*

technique, he found a rare Art Deco vase in an antique shop mixed in with the junk and priced at $35. Its retail value three years ago was $1,200. Add another $1,000 and you have its value in 1979. Luck was still with Fell when, eight years ago, he spotted a tall marble-topped iron stand in the Art Deco style at an estate auction. On viewing day, none of the dealers (including Fell) had found a signature. "My wife and I carefully went over the stand. It was so beautifully handcrafted we figured there had to be a signature somewhere. I bought it without much dealer competition for $200. At home, we cleaned it up and found a signature on the underside. That upped the value immediately. Today it is worth around $3,500."

In the paintings and prints category, the most famous rediscovered *artists of the Art Deco period*, Icart and Mucha, have gone from the low hundreds of dollars in the last six years to several thousand for an original drawing. Even prints are selling for several hundred dollars. Original magazine illustrations by such highly stylized *Deco illustrators* as John Held, Jr., Henry Raleigh, and Joseph Coll could have been purchased for under a thousand dollars two or three years ago. Prices are slowly rising.

What makes the analysis of what is a good antiques investment so challenging is that everybody seems to have a strong opinion often differing from that of another expert. Chase Gilmore, owner of an auction gallery in Chicago that bears his name, remembers a South Side auction in 1958 when a Tiffany laburnum floor lamp sold for $17.50. "$18,000 would be a reasonable price today. These days the Tiffany name means money in the bank. Look what happened at the April 1979 Christie's auction in New York. A small Tiffany spider-web lamp brought $150,000. A lavalike glass Tiffany vase established a new auction high in its class at $19,000. The sum of $150,000 was more than twice the previous record at an auction for a Tiffany and an Art Nouveau design."

Gilmore also said, "The serious collector doesn't invest heavily in *Depression glass* (the mass-produced glass sold in dime stores in the 1930s, to early 1940s). Just because something was made in the 1920s and 1930s doesn't make it good. There should be the element of good design." He pointed out that as recently as two years ago, finely designed Art Deco glass items by quality designers could have been purchased for several hundred dollars; he noted one example by C. Fauré Limoges that was sold at that time in a New York S.P.B. sale for $400. "If it were to appear now in that same New York market, it would probably go for $1,200."

Try and tell members of the Depression Glass Club that their collections aren't investments, or the hundreds of dedicated collectors of Depression glass who are watching their modest investments escalate. "It may not make it to Sotheby Parke Bernet, but who cares?" said one Des Moines, Iowa, collector. Years ago, she went "junking" every weekend. She'd buy a single piece or sometimes a complete dinner set at a modest price. Later, she got fussier and began looking for the "more elegant pieces." Ice buckets, decanters, and pitchers that once cost next to nothing, now have values of $50 and up. Recently her collection was appraised by a fellow collector at $8,000. Of course, there are hundreds of pieces in her collection. Perhaps another collector might suggest she would be smart to sell now and invest that $8,000 in several fine pieces of art glass.

You don't hear much about *stein collections* as investments. As in many areas of collecting, members are positively paranoid about the possibility of theft. They go about their collecting, buying, trading and selling as quietly as possible. As a newsletter from Sotheby Parke Bernet observed, "Auctions of steins are a very infrequent occurrence; the usual method is buying and selling them through advertisements in the various collector's pamphlets." However, Sotheby Parke Bernet managed a coup a few years ago by managing to have an auction of steins during the week the Stein Collectors International held their convention in New York City. Offered were Mettlach steins, made in Germany between 1890 and 1910 and considered choice. At that time, the pre-estimates ranged from $50 to $1,500.

Those who began collecting fifteen or twenty years ago may recall spending $5 or $10 for steins that today bring as much as $1,000. Among the most expensive steins in today's market are the earliest types known as *Kreussen steins* and *tankards*. The most elaborate pieces with polychrome designs are valued at as much as $10,000. Popular with collectors but not as high-priced are *Regimental steins*. Until 1914 they were presented to German servicemen upon completion of their duty in the military reserve. Prices range from around $150 to over $300, depending on the scene depicted, especially those with scenes lithophaned on the bottom showing nudes. If a truly important stein collection were put up for sale, chances are it would never reach the general public.

Steins have a loyal following of collectors. Old and/or rare steins from Germany and other countries are considered serious investments. You'd probably pay $150 for this one.

CREDIT: *National Arts and Antiques Festival*

I'm a great believer in reading anything and everything I can get my hands on that will point to trends in the antiques and the collectibles market. A suburban newspaper may be the source that reveals what's happening. One article in the September 1978 Pioneer Press papers of Illinois was entitled, "Toys: The Investment Playground." The writer covered flea markets and shows, shops, and collectors for her facts and showed what was happening in just one category in the affluent suburbs of Chicago. A Buddy L. standard-gauge train set with five cars was sold there for $1,200 and a ten-inch walking doll and cart brought $1,000. The article went on to point out that the main problem with investing in antique toys or trying to figure the value of toys in a collector's possession is the "specialized and scattered market in the *antique toy field*. In other words, locating the potential buyer, who is out there somewhere waiting to be found." The article included interviews with several collectors and dealers who all had their own opinions on how to sell for profit. All agreed it would be "unusual for a person to get involved in antique toys solely for their investment potential. The most popular collectibles seem to be dolls, trains, metal cars and trucks, windup toys, and banks, especially mechanical ones." The key is to find the buyer when it comes time to sell at a profit. One shop had an early *1920 toy back-up truck*, with the name of a still-existing business painted on its side. Originally, it sold for $8; recently, its owners turned down an offer for $500.

Why toys? Although collecting usually begins as nostalgia, it ends up as a fascination. What about condition? Naturally those that work are prime. However, a rarity, even in bad condition, will always find a buyer. One collector noted, "It's not like real estate or the stock market, where you can predict with a fair amount of certainty what your investment is worth on a given day." You can really play Russian roulette in this field if you don't take the time to know what you're doing.

Let's take a look at what's been happening to toys during the past few years. At a Butterfield & Butterfield auction in San Francisco in 1977, a *1937 Lionel Hudson-type steam locomotive* sold for $1,700. One of the factors that made it a top bid was its being the first model ever built to scale. At the same sale, an 1875 brass-and-wood sixty-six-inch long model of a steam locomotive, hand-painted, went for $3,400. At the sale, other trains sold for far less, such as a *Lionel #717 New York Central lighted caboose* for $130. Similar items came to market in 1979. Prices were about the same for the more common pieces. But as one collector told me, "Any first scale models or rare hand-painted nineteenth-century trains probably would go for double. They could be considered an established toy investment."

Dolls don't have to be old to be good investments. Consider that in 1975 prices were beginning to rise on twentieth-century composition dolls. Two boy dolls dating around 1910 were selling at between $40 and $50, priced higher than the girl dolls because fewer were made. By 1979 prices had sometimes tripled, as always depending on the demand. Even *Barbie dolls*, sold in the 1950s for $3, have found buyers today in the $200 to $500 range at auctions around the country. There is, of course, a current up-trend on *Elvis Presley dolls* that once cost $5. Some buyers will pay as much as $1,500. Antique dolls still bring in the best constant price. A French nineteenth-century *Jumeau doll* sold at a 1978 P. B. Eighty-four auction for $3,250. On the other hand, *character dolls* of once-famous celebrities like Sonja Henie sold for $145. A Shirley Temple doll, twenty-five inches high with original dress, sold for $225 in 1978. A set of quintuplet dolls from the 1930s in original clothes found a buyer at $300. The majority of nineteenth-century dolls bearing such names as Heaubach and Kestner seemed to have stabilized in the mid hundreds. Gaining in price and popularity are *Madame Alexander dolls* made from the 1920s on. A *Princess Elizabeth doll* from the 1930s was up to $75.

The upper echelon of dolls and toys find their way to the big auction houses at even bigger prices. *Automata* have always commanded good prices. At the May 1979 "Collectors Carousel" held at P.B. Eighty-four, fifty were offered. Prices ranged from the hundreds to several thousands.

Folk Art has been climbing in value for the last eleven years. In 1979 an important collection, the Stewart Gregory assemblage, was sold at record prices during a S.P.B. two-session sale. A preauction estimate was $800,000. For individual objects, a Wilhelm Schimmel eagle had a presale estimate of $6,000 to $8,000. It brought $14,000. Gregory had spent more than half his lifetime as a folk art collector. When he began collecting over thirty years ago, not many were buying such items as *hooked rugs*, *weather vanes*, and *ancestral portraits*. Yet the auction attracted 1979 bidders from all over the United States. When it was over, the gross total for the sale was double the presale estimate at $1,340,450.

Is it a jumble of wood sticks and junk or an antique doll house? As a jumble, it would be worth about $20. As a hand-made Victorian doll house, the value would be over $100. As they say in the trade, "It needs restoration, but not too much." As an interesting example of handcraft, it has investment potential. It is similar to the many birdhouses made around the turn of the century.

Middle European folk art carvings haven't found much of a market in the United States. Prices have been substantially lower than for comparable American pieces. As the interest in folk art from the nineteenth century continues to grow, it will probably encompass its counterparts from other countries. Pieces such as this Polish carving can be expected to go up in value, just as Russian items have.

CREDIT: National Antiques Show

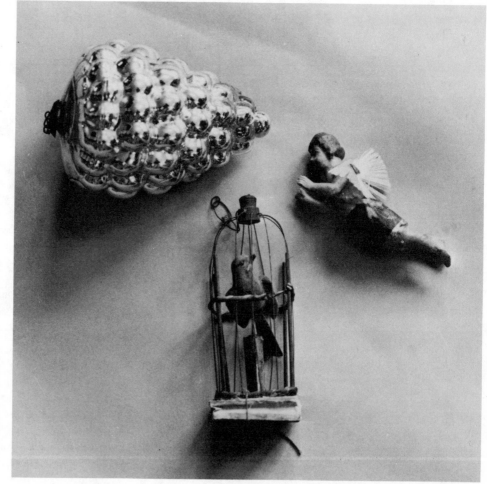

Christmas-tree ornaments are a rising market. The hand-painted chalkware bird is valued at over $150. The rare wax angel goes for $75. The large silver cluster of grapes is known as a Kugel. It was sold to me for $20. Research proved it to be possibly a nineteenth-century American piece and worth over $100.

An interesting survey of who the buyers were showed that 69 percent were private collectors; 29.5 percent were dealers, some of whom were buying for collectors; and 1.5 percent were purchasers for museums.

The sale is doubly interesting because so many purchasers were private collectors who had become knowledgeable enough to have the confidence to bid against dealers in a collecting area that had only recently developed. It also shows that they had been keeping track of the growing prices for American folk art and were willing to take a chance investing money. With prices of $700 for a bandbox and $12,500 for a decoy, they had to have a combination of confidence in the market and knowledge of the importance of the pieces they bid on. Another influence on bidding was doubtless an eastern museum exhibit "Flowering of American Folk Art" that stimulated general public interest.

In the 1978 S.P.B. folk art sale, a single watercolor portrait painted by S. A. and R. W. Shute was sold to a collector for $42,500. It established an all-time high for an American folk art watercolor. Even more interesting were prices for unknown artists; they ranged from $125 to $350 while those with attributions went for from $550 to $600. The more naive the technique, the more enthusiastic the bids. However, one New York dealer said, "I'm not advocating folk art for investment, but for pure aesthetics I think it gives a good return."

And to think that the dog probably slept on this rug! These days, hand-hooked rugs are rating a second glance from Americana collectors. Along with quilts, coverlets, and samplers, examples of American twentieth-century textile design are quite collectible. Because they got such rough treatment, there aren't as many around as you might believe—hence the rise in price.

Nevertheless, one year later, the lowest preauction estimate for folk art paintings at the S.P.B. Stewart E. Gregory sale ranged from $700 to $900 for an unsigned oil. Should that dealer be eating his words?

In the Midwest, except for very small groups of collectors, the folk art market isn't very active. "If a painting isn't signed and by a nationally known artist, forget it," one dealer said. "I've passed up dozens of American primitive paintings at estate sales with prices of ten to fifty dollars. You can still pick up an early nineteenth-century ancestral oil by an unknown artist around here for one hundred fifty to two hundred dollars, the kind that are snatched up in the East for thousands of dollars. The people who do collect here buy in the East. Seems sort of foolish when they could spend a fraction of the cost by going to a Chicago house sale."

Another dealer specializing in museum-quality early nineteenth-century American antiques admitted, "There is a snob element in buying Americana. My customers like it to be not only from a famous name collector but at a New York auction house. They are the kind of people who don't mind paying more to get that social provenance."

Right here and now, let's take a look again at you, the budget-minded investor. If you can forego the snob trip, obviously you can build up a collection of folk art where you live.

You have to have faith in your own taste and knowledge, however. And never mind if nobody understands why you are buying a painting that looks as if your grandchild did it. Just for fun, let's trace the journey of one particular unsigned example of *American nineteenth-century painting* not naive enough to be classified pure folk art. The scene pictures a group of red barns and a country setting. I acquired it while talking to a dealer in her shop. This particular dealer specializes in Art Deco objects from Depression glass to old dresses. As I stood there, a pair of dubious-looking young adults came in with two objects to sell, one of them the oil painting. "I'll give you $15 for it," said the big-hearted dealer. The pair was delighted. To me the dealer said, "You can have it for $35." Delighted, I took it home and hung it on my overcrowded walls. A few weeks later, I called in another dealer to sell her some antique jewelry, which was her specialty. She spotted the painting and asked me what I wanted. Off the top of my head, I said, "How about $325?" The painting went into her very posh shop wearing a price tag of $450. I have no doubt that it will find its way to New York and find a bidder at $900. As such, it will be considered an investment. In another year, it may go up again in price. Whatever happens to it, it was a short-term investment for me.

Some of the most significant price increases this year have been with eighteenth- and early nineteenth-century *American country pieces.* In March 1979, a painted, decorated pine-and-maple blanket chest, New England (c. 1810) sold for $950 at Phillips auction house in New York. A *country-style Chippendale* tall chest-of-drawers sold at the same auction for $875. Two similar pieces were sold in a midwest antique shop for $200 and $250 a piece. What is considered an investment purchase in one area of the country can easily be classified secondhand furniture in another!

In January 1978, a set of ten New York Sheraton chairs sold at $10,500, slightly over the low estimate. Experts believed it indicated that a recent trend of increasing prices for sets had stabilized. At that same sale, a simply styled Chippendale desk sold at $2,300, not only under the retail price but also the estimate of $2,500 to $3,500. Does this mean that Chippendale was suddenly losing ground as an important American furniture investment? Not really. Perhaps the attending bidders already owned similar pieces or were saving their money for other items. This type of upset is why prices should never be gauged on a single auction price. A year later, if few Chippendale pieces had been at auction, this same piece might easily have gone over a $3,500 bid.

Purchased for $200 in a midwestern antiques shop, this Hepplewhite country chest-of-drawers was a good buy. A similar American piece might easily find bidders at an East Coast auction for several thousand dollars. The piece is cherry with pine drawers, beautifully dovetailed. Brasses are new. The chest is in its original finish, which isn't too bad considering its age.

While a down-trend like this, which should have been a good investment, can make a collector nervous, it shouldn't cause panic. The collector would do better to look at the overall picture of prices for similar pieces of Americana. For 1978 and 1979, it couldn't have been better.

The January 1979 issue of *Antiques World* reported on the purchase of a mahogany blockfront desk (1750–75) at a Christie's auction, noting: "It brought a record-setting $140,000, or $154,000 when the buyer's premium is added. Seven years ago a similar piece brought $120,000 at a S.P.B. sale. The $20,000 appreciation (or $34,000, with premium) over six years is about 3 percent (or with premium about 4 percent) a year. So it appears that even the value of the masterpieces of the eighteenth-century American furniture has not kept pace with inflation. Even so, blue-chip furniture seems to have fared better in that time span than blue-chip stocks."

A comparison of some preauction estimates from 1978 and 1979 S.P.B. catalogs of fine Americana of similar design shows one for a Federal inlaid mahogany bow-front chest-of-drawers with flaring feet in 1979 at $1,000 to $1,500. A similar piece of cherrywood with inlaid maple drawers in 1978 was $750 to $1,000. In 1976 a similar piece was $700 to $900. A quick analysis would show that *country-style Federal* is very slowly inching up in price. Logic would conclude that since fewer and fewer of these pieces will be on the market as time goes on, prices should go up. Yet, in 1978 a buyer might have purchased a *primitive painted-pine wall cupboard* (c. 1750–1800) for $800 to $1,200. By 1979 a similar piece had pre-estimates of $2,000 to $2,500. A 1976 estimate for a similar piece was $600 to $800. In about three years, the primitive cupboard had more than tripled in estimated value.

Sometimes only a year elapses before an owner wishes to sell. This was the case with a piece the 1978 S.P.B. catalog described as a "rare and important Queen Anne carved walnut step-top highboy, Mass., ca. 1740–60." Its provenance was listed as "Descended in the Weston-Sampson-Winslow family of Duxbury, Mass. to previous owner." The 1978 preauction estimate was $18,000 to $22,000. The identical piece, complete with identical provenance, turned up at the January 1979 S.P.B. auction, only this time its preauction estimate was $8,000 to $12,000. It sold for $4,250, quite a comedown, and not much of an investment for the poor soul who had bought it the year before. Now why do you suppose a piece with all that provenance, and seemingly a fine example of Queen Anne would take such a downturn? Perhaps somewhere along the way someone discovered it was a fine reproduction? It would be dismissing the event too casually to suggest that there simply were no interested buyers in the crowd that night, not when other examples of *American Queen Anne* were going for record prices. Interestingly enough, the S.P.B. catalogs give no clue to the great differential in price estimates. Could it be a little case of *"Caveat Emptor"*? At any rate, it pays to keep old auction catalogs. If another collector hadn't found out that this piece had turned up one year after its sale because he'd noticed the pictures in the catalog, who would have known? Now if the piece had come back to market at a higher pre-estimate in one year's time, that would have made it a really growing investment. Keep close check on items in the category you plan to buy into. You may be amazed at how many times pieces come back with prices that should have been higher.

Sometimes it depends on whom you talk to as to whether something is really appreciating. Obviously, the average dealer isn't going to tell you that his items aren't doing well. One of the country's top dealers in the eighteenth- and nineteenth-century *English antiques* is constantly quoted in trade publications as having said, "The

As public taste changes, so do prices. A decade ago, these investment-quality American pieces were neglected. They could have been had for a fraction of what they cost today.

While one-of-a-kind Steuben pieces are expensive, table settings are affordable. Pictured is a bowl which sold recently for $125. The candlestick has a value of around $100. The compote on the right sold recently at an estate sale for $100.

market for English antiques constantly goes up. In fact, we have such a hard time finding quality pieces that we try to buy back from our old customers." What he doesn't tell you is that English antiques certainly are going up in the United States, but not as much as American antiques. The English furniture market is a rather fascinating one. Like French eighteenth-century furniture, it was predicated on the snob market. Perhaps only since the Bicentennial have American-made eighteenth- and nineteenth-century pieces of furniture outstripped the demand for English and French. Call it national pride if you will. I am more inclined to think the rising middle-class collector got sick of worrying about the thousands of reproductions of English furniture and decided to take a chance with American-made antiques. Whatever the cause, the average Georgian chest-of-drawers or highboy has not kept pace with its American counterpart. If you don't believe me, look at all of the Georgian pieces languishing in shops around the country for from $800 to $1,500. Another event that has done much to slow down the English market is container sales. Hundreds of new antiques shops have been opening from coast to coast during the past five years stocked with antiques and would-be antiques from England and the continent—more antiques, as I have said many times, than ever existed in their period.

"It's becoming increasingly apparent to many former collectors of English antique furniture that they bought reproductions of reproductions," one professional appraiser said. "Even the very wealthy don't like to be gypped all the time."

Three years ago, one of the quality charity antique shows that had relied heavily on English antiques as a drawing card nearly decided to make that year's show the last. "People simply weren't buying," said one society matron, a veteran of five years on the committee. "Would you believe they seemed afraid of buying English pieces and porcelains? These used to be our biggest seller." Well, as more and more reproductions of English enamels, porcelains, and William and Mary pieces are battered and aged into premature senility, an age of enlightenment has come to many collectors. All you have had to do is follow the year-in year-out supply of Meissen, Sèvres, and Royal Worcester, along with Staffordshire figurines and Chinese Export pieces, to become a seasoned sceptic. As a result, Meissen and Sèvres didn't do too well on the American market. A happy S.P.B. newsletter announcement in March 1978 noted: "Porcelain did extremely well, particularly prices for Sèvres, which are making a strong comeback in the United States." One purchase by a New York dealer for a pair of Sèvres *blue celeste* vases and stands amounted to $20,000. Guess what that will cost the private collector! London dealers seemed to anticipate a ready market for Meissen figures, at that same auction. Even so, the highest price paid at auction for Meissen porcelain by an American private collector was $60,000 for a *circa* 1734 figure (thirteen and one-half inches high) modeled by J. J. Kaendler.

Are these good investments? Chances are, there will always be another buyer for these Sèvres and Meissen pieces. Only time will tell if they will go for enough in the next few years to make them a good investment. However, when you are dealing with buyers who pay $60,000 for a single figurine, perhaps the investment aspect isn't as important as it would be for the collector who spends from $10,000 to $20,000. Again, it *is* important to determine whether the pieces are reproductions to know how their future prices will hold up. In the status collecting crowd, the names Meissen and Sèvres have always been good names to drop, practically ensuring that, reproductions or no, there will always be another buyer waiting with cash. In the long run, that seems to be more important than whether something is what it claims to be. That's the only way to explain the year-in and year-out market for what has to be a reproduction of a reproduction.

1979 was a good year for a growing market of *American silver* that included 1920s silver from Tiffany & Company as well as a variety of *Victorian* and *Art Nouveau pieces*.

"We've seen prices for good silver from the 1950s keep going up. Companies like Jensen and Gorham that may have been the wedding silver of the post–World War II generation is being seriously collected," said Ernest Du Mouchelle of Du Mouchelle's Art Galleries Company, Detroit, Michigan. He pointed out that the same holds true for good sterling from the Victorian and Art Nouveau period. To date, silver plate is moving slowly, at least in Detroit.

"Victorian silver plate with unusual designs or from a good company has made gains since 1979," said Chicago auction gallery owner Chase Gilmore. "There haven't been any fantastic uppers yet, but I can see it coming."

It would seem that the still reasonably priced pieces of Victorian, when carefully selected, offer the medium-price investor at least a chance. It's highly speculative at this point. But then, weren't a lot of now high-priced objects a gamble?

Do you know a *satin-engraved piece* from a *chased* one? *Engine-turning* from *engraving*? If you do, you will be able to date your silver more easily. Above all, don't give up hunting for good buys. While most dealers and collectors are tuned in to the early sterling silver marks and Sheffield pieces, not all are that well informed. Get some good books on eighteenth-century American silversmiths and familiarize yourself with the various styles, hallmarks, and general types made. Chances of finding a rarity are better than finding the more commonplace, and that is where the money lies. Consider this fortunate collector who had been reading up on early American silversmiths: One day, while browsing in a good antique shop in the Midwest, she saw what appeared to be a double-shot glass in brass. At any rate, it was sitting, tarnished, on an upper shelf. The dealer suggested it might be Chinese and was most certainly brass. The collector recognized by the shape and manner of decorating that this was an eighteenth-century American church beaker. Not until many hours of silver polishing had been expended did a strange, elongated heart hallmark emerge and the pale look of old silver. The piece cost the collector $7. It is probably worth over $2,000. She hasn't had any such luck since then, but how many coups like that can you expect?

Should you find some unusual silver pieces marked "EPNS" or "EPWM" you have a Victorian silver-plated object. The letters stand for Electroplated White Metal or Electroplated Nickel Silver, made in England. American silver plate of the same period will have the words "triple" or "plate" or "quadruple." Pieces marked "Brazil Silver" were made by the Globe Nevada Silver Works of Birmingham, England, on nickel silverware. "African Silver," believe it or not, was also English plate made after 1850. Equally confusing are pieces marked "German Silver," which are really silver-colored combination of nickel, copper, and zinc.

It wasn't long ago that Victorian silver plate with embossed ornamentation (chasing) was passed by or sold for a few dollars. Even beautifully *rococoed teapots* priced at $5 couldn't raise an eyebrow. The same could be said for satin-engraved pieces. They were unfamiliar, unpublicized, and not of interest to dealers or collectors. Generally, they were blackened and in need of resilvering.

Now collectors are giving chased silver a second glance, and it's still cheap. The Victorian silversmiths revived the early art of hand chasing, which achieved popularity in the 1860s to about 1900. Sometimes the design was flat, other times raised, and it was a time-consuming art demanding special tools and years of training. Even in its day, it wasn't expensive; today, it is a relatively lost art. The satin appearance

American sterling silver spoons made in the early nineteenth-century can still be purchased for from $10 to $30, depending on size. This one, in the classic fiddleback design, was found in a box of junk flatware in a thrift shop for $2. It's bound to start rising in price, as everything and anything American from the early 1800s is doing.

was created using a circular wire brush on a lathe for the desired frosted, satin look, and a design was then engraved into it. Some of the early pieces will have B.C. stamped on the bottom. You'll find examples in old Sears Roebuck Catalog reproductions.

"As enthusiasm continues to grow for virtually all works of art dating from the late nineteenth and early twentieth centuries, so have the prices risen commensurately, in fact, to a point totally unexpected only a year ago," stated the writer of an article about a Victorian sale in the February 1979 S.P.B. newsletter. At the sale, an English Victorian silver Monteith bowl, London (c. 1878) had a pre-estimate of $1,200 to $1,500. It was sold for $2,900.

"New rules apply when you are collecting Victorian silver," advised one collector. "Don't rely on what others are buying. There isn't any established collecting criteria in this area. Collect what appeals to you."

On the other hand, if you have the cash you could put your money on the relatively safe silver market. At the $2,000-plus level for important American silver pieces, you will be in the upper echelon of auction bidders, museums, dealers, and wealthy collectors. There really isn't "room at the top" where antique sales are concerned. In 1978, for instance, the Thomas Jefferson Museum at Monticello purchased items in the $6,100 price area. At the same S.P.B. auction, a dealer paid $47,000 for an eighteenth-century American silver teapot by Peter Van Dyck, New York. Its preauction estimate was $14,000 to $18,000. This was a record for any silver teapot and the second highest price for any piece of American silver. You can imagine the fast and furious bidding that brought the price up so high.

Another group of collectors have been following the downs and the current ups of *Georgian silver*, which has gone up to ten times the value it had nine years ago. The 1978 *Official Price Guide to Silver-Silverplate* by Carl F. Luckey lists a set of four bedroom candlesticks, silver-gilt with a Paul de Lamerie maker's mark, at $3,850 to $4,700 per set. In 1976 the Lion Mark offered a pair of Corinthian column candlesticks made in London in 1762 by Emick Romer for $2,150. These days, you can expect to pay between $4,500 and $5,500. Currently, you will pay $11,000 for a set of four candlesticks by an equally fine Georgian silversmith, Ebenezer Coker. Yet a Kovel price guide for 1978 prices a pair of Corinthian column Georgian candlesticks signed by Thomas Law at $350 a pair.

Generally, but not always, the finest pieces, be they of American sterling or English "plate" sterling, are found in the finest shops. The trick is to recognize an unfamiliar but rare hallmark ahead of the dealer. It could be a rare French eighteenth-century piece of flatware. One collector recognized the French mark and paid a fraction of the value for a pre-French-Revolution silver spoon. So much silver was melted down during the French Revolution that remaining items are scarce.

One of the most popular areas for investing, *Oriental antiques*, never seems to lose its stride despite the fact that so many items that reach the market are reproductions not only from the nineteenth and early twentieth centuries but "made yesterday." It's fun to look back to the auction years of 1970–71 and the *carved snuff bottle*. Those of jade found high bidders. A *Canton enamel bottle* sold for a high of $8,416. Yet, jade carvings, which had been on a popularity high for several decades, took a downturn, and very few prices were bid in over $10,000. Then a slight interest in *Japanese pottery* and *porcelain* emerged. Lacquer items found new collectors willing to pay as much as $6,720 for a domed, lacquer coffer with designs in mother-of-pearl, gold and blue-gray lacquer. Around that time, a variety of other lacquer items from boxes to picnic sets sold for over $1,000 each. Getting highest prices for the 1970-71 auction

They're always digging something up in China these days, to the delight of collectors of Oriental artifacts. This archaic bronze cup is typical of the many bronzes showing up at market. This past year has seen a resurgence of the Chinese market, though not as great as several years ago. Items like this cup are good buys when compared to expensive porcelains.

CREDIT: *Butterfield & Butterfield Auction Gallery*

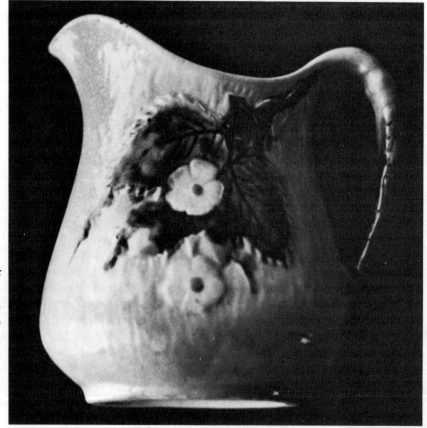

Still very underpriced are pieces of Victorian majolica. Once used as grocery premiums, the colorful pottery is now being seriously collected. At $20 to $50 for most pieces, it can only go up in value. This yellow pitcher with purple lining was made around the turn of the century. You would probably pay $30 or less for it in an antiques shop.

years were *Chinese porcelains*, with Ming period pieces at the top of the price list. One notable example was a fifteenth-century blue-and-white stemcup bid in at $105,600. A pair of late *famille rose* Mandarin vases forty-two inches high of the Chi'en,Lung period were sold for $21,420.

Contrast those auction room winners with the May 1979 S.P.B. auction of Chinese paintings, textiles, snuff bottles, and other items. There enthusiasm for the snuff bottle market was revived. A Peking painted-enamel snuff bottle, Chi'en Lung mark, and painted in *famille rose* enamels on both sides, sold for $17,000. A pair of late nineteenth-century *famille rose* enamelled vases sold for $2,100. Steadily appreciating in price and appearing at auction more often are *Chinese robes and textiles*. Highest price was $2,200 for a woman's ceremonial robe at the Chi'en Lung period. Peking glass, represented by a pair of yellow bowls with high-relief carving, was sold for $500. The highest price for any blue-and-white Ming porcelain was $2,800 for a censer. There, apparently, wasn't the quality of previous auctions to merit any high prices.

An April 1979 S.P.B. newsletter noted: "Additional sales of *modern Chinese paintings* were successfully introduced this season, with prices for artists sold for the first time in the fall doubling by the spring sale. There has also been an expansion of the market for Chinese textiles, and a new record was set for Sung jade ($75,000)."

There is life after an S.P.B. auction; in fact, dear reader, auctions that most people have never heard of can influence new trends and prices. Such was probably the case with a September 1978 auction held by Hemphill Auction Company in Fort Worth, Texas. It was a collection of *art pottery* including pieces by Roseville, Weller, and Rookwood. A Rookwood cookie jar was sold for $125, a Van Briggle bowl went for $152.50, and a Rookwood lamp sold for $380. This is an interesting auction to analyze, mainly because six years ago, only the finest examples of art pottery found buyers. The market has shown a steady but slow growth since then. The finest examples in Rookwood and Weller have nearly doubled: the average designs of trays and bowls and vases have gone from around $15 to $30—not spectacular, but enough of an advance to find more serious collectors.

"People seem to like anything Russian," Ernest Du Mouchelle observed. "*Icons and Russian bronzes* always do well, especially in 1979, which was definitely a seller's market. A small Russian bronze sculpture sold then for $1,600."

If this was a time to unload at a profit, how could anyone lose?

"To have a successful auction from a seller's standpoint, you have to have enough like items to draw in the collectors," said Du Mouchelle. "If, for instance, the auction is specializing in Oriental objects and there are a couple of American Indian rugs in the sale, they won't do well. This happened with a fine Navajo rug that sold for a quarter of what it should have. Yet American Indian rugs are an important investment. It was just one of those unfortunate things."

Investors have certainly bought the theory that art is a good investment. Everything from bronzes to oils, from watercolors and prints set records from Detroit to New York at auction. For example, there has been a good market for the sellers who had been buying *late nineteenth-century oils* by American painter John George Brown. As recently as five years ago, a good Brown painting could have been purchased for from $3,000 to $5,000, even at the S.P.B. auctions. 1979 became a seller's market for works by Brown, the record set by "Boy with Rabbit" at $40,000. If you had bought a print of Winslow Homer's "Eight Bells" in 1971 for $8,000, you would have found ready buyers for it in 1979 for $16,000.

While others were spending high thousands on already established markets for old

During the past two years, Russian antiques of the nineteenth and early twentieth centuries have become popular with collectors. Icons keep going up in price, even though many are not as old as they seem. Icons such as this one can cost from $500 up, and their relative scarcity makes them good possibilities for long-range investing.

master paintings and modern Impressionists, a few were looking at another type of artist, *the illustrator-painter*. Everett Shinn's painting "Spoiling for a Fight, New York Docks" had an estimate in 1976 of from $10,000 to $15,000. It went for $27,000, establishing a record price. "Garden of Allah" by illustrator Maxfield Parrish was painted in 1918 as a decoration for gift boxes of Crane's chocolates. It more than doubled a preauction estimate of $15,000 to $25,000. By 1978 other original illustrations by Parrish went to buyers in the $22,000 to $28,000 range. It is interesting to note that they were bought by private collectors. "The Courtship of Miles Standish," an illustration by another illustrator-painter, N. C. Wyeth, had a pre-estimate of from $7,000 to $10,000. It sold to a dealer for $16,000. The previous record in April 1978 for an N. C. Wyeth illustration was $13,000: a small gain, but again, 1978 was clearly a time to get in on the growing market for *original book and magazine illustrations*. In May of that year, a Norman Rockwell oil sold at Sotheby Parke Bernet for $35,000. As ghoulish as it sounds, Rockwell's death in late 1978 automatically assured the rise of his already popular paintings and illustrations.

By January of 1979, David Rogath of Vermillion Gallery, New York, who had a large collection of *Rockwell lithographs*, felt that prices could climb as high as 15 percent a month at first. "It would peak in about six months, after the profit takers have finished buying, then build again at a more gradual pace. That was the pattern with Picasso," he said. "The people who are buying now will sell at a profit later, but not at a great profit." His advice was to buy the lower-priced Rockwells. Prices by January for originals had even hit the $100,000 mark, and lithographs were selling sometimes triple over 1978. Probably the biggest jump after Rockwell's death was in the limited-edition field, where greedy dealers began selling Franklin Mint silver Christmas plates with Rockwell art for $800. In 1970 the price was $100 each. I'm happy to say the demand was sparse.

I don't have to tell you about skyrocketing prices. By now, you know how the market works. The question is how you can possibly put your money into it and come out with a profit. Many of the aforementioned auction records are flukes, while others are predictable. At one time, to make investing decisions, you could definitely observe who was spending money in an area you were interested in. For instance, if an art museum were buying heavily into a certain artist not previously doing well, chances were dealers would follow the lead. It meant there would probably be an important exhibit of that artist or of contemporary works which in turn would generate an interest among the general public. Those who had the means could be expected to scramble for similar works before prices jumped beyond their reach. In the meantime, dealers would make quick decisions as to whether they should start building up their stock of that artist or period in anticipation of the rush. Well times have changed. Even in the art market, the private collector has to have the courage to take matters into his own hands and battle it out on the auction floor, as long as his cash holds out.

The Nelson Rockefeller Collection of *art replicas* presented a current problem to art dealers and most likely a future one for collectors. In an editorial in the April 1979 issue of *American Collector,* a dealer was quoted as feeling threatened by replicas that cost in the thousands of dollars. "Dealers are hard pressed right now to find support for art from the middle class. If people are buying replicas from Rockefeller rather than originals from galleries, the dealers see another chunk of the market going down the drain." However, the writer proposed that the replicas would eventually increase in value, but that's another story. The problem is now, and the question is: should you or shouldn't you spend on replicas. One private collector who spent $2,000 on a small Rockefeller replica feels he made a wise decision. "I couldn't afford the original. Why shouldn't I make this addition to my collection? It can only go up in value. Meantime, I can enjoy it." Score one for the private collector. I think most of the grapes are going sour in the dealer's vineyard.

At the other end of the investment scene are *nostalgia items*. For all of them, 1979 seemed a very good year. "Ours is a sensitive market," one collector of advertising items said. "While I have seen my collection triple in price in sixteen years, I know what could happen in a recession. Most of the collectors I know are in the middle-income group. A serious recession could cause a panic and the dumping of quantities on the market. However, even in the tin market, there are established early pieces that will probably always hold their prices, because they are that scarce." Considered choice are the *Roly-Poly tobacco tins* dating from the early 1900s. Collectors will pay from $350 up for those tins, provided they are in mint condition.

In comics, another popular collecting field, prices show a wild division between first and more recent editions. As of March 1979, some buying records were established for Number one *Batman* at $1,800; Number one *Action Comics* at $5,250; and Number one *Wonder Woman* at $270. On the other end, but still considered good speculative investments, are Number one *Howard the Duck* for $15.00 and a 1955 *Dumbo* (Disney) for $2.50. It may not sound like much of a deal, but collectors will point out that in 1975 that same Dumbo had an evaluation of ninety cents. There is even a comic book price guide issued every year. Ah, but collectors will tell you the big money is in collecting of original pages. The more popular artists are always more expensive.

Paper items, aside from comics, post cards, and sheet music, have devoted collectors who feel their *original catalogs*, *paper dolls*, and *silhouettes* are investments. To be sure, each of the many areas of paper collecting have their high prices, the highest being gathered by silhouette artists such as Auguste Edouart and William H. Brown. An Edouart went last year at auction for $250.

Another field that is recently appreciating is *calligraphy*, drawings done in the Spencerian pen-and-ink style of the mid-nineteenth century. These once commonplace exercises in penmanship can go for as much as $1,200 a piece. Only a few years ago, the going price even at an S.P.B. auction was $400 for a good example. When they show up at sales and auctions in the Midwest, they seldom go for more than $50 (unless there is a savvy dealer or collector in the audience). Not long ago, an entire book from an estate showed up in an antiques shop in the Midwest. It was from Pennsylvania, dated from the 1830s, and once the property of a teacher of penmanship. It was sold for $700 to another dealer in primitives in the area, who in turn sold it to a collector in the East, who probably sold it by the page and came up with a profit of from $5,000 to $10,000. Unlike the old chain letter, in the antiques business it is the last person who reaps profits of purchase.

So you see, any analysis of the antiques and collectibles market depends who wants what, when and where; who is knowledgeable enough to spot a bargain or a trend; and who knows when to unload before a fad or trend passes him by.

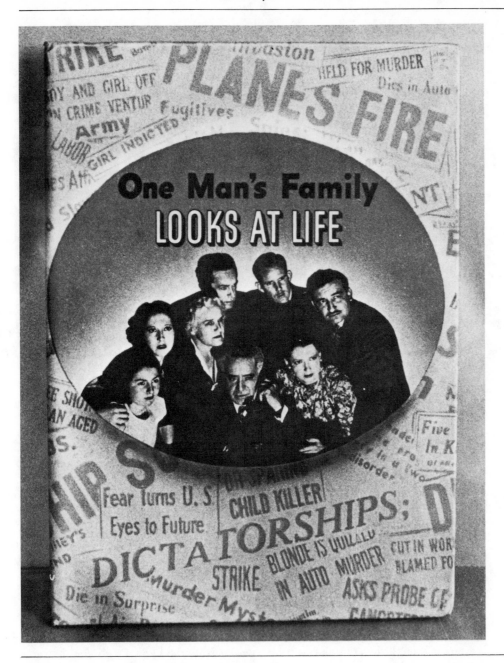

This radio script from the 1930s has a retail price of $15 or $20. It is the type of item which could easily jump to $100 as part of an important collection at auction. It is a perfect item for beginning collectors.

5.
What's in a Name?

Trumpets blare. TV newscameras cover every inch of ground not occupied by hundreds of human beings. Is it a Hollywood premiere? Is it the Queen of England riding down Fifth Avenue with President Carter and Frank Sinatra? Heavens no! It's just another name auction done the Sotheby Parke Bernet way. Whether it's Gypsy Rose Lee's G-string or Henry Ford's French furniture, you can bet there will be enough preauction hoopla to pull in bidders. Does it always work?

In 1978, when a duo of names, *Gypsy Rose Lee* and *Joan Crawford,* were offered by Sotheby Parke Bernet in a memorabilia auction, the total was $40,150. Gypsy's friends and fans, according to news reports, accounted for $29,700. Her mink G-string (a first worn by Gypsy) went for $500 to a London Banker who claimed to be a fur collector.

On the other hand, a sale of the late *Judy Garland's* effects found underbidding. Students at Goshen High School in Goshen, Ohio, pooled their money to buy the red shoes Judy wore in the *Wizard of Oz* for $375. The school uses them as a symbol in its campaign to find high school seniors in the performing arts "who might be able to fill Judy Garland's shoes."

The 1978 S.P.B. sale of *Henry Ford* collections totaled $2.2 million. Yet, many of the pieces brought less than he paid for them, despite the hype. One example was a signed Louis XV ormolu-mounted lady's lacquer desk that was sold for $47,500. In 1967 it went for $51,800. Another writing desk that had brought $11,200 in 1967 was sold at the Ford auction for $10,000. Though a Louis XV ormolu-mounted tulipwood and kingwood *secretaire à abattant* was the highest-priced bid at $195,000, it was still quite a bit under the presale estimate of $200,000 to $350,000. It was quietly suggested that Ford had paid too much in the first place. While prices for most items in the collection showed the stability of the market for French furniture and elegant objects of virtu, others went back to their proper level—if the name of the owner were Smith.

114

In Mentmore Towers, Buckinghamshire, Britain, over 7.5 million dollars worth of antiques and objects d' art *were auctioned for well over preauction estimates. Record highs were established in many categories, from Victorian silver at $22,100 to Sevres· porcelain at $102,000. Could the collectors name, Rothschild, possibly have helped?*

CREDIT: Sotheby Parke Bernet

Pictured are several pieces of Joan Crawford's jewelry that sold for well above their preauction estimates.

Would you pay $75 for this limited-edition collectors' plate, even though actress Elke Sommer hadn't painted it? Only time will tell "what's in a name" as far as Sommer's art venture is concerned. This plate, Hawaiian Wedding, *produced by Viletta China Co., has a total issue of 5,000.*

Contrast that name with *Elvis Presley*. The *National Enquirer* September 1977 issue covering Presley's death sold 6,688,563 copies out of a total press run of 6,731,851. In a week, it had become an investment, selling for as much as $50 a copy. Another Elvis item that has found buyers is a set of Elvis bubble gum cards circulated in 1965. In 1978, they were listed in a collectibles price guide for $200. At an auction of Elvis memorabilia in West Palm Beach, Florida, in 1977, a bidder paid $150 for soiled Presley linens (pillow cases, sheets, towels). In another fifty years, who is to say those linens won't make it to an S.P.B. auction? After all, they have provenance.

Names from Presley to Von Hirsch attract bidders and big money. Now you probably know who Presley is, but who is Von Hirsch? Well, Sotheby Parke Bernet did its best to let the collecting world know—in three languages in their fancy publicity

Would you be surprised to learn these two school pencil boxes made of tin would cost anywhere from $15 to $25 each? The names and faces of old-time movie stars Charlie Chaplin and Jackie Coogan are the reason. Their original cost was probably a dime.

CREDIT: *Dennis Todaro Collection*

catalogs—that Von Hirsch was probably the ultimate collector. He went from collecting Impressionists and old masters to Continental furniture, carpets, medieval works of art, and Meissen porcelain.

There are many fine auction houses in a city the size of Chicago, but when it comes to selling big-ticket items, the bid goes to big-name New York auction houses like Sotheby Parke Bernet and Phillips. One of the reasons, of course, is the status of having your things on the eastern block. Another, as one brokerage executive told me, is, "Prices are higher. Plus, chances are better of selling at least at the preauction estimate because there is such an international clientle." Many monied collectors who would never think of bidding on or even attending an auction in their home towns of St. Louis, Chicago, or Milwaukee think nothing of phoning in bids or jetting in for an important S.P.B. or Christie's auction. "I know if I buy something at any of the big eastern auction houses, I can always sell it because of the provenance," said one collector. This is true. If you don't believe me, thumb through any of the S.P.B. catalogs and you'll find asterisked items noting "previously sold at S.P.B. in 1949" or "formerly in the collection of J. Hepplespoon, sold at S.P.B. in 1973." Now if that doesn't give a potential bidder confidence in the item, I don't know what would. Psychologically, the bidder-to-be reasons, "If it were good enough for Hepplespoon, then it's good enough for me."

But picture this hypothetical situation: J. Hepplespoon decides to sell his authentic photographic collection of "Views from Mount Rushmore" at a local auction house. Several years later, the next owner of the collection decides to sell part at the local auction house and send the rest east." Those sold at the local auction house bring 10 percent more, but they are sold as "the famous Hepplespoon collection." The others don't make it to Sotheby Parke Bernet but down the street to P.B. Eighty-four, where the not-quite-so-fancy items go and where the catalog is generally a sparsely illustrated booklet. There, the photograph collection comes under the heading of "Items from Various Collections." It is picked up by a sharp-eyed collector who doesn't care who the previous owner was. He pays about the same 10 percent increase as the buyers in the local auction house, but the difference comes when he decides to sell the collection the following year. Because he is a well-known hair dresser in Manhattan, the collection is finally accepted by Sotheby Parke Bernet, and the unknown Hepplespoon photographic collection becomes "the rare views of Mt. Rushmore photographica from the collection of Mr. LeRoy, noted hair stylist." Guess what! A new auction record is established as friends and customers of *Mr. LeRoy* all but stampede the auction gallery. The collection has nowhere to go but up from there on.

It is a common practice for dealers and collectors to plant items in sales with famous names for come-ons. Often, items they have been trying to unload for years will go for double their value simply because they are associated with a famous-name auction.

You can figure if there is an important museum show traveling or about to travel the country such as the Tutankhamun treasures, there will be a revival of interest in ancient Egyptian antiquities. Sure enough, Sotheby Parke Bernet managed to come up with a timely collection or two. Most amazingly, prices were less than you might expect for such antiquities. For instance, a bronze group eight inches high of Isis seated with child Horus on her lap had a presale estimate of $1,500 to $2,000. Most were estimated at under $1,000. This also signaled the time to sow the seeds for future auctions of Islamic art dating from the thirteenth century, for a couple of pieces were included in the Egyptian auction. The actual reason for the sale was probably the timely decision of the Lannan Foundation to dispense of many pieces of Egyptian and other ancient art they had been collecting from other S.P.B. sales since 1958.

This seven-foot oil by Rosa Bonheur had a hefty preauction estimate of $25,000 to $50,000 because it was part of the Geraldine Rockefeller Dodge collection.

CREDIT: Sotheby Parke Bernet

This German silver-gilt model of a leaping stag (c. 1600) was sold in 1975 at a Sotheby Parke Bernet auction for $20,000. It had belonged to Mrs. William Randolph Hearst, Sr.

CREDIT: *Sotheby Parke Bernet, Los Angeles*

Tut wasn't the only name dropped for that auction. A limestone relief of a lion-headed deity once owned by *Cole Porter* was included in the show. You will note the word "once." To trade further on the Porter name, one S.P.B. newsletter devoted two paragraphs to Mrs. Porter's friendship with *Lord Carnarvon,* who was a friend of *Howdrd Carter,* whose excavation at Luxor in the Valley of the Kings was sponsored by Lord Carnarvon. The newsletter further noted that the last big antiquities excitement was in New York in 1972, when "the sphinx in turquoise-blue faience of Amenophis III, once owned by Howard Carter, sold for $260,000." The whole affair was almost as cosy as reading the pages out of a private diary. I had truly been let in on friendships and trips of the famous, and at last I would be able to bid on an object that had once belonged to the Cole Porters. Would this intimacy make for new record sales? The head had sold for $17,500, but in 1971 it sold for a mere $1,800, and in a post-sale newsletter, Sotheby Parke Bernet noted a 70 percent increase in value per annum of ancient art.

Not much was happening in bronze sculpture in the 1960s and early 1970s. In fact, there was an interesting analysis on bronzes in the 1970–71 *Auction Antiques Annual* by the editors of *Auction* magazine. "Bronzes are traditionally regarded as a perilous field, since it is so often difficult to know whether a work is unique, by or close to the hand of the master, or a later (sometimes much later) reduction. There are always a great many bronzes sold at auction, a lot of them for only a few hundred dollars. The nineteenth-century Animalier bronzes by Barye, Mene, the Bonheurs, and others, for instance, come into this class, and large numbers of them were priced at only $200 to $300." It seemed nothing was deader than bronzes. Then along came two magical names *Geraldine Rockefeller Dodge* and *Rothschilde Rede.* At the Rothschilde sale six months before the Dodge auction, a Renaissance bronze horse brought $375,000. Interest in Bronze sculpture among the monied was revived. When the Dodge sale offered nineteenth- and twentieth-century American bronzes, a primed group was on hand. Overnight it seemed that high prices had returned. People who had either forgotten or never knew names like Charles H. Humphries, Cyrus Edwin Dallin, and Charles Russell became aware that a new investment market had awakened. Or so it seemed. As the bidding became more intense, auction records zoomed beyond expectation. Private collectors, museums, and dealers vied for works by almost forgotten names. As a result, today most antique dealers on the lower level of the business are as convinced as their fancier counterparts that any bronze sculpture with a signature is automatically worth thousands of dollars. Pay no attention. Instead, study up and decide which names are really worth investing in, if bronzes are your thing.

In 1975, after the Dodge sale, John Marion, President of S.P.B., admitted, "Some allowance has to be made for a name like Dodge, which tends to attract greater attention than do normal auctions." Caution was advised in anticipation of what could have become a wildcat bronze market. "Price levels for bronzes could rise dramatically, because with some exceptions they had been depressed for so long."

1977 proved that there was finally a stable market for American bronzes. During a sale that year, many of the prices went way over estimate, "outstripping those fetched by similar examples in the landmark Geraldine Rockefeller Dodge auction." A thirty-one–inch version of Augustus Saint-Gaudens' "The Puritan" nearly doubled the $7,000 paid at the Dodge sale for a similar version only one-half inch smaller. The September 1977 S.P.B. newsletter admitted, "The Dodge prices were thought by many observers at the time to be greatly inflated because of the attachment of the Dodge name. Nor had there been a significant market in recent times for bronzes of this era of American art. The bronze market is clearly now an important feature of the American art collecting scene." In all, the sale was nearly $100,000 over the highest presale estimate of $322,845.

This twelfth-century ivory Bible cover fetched over $190,000 at the 1979 auction of the Brummer collection of medieval and Renaissance art. Its preauction estimate had been $120,000 to $180,000.

How about $29,000 for a pair of Chippendale chairs that belonged to George Washington? That is the ultimate provenance for any investor. If the chairs had no provenance, only their authenticity, the price would have been half of this SPB bid.

CREDIT: *Sotheby Parke Bernet*

Arthur Rubloff purchased this seated bronze of Abraham Lincoln by sculptor Gutzon Borglum for over $40,000. The brown patina bronze is a reduction of the heroic-size seated figure of Lincoln that is situated in front of the Essex County Courthouse in Newark, New Jersey.

Probably one of the best years for making the most of names was 1976, when some of the names to make money on were *General Lafayette* and *Martha Washington*. The year before the Bicentennial, the Smithsonian Institution paid $12,500 for George Washington's Valley Forge camp stool. Now that's really "high camp." The preauction estimate was $2,000 to $2,500. More in line were Martha Washington's tortoise shell spectacles for $650 and her diamond ring for $2,000, both purchased by private collectors. The needlepoint chair cushion that Mrs. Washington had stitched herself went to a dealer from Springfield, Illinois, for $1,300.

Names are equally important when they are the names of silver makers. *Hester Bateman*, English silversmith of the Georgian period, is very important to the status collectors of Georgian silver. To those on the inside of the Georgian silver market, it is a name to drop only in the sense of "eliminate it." Yet, many a silver buyer with an eye to investment will buy anything that bears the Bateman hallmark. "Bateman is bought by the insecure collector," observed Virginia Packer, Georgian silver dealer. "If people only realized the premium on fixing up Bateman pieces. The buyer looking for instant status looks to the currently popular name—Bateman. Little do they realize that out of the hundreds of pieces of silver made by quality silversmiths during the long Georgian period, Hester Bateman is the most run-of-the-mill. The serious, knowledgeable collector doesn't want pieces by the best-known silversmith but the finer lesser-known works by the general public silversmiths. We try to educate our serious customers to names like *John Scofield* and *Richard and David Hennels* from the end of the eighteenth century. You can count on them for consistently good work. Sure, Hester did some good things. Unfortunately, the majority were so-so."

Packer pointed out another problem that occurs when a silversmith becomes a fad. "There is a lot of fakery with Bateman and *Paul Storr* pieces. A collector really has to know what pieces from the individual periods look like design-wise. Otherwise, they might buy a late Victorian teapot that is out of the historical design context with a Bateman or Storr hallmark. Don't be afraid to carefully examine dubious pieces. After all, this is an investment."

The name *Paul Revere* is important to collectors of American silver. With prices in the thousands of dollars for a single good example of his work, a smart collector knows his work has been heavily faked. The problem comes when a collector must decide on a potential purchase. Is it authentic? Since pieces attributed to Revere do come up periodically at auction, it is a good idea to give them a close going-over before bidding. Only careful study of other pieces of the period and knowledge of the types that have been forged can protect you.

One of a collector's biggest failings is the assumption that the initials P.R. on a piece of silver in an eighteenth-century design automatically means Paul Revere and thousands of dollars. On the contrary, forgeries of Paul Revere pieces have been made for over a century, and chances are you will be buying another collector's mistake. Consider, for instance, why important museums and famous monied collectors haven't fought you to the death to bid on the piece. How come there's only a lady from Flamingo, Utah, bidding against you? Now coming upon what seems to be a Paul Revere serving piece in a small, out-of-the-way shop doesn't mean your chances of having spotted an authentic Revere are any better. More likely, it only means that you have spotted a "plant." Be even more suspicious of the dealer who plays it cool when your eyes bug out at the sight of the initials P.R. He may have gotten stuck with it himself. Collectors who buy by name often strike out. Consider all the objects from silver to pewter and brass that were originally made by quality craftsmen: if they were good enough to have endured, they were good enough to be forged or reproduced.

Another example of the perils of buying names is the famous porcelain sculpture by

J. J. Kaendler, chief modeler at Meissen in 1733. How often do sculptures with his mark and designs appear at auction for thousands of dollars? Anybody who collects fine European porcelains knows the importance of the name Kaendler. Yet, how many of the objects are the real thing and not reproductions? Apparently, not too many collectors and dealers worry about such details. After all, they reason, if they buy an object listed in a catalog as a Kaendler, then it must be one. For them, all that counts is owning the name. What else could it be but status when they keep buying these famous-name porcelain reproductions, from Sèvres to Worcester?

If the name is *Rembrandt* or *Durer,* you'd better believe buyers will be scrambling. Can it be that they aren't concerned with the forgeries that have been committed for several hundred years? Heavens no! These days, old forgeries count for something too! Not only have professed forgeries become collectible in their own right, but by now who's around in the average gallery or auction house who would know the telltale clues if he saw one?

The very fact that a so-called antique or collectible lacks any signs of age is what should make a knowledgeable collector wary of its authenticity, and yet if a piece has a few chips or, in the case of a Rembrandt print, some (God forbid) stains, the object is rejected. Nobody wants an antique that looks old. Does that sound strange? Some collectors don't stop to reason that if a print is hundreds of years old, it should show a bit of age, at least a couple of age spots. It is this longing for antiques that don't look that old that keeps the fakers in business. Consider dealers who specialize in Audubon prints. All their offerings are on snow-white paper, yet all profess to be over a hundred years old or more. You, the collector-investor, are asked to believe that they have remained in this pristine condition, despite the lack of storage facilities of a century ago. I recall trying to put up an interesting eighteenth-century French aqua-tint at auction. It wasn't accepted because it was a "bit wrinkled." Nobody would buy it was the concensus of opinion. But the so-called Rembrandts, Audubons, Durers, and other names sell as though there were a scarcity!

In the world of the Oriental art collector, some of the magical buying names are *T'ang, Sung, Ming,* and *Ching.* Proof of the magic in the T'ang name can be seen in the publicity given to a large T'ang tomb figure of a horse, supposedly the largest discovered, to be sold at auction. What collector of names could pass up such bait— not only a T'ang (c. 618–906) but the biggest? Now if a collector had bothered to avail himself of a book by Otto Kurz entitled *Fakes,* he might not have been so eager to part with his money. Kurz wrote that while the first T'ang tomb figures from the first excavations were brought to Europe in 1909, by 1912 a factory at Peking was busy making hundreds of copies. "Of course, one might designate such objects rather as reproductions than as outright fakes, but as they are being passed off as originals, the difference is purely theoretical." Kurz noted that as of 1912, "This successful industry is still flourishing, and everybody who takes the trouble to look around has ample opportunity to see numerous examples of its production."

Kurz also mentioned that Sung wares (c. 960–1279) went to Europe in the second decade of this century, and Imperial Ming table porcelain also appeared "only after 1920." He also mentioned the Sung copies that were made in the eighteenth century.

Two names important to furniture collectors are *Boulle* and *Riesener,* the master *ébénistes* of eighteenth-century French furniture, but names that don't come to auction very often these days. When they do, they will be part of a super-name auction like Mentmore. What many collectors don't realize is that the earliest imitations of French eighteenth-century furniture were made in Russia, only a few years after the originals. By now, most of these pieces have been scattered to the winds and some to millionaire investors. However, such reproductions can stand as investments on their

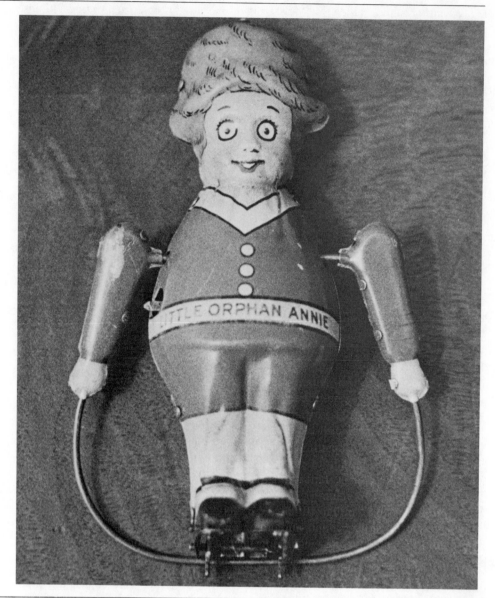

This Orphan Annie wind-up toy is currently popular because of the musical, "Annie." The entire tin toy field should continue to go up in price during the next few years.

CREDIT: *Dennis Todaro Collection*

own. As one collector observed, "It isn't a matter whether the piece is a reproduction, but *which* reproduction. So many people have signed Riesener's name to pieces, only a real expert can tell. After all, do you know what his signature really looks like? Maybe he had a bad day when he signed a piece and it looks different."

Not all names have shadows of origin hanging over them. If you are dubious about old master prints, consider some drawing card names of more recent interest. In the field of western art, *Thomas Hart Benton* will always find eager investors. At a S.P.B. auction of nineteenth- and twentieth-century prints, "Frankie & Johnnie," a print by Benton, had a presale estimate of $2,000 to $3,000. It sold for $3,600, establishing a new high for this print. *Toulouse-Lautrec*, another popular name in the art world, captured a $51,000 bid by a Michigan collector at the same auction. His lithograph "La Partie de Campagne" nearly doubled its presale estimate.

Sometimes a name becomes important to a sale because of the collector-owner's knowledge, not his social standing. Such was the case when a well-known collection of toys came to auction in the Midwest. For years, the former owner had exhibited and lectured around the country about his collection. He had also written articles on the subject for local papers. When he suddenly died, his widow put the collection up for auction. On the strength of his name as a collector and his years of research, buyers flocked to buy. They had faith in the collection and its former owner as an authority. That was all the provenance needed.

Names are used at important charity antiques shows to lure people. *Dr. and Mrs. Henry Kissinger* were used to promote an important New York antiques show. In Chicago the appearance of *Illinois Governor James Thompson* and his family is an expected happening at every important antiques show. These names are then used in other ways. Imagine the status for the dealer who can say, "Well, Mrs. Kissinger just spent twenty thousand in my booth for a little Oriental rug for a wall hanging." Instantly, the word is passed along, and customers and dealers become aware of who is here and what they are buying. It is the fond hope of the dealer that other customers, hearing of the Kissinger's purchase, will figure, "Well, that must be a good place to buy small Orientals." Or, "I bought my Turkish water pipe from the same dealer Henry Kissinger bought things from." The story may be further embellished to become, "I was standing right next to Kissinger when he bought that Oriental." There is nothing quite like a name to stimulate buyers, but unfortunately, it doesn't do much for serious investment in antiques. It may even generate sales of objects that aren't of investment quality.

Certain names in the antiques world hold up better than others. For instance, no matter when you purchased your collection of *Wedgwood, Derby,* or *Chelsea English* porcelain, it will find a buyer at more than you paid for it—providing, of course, that it was authentic, in mint condition, and contained rare examples. If you are a

These are pussy cats with pedigrees, a partial collection of fine early nineteenth-century porcelains. With names like Staffordshire and Spode on their identification tags, they are worth a small bundle.

collector of English or American clocks, names that are marketable are Englishmen *Thomas Tompion* and *Daniel Quares*, both eighteenth century, and Americans *Simon Willard*, *Eli Terry*, and *Joseph Ives*. The problems with these and other famous clockmaker names are fake labels. The names don't mean much if you don't know characteristics of design and type of works used for the appropriate period.

Collectors of English and Continental silver will want to remember the following names: *Paul de Lamerie* (George II), *Paul Storr* (George III and IV), and eighteenth-century American silversmiths *Paul Revere*, *Myer Myers*, *Jacob Hurd*, and *Jurian Blanck*. These names are as good as gold.

In silver, a few new names that bear watching: *Georg Jensen*, *Gorham Company*, *Tiffany*, and *Samuel Kirk*, all from the twentieth century. By watching any additions to important S.P.B. auction catalogs, even a beginner can see new trends. Only recently have twentieth-century silversmiths begun to appear with any regularity and achieve high bids.

In furniture, some newly appreciated makers' names are *Charles Rohlfs* (c. 1902–03), *Harvey Ellis* designs for the Stickley workshops, and other furniture with the name *L. & J. G. Stickley/Handcroft*. Similar furniture was designed in the *Roycroft* workshops along with decorative accessories. Roycroft pieces were marked with an orb-and-cross on the Roycroft name. All the above-mentioned designers and workshops were at their zenith from around 1902 to about 1913. Most of the furniture, made of oak in cleancut, straight lines, is referred to as mission oak. While a great deal of it may seem plain and uninteresting, many of the more interesting elaborate pieces have inlays of wood, copper, or pewter. Mission oak has a small, devoted group of collectors that has been following its slow rise in price. Choice examples have copper hardware.

Decorative arts from the same period such as candlesticks, picture frames, and inkwells feature hammered copper combined with other metals. These pieces are generating new collector interest. *Karl Kipp* and *Frederick Kranz* are two names worth remembering. They are among those who designed items for the Roycroft workshop and catalogs. Roycroft was set up as an artistic community in East Aurora, New York, by Elbert Hubbard, a publisher. The community evolved from printing books to every facet of decorative arts, all of which should be considered by serious investors.

In 1972 the Art Museum of Princeton University put together a traveling exhibit, "The Arts and Crafts Movement in America," which alerted many collectors to a new potential for collecting and investing. Yet, eight years later, there still is only brief action regarding Arts and Crafts in the influential auction houses. Prices haven't shown any dynamic growth, and only recently have collectors been buying examples of the Arts and Crafts books with their Gothic revival imitation of medieval manuscripts. These books are memorable since they were produced by hand methods with heavy impression and inking. The style was a drastic change from other turn-of-the-century printing styles. Names for collectors of books to remember are the *Elzevir Press*, Boston; *De Vinne Press*, New York; and *Copeland and Day*, Boston.

Book designers to look for from these publishing houses are *Bertram Grosvenor Goodhue*, *Daniel Berkeley*, *Updike*, and *Tom B. Meteyard*. Many were made in limited editions. Lucky is the collector who comes across one of the ninety copies of *The House Beautiful* designed by *Frank Lloyd Wright*. It is such a superb example of the emerging genius of Wright and shows his own touch to the Arts and Crafts decorations.

While the names of *Rookwood*, *Newcomb*, and *Van Briggle* of the Arts and Crafts period are familiar, there are others. *Dedham Pottery*, *Brouwer Pottery*, and *George*

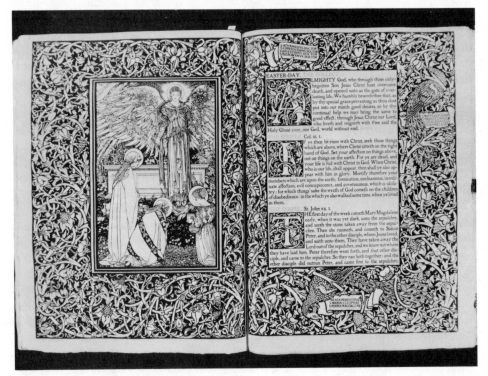

"*The Altar Book,*" *produced in 1896 by Merrymount Press, Boston, was designed by Daniel Berkeley Updike. It is typical of the fine type of hand-produced bookmaking that was redeveloped by William Morris. These Arts and Crafts books were done on fine, crisp, white, laid paper contrasting with heavy black ink and red accents.*

Book illustrations do well if the artist is either well known or currently being rediscovered. Arthur Rackham is enjoying a new wave of popularity and his original illustrations are increasing in price.

CREDIT: Sotheby Parke Bernet

E. Ohr, along with *William Grueby* worked in a variety of mediums, and for the collector there are vases, tiles, and small decorative objects. *Fulper pottery* has already found serious collectors. While many dealers are already getting several hundred dollars for choice pieces, there are others in the affordable $25 to $50 range. The name of *Moravian Pottery and Tile Works* of Doylestown, Pennsylvania, may not be familiar to you, but there are collectors on the lookout for the many tiles they turned out around 1910.

Names are very important if you are a collector of bookplates and autographs. To date, the average bookplate hasn't risen much in value, exceptions being famous names such as *Charles Dickens, Franklin Delano Roosevelt,* and *Winston Churchill.* This isn't to say that one day prices won't go up. Collectors look for unusual designs, famous names and especially famous names with famous owners' signatures. The field of autograph collecting is a separate, specialized category. Prices are based on rarity, popularity, and age. Two of the best-known dealers, Charles Hamilton and Joseph Rubinfine, point out that with big money riding on many a famous name, forgeries are a serious problem. As in furniture, with a little practice anybody can sign a famous name. It really takes a specialist to make certain a signed piece isn't a forgery. The same problem is faced by art collectors, especially where engravings and prints are concerned. If you aren't absolutely sure, don't spend your money. A favorite trick employed by a friend of mine who teaches antiques classes is to show his students a very ordinary glass bottle with the name Tiffany on it, and a small table in Chippendale-style with the name Chippendale on the bottom. Once the students are duly impressed, he admits that he signed all the names. "You didn't know the difference," he tells them. "That is precisely why you shouldn't buy for the name alone."

Are you familiar with the name *L. Gratchev* or *M. Koslovska?* Knowing who they are will help if you are interested in buying bronze figurines, especially since bronzes made by these two Russian sculptors will find buyers for thousands of dollars.

One name that meant little years ago but that has now become a synonym for quality is *Chinese export porcelain,* once known as Lowestoft. About thirty years ago, when antiques writer Carl Dreppard wrote *Primer of American Antiques,* this ware didn't enjoy its current high status or prices. Indeed, it was considered "Chinese lowstuff" and was still available in quantities. Dreppard pointed out, "The finer armorial and initialed pieces were special orders for which the customer waited often for as long as several years." Chinese export porcelain was imported on a large scale during the period from 1800 to the 1840s. Dreppard noted that the more common pieces were once owned by almost everyone in America.

Here's another example: a carving by Schimmel done with a jackknife costs thousands of dollars. Not always so. In 1948 Dreppard noted, "Very few people gave a second thought to jackknife carvings as possible candidates for the accolade of antiques until somebody discovered, and promoted, the work of one Schimmel, a German hobo. Happily, Schimmel and other such discoveries are not taken too seriously as yet. Schimmel and Mountz are not necessarily names to conjure with. They just happen to have had the best publicity to date."

Nevertheless, at that time, Dreppard advised collectors to "seek far better carvings by carpenters and cabinetmakers. You can have much fun in this field, and it is still wide open." You may ponder on another Dreppard comment: "Eagles were his [Schimmel's] specialty, copied mostly from the cast-iron eagles decorating building facades." Then came 1979, the place was Sotheby Parke Bernet in New York, and the event was the highly publicized folk art collection of Stewart E. Gregory. Included were several carved eagles referred to in the catalog as "Fine Carved and Painted Wood Figures of an American Eagle, Wilhelm Schimmel, Cumberland Valley, Penn-

The name Stewart Gregory drew crowds when his folk art collection was auctioned by Sotheby Parke in 1979. This painted wooden bust of Captain M. Starbuck set a record for American carving when it was sold for $30,000.

CREDIT: Sotheby Parke Bernet

sylvania, c. 1870." A presale estimate was between $6,000 and $8,000. Time certainly changes images.

If you aren't familiar with the names *Hans Popper* and *Hokusai*, you have no business buying a Japanese print, especially if you think you are buying a nineteenth-century print. When Popper, a collector of many things, visited Japan in the 1940s, he became interested in the beauty of Japanese prints. While there had been collectors before Popper, none had been as discriminating. Quantity wasn't as important to Popper as quality. Despite the fact that by the end of World War II, the best prints were supposedly in private collections and museums, in 1972 Popper's acquisitions made auction history. Who would have believed that a print by Utamaro could cost as much as one by Dürer? Indeed, at that auction, a polychrome print (c. 1793) by Utamaro was bid in at $37,000. The general mass of collectors were acquainted with the art of the Japanese woodcut print through two books, one by Jack Hillier and the other by James Michener, that came out in the 1950s. At that time, masses of eighteenth- and nineteenth-century prints were sent to the United States and sold in

Typical of the little baubles that found buyers at the Mentmore auction was this automaton. This Louis XV singing-bird and orange-tree musical automaton by Richard of Paris sold for $153,900. Made around 1757, it set a record for musical automata.

CREDIT: *Sotheby Parke Bernet*

such unlikely places as Marshall Field for $10 and $20 a piece. True, there were names like Hiroshige and Utamaro, and the prints were in various conditions. Most were quite faded. Currently, even the lesser artists from this same sale are selling in shops for from $100 to $200.

Since the Popper sale, prints from his collection have turned up over the years at auction. It was easy for Sotheby Parke Bernet to do a study on the results of these auction sales during the period of 1971 to 1979 because the same prints kept coming back to auction. The average annual increase in price per print was 19 percent. It showed that the top prints on good subjects by such names as *Utamaro, Hokusai,* and *Harunobu* had risen about 27 percent. However, the landscape prints of *Hiroshige* were way up. That was quite a track record for the Hiroshige print "Seba." At the Popper sale in 1972, it brought $8,000. In 1975 it sold for $15,000 at Sotheby Parke Bernet. At the May 1979, sale it brought a record $26,000.

While recently rereading some results from the fabled Mentmore sale, I was struck by the many times pieces were labeled "attributed to" or "in the manner of." That's name power at work. I didn't think they would have to bother dropping any famous names at that auction; buying anything at all should have been status enough. Yet, in Lot 444, a Louis XVI ormolu-mounted table de toilette was "attribed to J. H. Riesener, c. 1785." But get this: "This table bears a label indicating that it came from the home of Philippe, Duc d'Orléans, known as Philippe Égalité, cousin to Louis XVI and father of King Louis Philippe." Apparently somebody was impressed—to the tune of $44,460.

In Lot 621 one reads the words "probably" and "reputed to be." The item read: "Model of a dwarf in seventeenth-century attire (probably Iberian, c. 1840). Reputed to be a model of the celebrated dwarf of King Charles I and Queen Henrietta Maria." A London dealer paid $18,810.

There is one bright note to the Mentmore sale, aside from the records, of course. Lot 2883, a laundry basket and miscellaneous pans and kitchen utensils may have established some kind of record. Its presale estimate was between $9 and $17. It was sold for $13.68. Think of the ultimate name drop: "A laundry basket formerly belonging to the downstairs maid in the Rothschild estate, Mentmore Towers."

6.
Gambling on the Art Market

Once you realize that a large portion of the art market is built on guess work, you have a fighting chance to do well in it. The other portion is divided evenly between public relations and show biz. Thousands of dollars are spent monthly by galleries and auction houses to promote art and artists. Each work is touted as a new (or old) art investment. There is no place quite like the art world for speculation. Take your choice: antique prints, old master paintings and graphics, eighteenth- and nineteenth-century European and American oils. There are sporting prints and paintings, American Indian art, folk art, original cartoons and illustrations, and, lately, photography. There are even old quilts and secondhand clothes being promoted as wall hangings.

Often, what no one bothers to say is that to make money in art, you must have plenty of it to spend. For every dollar made in art investments, many more are lost. Guess who takes the biggest losses. The little investor. When you compare the percentages lost in relation to the income of Mr. Millionaire and Mr. Average, you'll find that the average investor spends as much but loses more.

Let's begin with the worst possible place to buy art and work our way up: without a doubt, it's the *motel art auction or exhibit*. Yet, these art traps are obviously making it pay off for themselves, considering how much it costs to buy an ad on television or rent a motel room. Your purchases are paying for it. No matter what you pay or what you buy at one of these events, you'll be paying at least double its value. These original oil paintings are usually done on an assembly-line basis in Taiwan and Mexico. In Haiti they do it with numbers. Sure, they're oil paintings, but are your mother-in-law's paintings investment worthy simply because they're done in oil?

However, here is a rather fascinating example of buying mass-produced oils that somewhat contradicts what I just said. During the last years of the nineteenth century, Americans wishing to flaunt their new affluence wanted the ultimate status symbol on their walls: an oil painting. As a result, painting factories sprang up all over the major cities of the United States where artists painted similar scenes of boats and forests over

134

and over again. These paintings were then hawked by traveling dealers or advertised in the cities. Prices were low compared to paintings by professional painters, business was good, and the need for an oil painting on the wall was satisfied. Now, nearly 100 years later, these paintings turn up in auctions and shops at high prices because they are old and because they are oils. Sometimes, when they show up at fancy auctions, their attribution will be something like, "In the manner of the famous nineteenth-century painter Waldo Dipp." Wild-eyed bidders may end up paying a thousand dollars or more for technically inferior works of art. Now if you can hang around another 100 years, your motel art may appreciate to the level of valuable art investment. Nevertheless, in the realm of true art, one of the major problems is that price doesn't necessarily correlate with quality. Consider some of the prices on limited-edition prints by such big names as Chagall and Leroy Neiman. Unfortunately, they were *overproduced works*, and as many who have tried to sell them have discovered, they are currently worth zilch. Like the motel paintings, they will have to age a little.

Another big problem is *fakes*. There is something about human nature that can't resist the magic of an important name like Rembrandt or Michelangelo. This goes for buyers on every level, including museums. Not too long ago Swiss art historian Alexander Perrig raised the hackles of many a museum art curator by claiming that 90 percent of all Michelangelo drawings are forgeries. For the past 24 years, he has been studying Michelangelo's works, and he discovered that only 10 percent were actually done by the master. The others were turned out by students, followers and copyists. Perrig points out that only about ten large-size drawings were found in

Is Mickey Mouse art? To a collector of industrial comic art, both the wooden toy and the blownglass figurine are serious art investments. They point to the rising prices for Mickey Mouse and other popular comic characters.

CREDIT: Dennis Todaro Collection

Michelangelo's home after his death. How does he account for the other 690 extant drawings? "It was in the seventeenth century that Michelangelo became so famous and his works so sought after. Conveniently, at that same time, a large number of Michelangelo drawings 'came to light.' " If Old Master drawings are your weakness, keep in mind that many have been and still are being forged. After all, why should the art business be any different than the antiques business?

Unless you know what you are doing, the *field of graphics*, especially print collecting, can be a financial disaster. Since not only authenticity but condition are important, learn a few sad facts. Again, if you are a "name" collector, you had best know that famous names such as Pablo Picasso and others have been forged. Serious collectors study the paper, measurements and the original number in instances of numbered editions.

While *restrikes* aren't technically fakes, neither are they as valuable as prints made from first impressions. There is quite a difference between a Currier & Ives restrike price and one from the original printing. It's a poor purchaser who doesn't bring a jeweler's loup or magnifying glass to discover any telltale large dots like those that appear on comic strip pages. They are the clue to a restrike.

Sometimes you may come across what appears to be an original drawing by a famous artist for a very low price. Unless you are a super expert on that artist, pass it up. It has been quite common, for instance, to find *signed drawings* with names like Whistler and Charles Dana Gibson in small shops and flea markets. I did a newspaper story on buying original Gibson drawings and received dozens of letters from people who had them to sell. Many took the trouble to Xerox their drawings. Guess what? All were either outright fakes or copies of popular Gibson drawings. I couldn't convince the sellers that they weren't the real thing. Doubtless someone else bought them for the asking price of $200 and up. As one seller said, "But even if they're copies, they're old copies." I can only say, wait about 300 years and nobody will know the difference.

Many print collectors buy the *Print Collector's Newsletter* for current listings of fakes. Even better are back issues. A fine reference book for collectors is *Fine Prints: Collecting, Buying and Selling* by Shapiro and Mason. Some dishonest print dealers of my acquaintance think nothing of patching up torn and tacky prints. The repairs are then hidden under the glass and frame. Close scrutiny is a must when buying prints.

A currently magical name in art for collectors and investors is *Norman Rockwell*. His work affords a good chance to follow what can happen to an artist's work. In 1979 a Norman Rockwell painting sold for $42,000 at a Christie's auction in New York. The painting was the original art for a 1925 *Saturday Evening Post* cover and was titled "Self Portrait." A few years ago, it would have been inconceivable to have a Norman Rockwell painting sold at a Christie's auction. While prices for Rockwells have been steadily rising, they seem to be peaking in the years following his death. Does this mean they will continue to double in value or will they level off in a few years? Many collectors of American illustrators have been picking up Rockwell paintings whenever they could, for years. They never were exactly cheap, usually several thousand dollars. These collectors rightly figured that at Rockwell's advanced age, his days of painting would shortly be over. And, as with so many artists, his works would soar during the years after his demise. It was something of a gamble, but how far off could a Rockwell buyer go?

One buyer, Judy Goffman, remembers buying a Rockwell oil several years ago for $10,000. In 1979 she sold it for $30,000. Rockwell and other American illustrators were the impetus for Judy and her husband Alan to open a specialized art gallery on

This J. C. Leyendecker Saturday Evening Post *cover painting could have been bought for $2,000 a few years ago. Today it would cost around $15,000.*

the outskirts of Philadelphia. What began small has now become a serious art business, an investment in a new area of collecting that is paying off.

"For a young collector, the field of *original American magazine illustrations* offers affordable opportunities," said John Evans, sales manager of Manhattan's Grand Central Galleries. "The market is slowly rising, and you can still get excellent quality pieces for as low as $500." The gallery, founded in 1922, recently had an exhibit of American illustrators. "There is such a built-in resistance to thinking of illustrators as fine artists that we decided to treat the exhibit as a fine art exhibit. We were very pleased to see that prices in many instances were double what we had expected, and sold." Evans observed that illustrator *J. C. Leyendecker* is becoming very popular. "One owner refused to sell for $10,000." Lesser-known illustrators from the 1900s to the 1930s such as *Frederic Gruger* were finding buyers at prices from $700 to $1,500

In Detroit's Du Mouchelle Galleries, this Norman Rockwell painting for a Saturday Evening Post cover brought $60,000 in March, 1979. Considered typical of the Rockwell genre, it is appropriately titled "In Need of Sympathy."

CREDIT: Du Mouchelle Galleries

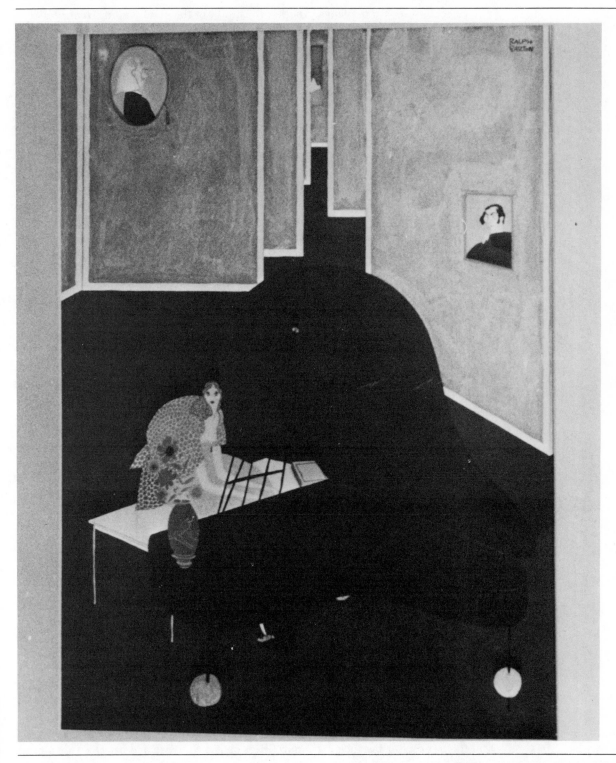

Did you ever hear of Ralph Barton? In the 1920s and 1930s he was a top il- lustrator known for his social satire. New Yorker covers and book illustra- tions for such works as Gentlemen Prefer Blondes made him famous in his day. Now his work is being reev- aluated and sought by collectors.

for pencil-on-board drawings. Another illustrator of the same period, *Henry Raleigh,* found interest in the $800 to $1,200 range for pencil-and-color wash drawings done for the *Post.* A *Howard Chandler Christy* on loan had offers from hopeful buyers for four times the owner's purchase price.

Author-illustrator *Walt Reed,* who has been dealer and collector for many years, said, "There's no doubt that the American illustrators and their work are finally achieving recognition. Now that original Rockwells are over $65,000 (June 1979) collectors are turning to other magazine cover artists. Stevan Dohono's covers are now $5,000 and up. Still underpriced are the illustrators for the 1940s and 1950s. They offer the beginning collector an opportunity to build a good collection."

Rosalind Mikesell, owner of Webberly Gallery in Chicago, sees Rockwells going up "just as surely as real estate appreciates." However, she feels that one of the best current art investment opportunities would be artists from the *Barbizon School* (1879–1900s) such as *Corot.* "Prices are low because of the French currency control. Also, artists from this particular school worked in somber and now unpopular colors, although they verge into the Impressionist school." Right now Mikesell feels that the ash-can artists such as *Shinn, Potthast,* and *Bellows* will go continually higher. She points out that many of their works could have been purchased for from $5,000 to $10,000 a few years ago. Now they are in the range of $25,000 to $50,000.

"There is a vast difference these days as to what sells in England and what does well in the United States," Mikesell observed, "but that wasn't always so. The United States collector was more impressed by English and European art and artists until the last ten years or so." What she didn't say was that until recently, it didn't even matter who the artist was or how good the subject was if it came from England or the Continent. This attitude was a hangover from the early feelings of inferiority when American craftsmen from silver to furniture and art weren't considered as good as European craftsmen. As other art dealers have noted, the Bicentennial did a lot for the American artist.

As for current trends in England, Mikesell sees a growing interest in *Victorian oils* (the pre-Raphaelites). Artists she is keeping her experienced eye on are *Alma Tadema, Oman Hunt,* and *Rudolph Ernst,* all from the pre-Raphaelite period. "I sold one to a London dealer for $4,000 who in turn sold it to another dealer in London for $6,000. When I lást heard, that dealer had a price on it of $10,000. But that's in London," she told me. She also sees a trend toward a return to realism. "Abstracts seem to be going down. People have grown tired of them."

She has some advice for new art collectors. "Buying at an auction can be risky. Dealers always take what they can't sell and put it up at auction. Never, never bid on art at auction without seeing and studying it." The great collections amassed by people like Rockefeller are always purchased with the aid of a knowledgeable dealer, according to Mikesell. "Of course, you have to first find a dealer you can trust and then put yourself in his hands. This way, you'll probably pay a 10 percent commission to build a collection. The other way is to do a lot of leg work yourself. Study auction catalogs and ads, and hopefully you'll begin to develop some kind of selective powers. Selecting good work by good artists is the starting point. It also helps to keep ahead of the trends. For instance, right now prices on Art Nouveau and Art Deco are almost topping out." She thinks these are faddish things and advised: "If I were just beginning to collect, I would look to the *Arts and Crafts movement* that took place between the two World Wars. There are many good artists from that period yet to be reappreciated. By the time there are exhibits and books about them, it will be too late to buy them for modest prices. The same could be said for the signed porcelains from that period. It is certainly something to watch."

Another dealer noted that investors pay through the nose when they put their money into artists who are momentarily popular. She called attention to *Andy Warhol's hand-colored silk screens on canvas* and *Willem de Kooning paintings* that can cost you dearly. Another dealer recently realized a nifty profit when he sold a de Kooning painting for just under $1 million.

"Buy from the innovator not the person who copies from the original style," advised another collector. "And buy from the artist's peak period."

If there is one lesson to be learned from the art market as well as from the antiques market it is: Pay attention to the trends. For instance, one 1971 Sotheby Parke Bernet newsletter noted: "American art has become increasingly popular, particularly over the last ten years. Suddenly greater success of auctions this year in relation to other years might reflect the consignment of finer-quality material and the willingness of collectors to pay more for it." The article noted that the Americana boom was reflected in record prices, in higher volume of trading, and in higher valued lots. "It makes few exceptions for schools, periods, or particular styles." At that time, a *Winslow Homer* print set a record at $8,000. *Thomas Eakins'* "Cowboys in the Badlands" became the record price at $210,000 for any painting by an American artist. This during a year of recession. Now if you were a trend watcher, this information would

Once-famed illustrators such as Henry Patrick Raleigh, a lesser-known contemporary of Norman Rockwell, are being reassessed by collectors. This Raleigh magazine illustration done for the Saturday Evening Post *in the 1920s cost $50 three years ago. Today it would cost $800.*

have been a signal not only to buy other Homer works but western artists and subjects as well. The proof is the sale of a Winslow Homer oil at the Detroit Du Mouchelle Galleries in 1978 for $275,000, a record high. Several years later at a Sotheby Parke Bernet auction, Thomas Eakins' "The Archbishop William Henry Elder" set a new record price for the artist of $265,000.

By 1977 the boom in American art was in full swing. "It is interesting to note," said Warren Adelson, director of the Coe Kerr Gallery in New York City, "that two collectors of Impressionist paintings, Mary Lasker and Frank Sinatra, have recently shifted the emphasis of their collections to American art." He further noted strong interest in the *Hudson River School of Landscape Painting*, which includes the artists *Bierstadt*, *Church*, and *Cole*.

Actually, the Hudson River School wasn't a school at all but a sarcastic term coined by a critic who derided the nineteenth-century American landscape painters for their "provincialism and geographical limitations." Many artists were influenced for the

Even late nineteenth-century oil paintings by unknown artists have escalated in value. This painting dates from around 1870 and is unsigned. It was originally purchased in an antiques shop for $35, then sold to another antiques dealer for $250. She in turn sold it to a customer for $450.

first time by the native beauty of the American rather than the European landscape. Choice years for Hudson River paintings are from 1825 to the late 1870s. Some of the names that have come to represent art investments are *Jasper F. Cropsey, George Inness*, as well as Cole, Church and Bierstadt. Sure enough, as the Hudson River paintings began to flow to auctions, mainly in New York, prices rose like high tide. They still are.

Adelson also mentioned that there was a growing interest in the *American Impressionists* such as *John Singer Sargent, Mary Cassatt*, and *William Merritt Chase*. The American Impressionist period lasted from 1880 until 1930. They were a direct outgrowth of the French Impressionists that influenced art throughout Europe and America during the late nineteenth century.

While prices had never been exactly low for American Impressionist paintings, they were clearly reaching new highs by the end of the 1977 Sotheby Parke Bernet auction year, when a record was set by the sale of *Hans Hofmann's* "Rising Moon" at $220,000. By 1979 an oil by *Childe Hassam*, "Just Off Fifth Avenue," brought $105,000. Only a few years ago, Hassam and other important American Impressionists could have been purchased for $60,000 and up—not cheap, but within the range of an upper middle-class collector.

In 1977 the stage was being set for what John Marion referred to as "the quietly booming market for tangible assets" like art, antiques, and other collectibles. He attributed the growing interest at that time to "Sotheby Parke Bernet's marketing policy of attracting more bidding from private collectors, especially those from outside New York." But, there was plenty happening in other areas of the country. By June of 1979, San Francisco's Butterfield & Butterfield auction gallery noticed a new art trend when works by *California and western artists* began to appreciate. "Saddling the Horse" by *Virgil Williams*, dated 1893, had an estimate of $700 to $900. It sold for $3,575. There was also a strong market for *European paintings*. A *Claude Monet* went for $66,000. *Marinus Kruseman's* "Winter in Holland," purchased six years before for $150, sold for $44,000. Its estimate was $7,000 to $10,000.

The gradually rising area of American folk art paintings really took off in 1979 with the Stewart Gregory sale of folk art. However, the year before it had become an important contender for art investors' dollars. Sotheby Parke Bernet established a record in this area for a naive portrait by *S. A. and R. W. Shute* at $42,500. Pictures by *Joseph H. Davis*, a popular early folk artist, sold for $5,000 and under.

You may ask, who were the Shutes and why are they worth $42,500 to a dealer? For one thing, the buyer, who had also bought another Shute the year before for $22,000, doubtless knew that the New York Museum of American Folk Art was planning a traveling Shute exhibit. As we all know, nothing helps to boost up prices like a museum exhibit. It remains to be seen what will happen to his purchases. From any standpoint, they can only increase in value. Just how much depends on a variety of factors, most importantly public taste. As far as the average $500-to-$2,000 collector of folk art paintings is concerned, this investment area may seem almost too late to enter. Not really, though. There are so many areas and so many artists that a sharp-eyed collector can still purchase good examples in the medium-price range. Keep remembering that different areas of the country have different types of art preferences.

Probably because of their simplicity, folk art paintings have been choice fields for forgeries. The Joseph Davis style is one example of busy fakers. Therefore you the collector must work doubly hard on details before buying. For example, pay attention

This fine example of American folk art is typical of the type of painting that has more than quadrupled in price in the past eight years. Even unsigned and undated examples will find serious collectors paying thousands of dollars.

to the material the art is painted on. Some of the fakes I have come across have been painted on twentiety-century canvas board. Yet the technique appears to be early nineteenth century. Once your eye becomes accustomed to the look of an authentic primitive style, you'll recognize an affectation of it. Cracking paint is no guarantee of age as it can be faked. Another trap is country auction primitives, from paintings to furniture. After all, what could be a better place to get rid of fakes? Be especially wary when buying family portraits in mint condition for little money. Their growing popularity has made them wonderful fields for rip-off artists.

How does an area of painting suddenly manage to take off and become another art investment category? "We believe that it is the marketing as much as the market that influences auction results," reported S.P.B.'s John Marion in a newsletter. "It's not enough to obtain property. You must also assure sellers that your skills and energies in reaching buyers are also being efficiently and properly applied."

That's for sure. A touch of public relations and a lot of show biz can make the big difference in what happens, whether it is a King Tut carving or a Grandma Moses painting. Sotheby Parke Bernet isn't the only auction house to discover that marketing and promoting can turn a market. Just read the pages of such trade publications as *Antiques Monthly* and you can quickly get the drift of the next auction biggie. Dealers and auction gallery folk have become the star attractions along with the objects. Who can blame them, when apparently the public is waiting for their every word?

The last few years have seen not only Sotheby Parke Bernet but dealers and galleries from across the country smiling into cameras and pontificating on the importance of this or that item. Unfortunately this book is doing the same thing. Hopefully the difference will be in the final analysis of what really happens when a collection is unloaded at the marketplace, public relations or no. The upward spiraling of prices because of marketing in one geographic area can be of benefit to the collector who buys in another less important area. The small investor has quickly learned that by following the leads in such major markets as New York, Chicago, or Milwaukee, the "picking" will be easier in St. Louis, Minneapolis, and Fresno.

Some of the ploys used by Sotheby Parke Bernet are worth observing. Shortly before the Bicentennial, they began their "Heirloom Discovery" service. It was great for the owner of the discovery and even better for Sotheby Parke Bernet when it came to the auction block. S.P.B. missionaries were sent out to save antiques around the major United States cities. A wag has said the sun never sets on Sotheby Parke Bernet. I'm beginning to think its true. However, in fairness, the entire antiques and art industry has certainly benefited from the increased awareness of what's new and worth buying.

By 1977 dealers were discovering another spinoff from the S.P.B. marketing: American collectors were often willing to battle dealers to the bitter end. The missionaries had done well, and the flock jetted to New York from the hinterlands of Dallas, Milwaukee, and Indianapolis. American collectors had come of age. They had discovered they could successfully bid in competition with dealers and museums to secure the fine works they wanted—without paying higher gallery prices. Of course, these bidders weren't the average ad agency account executive or lawyer parting with $220,000. Granted, the majority had plenty of cash to spend, but more important, they had chosen to spend it with an eye to investing. Instead of buying another hotel or island, they were putting their money into important pieces of art. Does that mean they picked a sure thing for their thousands? Not necessarily. For the moment, American Impressionist paintings may be top dog, but not forever. Remember the thousands spent for years on abstracts? Remember the observations of the dealer who said the public has tired of them. Prices may be expected to start going down. Public taste is erratic. Today, it is enjoyable to have an Andy Warhol "Red Elvis" hanging on your wall to the tune of over $100,000. In another ten years, when you decide to sell and reap your profit, the public may have lost interest not only in Elvis but in Warhol as well. This is why it is nice to enjoy living with your purchases.

In the 1920s and 1930s, every fashionable American home had to have either *English sporting paintings or prints* on the walls. Country clubs usually had several sets of sporting prints dressing up their dark oak walls, and many still do, such as the Onwentsia Club in Lake Forest, Illinois. No art gallery of any importance lacked sporting art. By the late 1950s, hardly anybody cared about prints, much less the sporting type. They were considered old-fashioned by the post–World War II generation. Prices went down all over America, although the British market for them remained pretty constant over the years. Names like *Henry Aiken, George Stubbs*, and *Thomas Rowlandson* once bandied about at the "club" were pretty much forgotten. Restrikes and a general flood of sporting art had pretty well saturated the American market. Many dealers put them away to wait for a better time. Then, in December 1978, an article appeared in *Antique Monthly* that should have alerted buyers and dealers to a resurgence of interest. "Sporting Art Enjoys American Revival" was the headline, and reading it made me ask this question: Is this an effort to revive the market rather than a report of an actual revival? The article mentioned past collectors, but when it came to bringing the reader up to date, one learned that all of the great prices of $17,000 and up that year had been paid by English buyers, not American ones. If any Americans were battling it out on the auction floor, it was not mentioned: "When two Herrings crossed the block at Sotheby Parke Bernet in New York not long ago, they were both purchased by London dealers." It is not what you read but how carefully. Should this be the moment for all of us to rush out and buy up British sporting art while it lasts? Is anybody doing so? Actually, not much has been heard about sporting art as an investment since the innuendo was dropped in 1978. Apparently, Americans did not bite.

Another fascinating question for would-be art investors to ponder is *who buys what*, which can be just as important as the record price achieved. For instance, let's go back to that Norman Rockwell painting, "The Bookworm," which was purchased for $65,000 by a New York dealer, to the $42,500 folk art painting by Shute bought by a Boston dealer, or to the Frederic Remington bronze purchased in 1979 by a dealer who paid $90,000. These purchases can have two implications: one, the dealer was willing to pay the record price because he had a customer willing to pay much more for it, and two, the art may have been purchased to be held by a dealer who may have been planning to put it back on the block the following year, for perhaps double the amount. Don't laugh. By now you've become aware of similar price jumps in a year's time span. A collector watching from the sidelines can also interpret the purchases to mean that the market for these artists is obviously going to jump way up. What the collector may not know is that the dealer may have bought them for a fellow dealer who placed them at the auction to do just what they did—establish a new price record. This practice is not dishonest, just a little market manipulating. Maybe it will work, and at the next sale, the art will zoom even higher. Or maybe it won't work. It's simply a good idea for the collector not to be too impressed by the astronomical alone.

One field largely passed up by the American collector had been that of *old master paintings*. This may have been because they had always been expensive, and the practical American mind felt they had long since had their day and belonged in museums and mansions. Then along came a S.P.B. auction in January of 1978 featuring old masters, many from a private collection that had been collected in Europe but brought to America before and during World War II. With prices reaching over $500,000 for a single painting, it is easy to be intimidated by European dealers. In their follow-up newsletter, Sotheby Parke Bernet crowed: "Americans are buying old masters." Figures from the old masters sale do indeed reflect that 27 percent of the offerings were bought by American private collectors; European dealers, however, bought the bulk at 40 percent. American dealers invested only 15 percent; European buyers bought 17 percent.

The star painting, "Flowers in a Glass Vase" by *Jan Brueghel the Elder*, was sold to a Swiss dealer-collector for $560,000. In an attempt to stimulate American interest, the S.P.B. newsletter stated, "One American collector was very prominent in the bidding on the $560,000 Breugel," but no actual purchases, or their American purchasers, were named. Some names were dropped: "Many new American buyers were attracted to an old master sale for the first time, among them Paul Simon, the songwriter; and Alan Alda, the actor." They may have been attracted, but did they buy? Conclusions to be drawn from the newsletter seem to be that the private buyers bought lots of the least-expensive paintings, or that only a couple of private collectors bought several very expensive paintings. In other words, old master paintings are still

Early silent-film posters are a relatively new collectors' item. Reproductions can cost up to $20; originals occasionally go for hundreds.

Nothing has escalated in price in so short a time as posters. Posters such as this one by famed illustrator Howard Chandler Christy might go for as much as $1,500. Top subjects are war and western themes.

CREDIT: National Antiques Show, New York City

bought primarily by Europeans. Apparently the American collector likes to spend less and takes the chance that his purchase will appreciate. As one successful art collector told me, "I would rather speculate on a new market than compete on an established world market. There are too many problems buying old masters. In the first place, I don't think there are any surprises. If somebody suddenly discovers a new Corot, I automatically think it's a forgery. Let's just say I'm too late for this game."

One area collectors are enthusiastic about is *posters*. The field is still wide open and ranges from top-dollar items by such artists as *Jules Cheret, Alphonse Mucha,* and *Toulouse-Lautrec* to medium-priced originals by famous American names like *Harrison Fisher, Maxfield Parrish,* and *Charles Dana Gibson.* There are areas to specialize in from war posters to theater and travel. To have the most investment value, poster collections should be of a specific category of artist, historical period, or theme. One collector specializes only in mini-sizes as small as a post card.

Important art galleries have looked beyond the Alphonse Mucha and Jules Cheret posters to interesting *advertising art* by lesser-known names. One New York gallery offers them in the price range of from $200 to $3,000. Ten years ago, you could still find unusual posters in antique shops and art galleries for a few dollars. In those days, the sellers almost apologized for the poor quality of the paper as well as the ten-dollar price. Now among the most expensive advertising posters (at least in the galleries) are the early *automobile ads.* Is $2,000 too much to pay for one? Of course, you can always get a newly reproduced version of oldies for a few dollars, but they aren't yet in the league with the old ones and can't qualify as art investments.

Only recently have collectors begun to consider twentieth-century political cartoons as a form of collectible art. Names like Joseph Parrish and John T. McCutcheon, political cartoonists for the Chicago Tribune, have assumed new importance. An early McCutcheon cartoon might go for $800; a Parrish for several hundred dollars.

Certainly of investment quality are Art Nouveau and Art Deco posters by American artists like *Edward Penfield. Travel posters* of this period advertising the luxury steamship and the old railroad train are finding serious collectors. Who knows, those ad posters for theater and dance performances, music concerts, museums exhibits, and movies could very well be worth money one day. I personally like to invest in the *Christmas stamp posters* that are issued every year by the post office. You might want to specialize in famous people or inventions. Post Office poster art has been around for a few years, but I have yet to see it listed in the price guides. That gives collectors a chance to begin a collection inexpensively, sometimes for free. I discovered if I put my name in at the post office for whatever new poster hangs on their walls, I had a chance to get it free when they got a new one. Talk about art investments! This one can only increase in value.

Political cartoons have always had a few aficionados. Collectors tended to buy the old Daumiers rather than any twentiety-century pieces. Recently, along with the developing interest in illustrations, original cartoons have become popular. These can range from a *Helen Hokinson* "club lady" for $150 to a political cartoon by such contemporaries as *Fischetti* for $800. A recent exhibit in a midwestern art gallery showed prices to be on the rise, but still in the $250 range, for such famed cartoonists as Chicago *Tribune's Joseph Parrish.* The subjects can range from the humorous to the evils of war. Here again, the field is just developing, so a beginner can build a

Thanks to specialized collector-dealers like Cartoonerville in Huntington, New York, original cartoon art has become something to hang on the wall. Prices range from twenty to hundreds of dollars. This original comic book cover art for the Fantastic Four *is one of the many possibilities open to collectors.*

good starting collection for a couple thousand dollars. Even original turn-of-the-century cartoons can be found in shops for under $100. It all depends on who knows the new trend. Unfortunately, all it takes is one book or article on an artist or art form, with one price listed, to stampede dealers into raising prices. Most times the objects are overpriced.

Another interesting art field is *television news art*. Take a closer look at the drawings shown on your TV set that cover the important trials and other events where the camera isn't allowed. What wouldn't you give for a pen-and-ink colorwash drawing of events of the Chicago Seven trial or the Watergate hearings? I came across this new art possibility at the same midwestern gallery that held the cartoon exhibit. Prices ranged from $800 to $1,500. If you live in a metropolitan area that handles its own TV coverage of important news events, chances are there will be a TV artist whose name may appear on the list of credits. You might personally contact the artist and offer to buy some of his or her work. From what I have learned, once the art has been used, it is often tossed out or given back to the artist. Sounds familiar, doesn't it? The same thing happened long ago with the *Saturday Evening Post* original illustrations. You never know when one of these TV artists will go on to become an important artist in another medium. Because this is such a new area, you'll have to use your own judgment on what prices should be as well as what is really worth collecting.

The field of *sculpture* is also newly popular, but the problem for many collectors is space, unless they have large rooms or garden space—and lots of money. We have

The success of bronzes at the Geraldine Rockefeller Dodge auction set off a chain reaction for anything bronze and American. Contemporary sculptures by American Indian sculptors are being avidly collected.

This three-inch carved-ivory Eskimo sculpture was sold in an antique shop for $7 last year. It is an early twentieth-century piece and is unsigned. In a specialist shop, its price today might be $150.

covered the revival of interest in bronze sculptures of all types and its continual rise in price. The average collector is out of the picture except for purchasing small bronzes by contemporary artists. Two affordable possibilities, however, are in *contemporary American Indian and western sculpture.* Even here we are still talking about $1,000 and over. The same could be said for *contemporary wood carvings.* It is a speculator's market. Some of the gamble is eliminated if you put your money on those sculptors who are considered the finest in their line. By paying attention to art exhibits and by developing your own taste and knowledge, it is possible to build an important collection of contemporary pieces that will continue to go up in value. But you have to wait and hope that your decision was wise. You can't always go by the art critics. Remember, they didn't like Van Gogh or Matisse for many years. Nor can you make decisions based on marketing and public relations hoopla, especially if your art investments represent a financial sacrifice. A Ford or a DuPont can afford to make an expensive mistake. Most of *us* can't. Another Thou-Shalt-Not is to avoid following what everybody else is doing, because by then, prices will be up. Worse, the art may be expensive because it has gained current popularity, though it may not have lasting worth.

Explore new areas of art such as *textiles* and *needlework*. Eighteenth- and nineteenth-century *samplers* have been collected for a long time and prices continue to go up for the best examples, but only recently have *quilts, coverlets,* and *needlepoint* become appreciated as *wall hangings*. Historic, *signed woven coverlets* and quilts can cost from two hundred dollars to several thousand, depending on where you find them. Many collectors are buying good examples of contemporary *Amish quilts* and treating them as works of art. The humble *hooked rug,* even as late as from the 1920s, can be treated as wall art, especially if you pay several hundred dollars for it. Do you prefer a gaudy *crazy-quilt* for over $500 or a quiet *flower basket quilt* for the same price? Which will continue to hold its value or will both? In this area, such questions are often a matter of taste.

Several years ago, you could find a hand-embroidered late nineteenth-century *Chinese robe* at garage and estate sales for under $25. These days, a single cuff from their sleeves can cost $150, and the entire robe may be worth $1,500 or more. Framed it is a dramatic wall hanging—art, if you will. As lost art forms, these textiles can be considered art and art investments, and since they are still being sold by uninformed owners, there is a chance for a discovery. The danger to someone not familiar with the

Fine quilts like these are hung on the wall as art. Prices in the hundreds and sometimes thousands of dollars are common these days for unusual or historically important designs. The Centennial quilt is museum quality. The other quilt is important from a design standpoint.

look of old textiles and delicate stitchery are the new items coming in from the Orient. Their colors are often brighter and the look of age is missing.

Tapestries, real losers for years, are gaining in popularity. I'm not talking about the *Gobelins*, woven in the eighteenth century and priced today at $50,000, for which there is always a waiting museum or mansion wall. I'm referring to the area of the *Biblical tapestries* and partially *machine-finished tapestries* of the turn of the century for which the market has been dead at least thirty years. These tapestries found a waiting market in the nouveau riche of the early twentieth century. Hundreds were shipped from Belgium and France. By the 1920s and early 1930s, even Sears Roebuck was offering machine-made versions for a few dollars, but the colors were drab and lifeless compared to the fine early tapestries. Sometimes important people and events were worked into mass-produced tapestries. One was the flight of Lindbergh in the *Spirit of St. Louis*. For a long time, tapestries were the losers at conducted house sales and auctions. Nobody would buy what had once been a $500 tapestry for even $100.

Today there is suddenly a glimmer of a trend for all kinds of tapestries. Leave it to Sotheby Parke Bernet to get the ball rolling with its May 1979 newsletter building interest in a tapestry auction. According to S.P.B. expert David E. Tripp, "Tapestries are one of the most undervalued areas of fine art collecting. When you consider what one pays for paintings of the same period and that tapestries are a rather rare commodity to come by, it's a wonder that they haven't attracted a major following." Pre-estimate auction prices ranged from $30,000 to $50,000 and under. Now would be a good time to start picking up good examples of tapestry. Obviously, all forms are about to make a comeback. Rather than buying two $500 machine-made pieces, look for interesting needlework from the Art Deco period, or, if luck is with you, from the Art Nouveau period. Another possibility to consider is hand-embroidered towels and other linens, not only American but European, from before World War II. Don't worry that nobody else is doing it. Think of the man who specialized in collecting early photographs before anyone else did. His junking became a collection worth thousands of dollars, and that is what speculating in the art market is all about.

One final word involves *limited-edition plates* hung on the wall as art. Even Renoir paintings haven't escaped the limited edition-plate market. Last year, one of the offerings, "The Children of Renoir," was issued in a series of six plates by *Pickard China*. The edition was limited to 5,000 at an issue price of $50. Doubtless it has gone up in value since that time. The good news is that it brings the beauty of Renoir paintings into 5,000 homes that might not otherwise have become acquainted with them. You can't argue that this is art, even though in a new form, but how endurable an investment it will be is debatable. After reading what's happening in the limited-editions market in the following chapter, you can make your own decision. It is important to realize that plates are an art form that many thousands of collectors are investing in, and many seem to be making a profit. With hundreds of issues and companies, the problem is to choose *the* one in a thousand that becomes a lasting, growing investment.

This bas-relief porcelain plate, "Heading South," was designed by famed sculptor Hans Achtzinger. Of 10,000 plates fired, only 5,000 were issued in the United States, for $150 each.

CREDIT: Hutchenreuther

7.
The Rise of the Limited-Editions Market

One indisputable fact about the limited-editions market is that it surely is unlimited. You name it and there is probably a limited-edition issue of it—or about to be. From Tut to Towle and all of the Boehms and Beams, it is the one area of collecting that has something for every pocket and taste. Just when you think surely no one would dare use the word "limited edition" one more time, fifty thousand dealers and manufacturers do.

To get to the truth of the matter, any "chip" in the porcelain market is next to impossible. According to dealers and collectors (the latter starry-eyed), limited-edition anything is the perfect collector's investment. All hasten, by rote, to advise, "Most people don't buy these for investment but because they love them." Old-time collectors and dealers point out that "the plate" made by Bing & Grondahl back in 1895 to commemorate Christmas originally cost fifty cents. As of June 30, 1979, it was quoted at $4,000 in the Bradford Exchange current quotations.

The one morsel of truth I managed to get out of at least one dealer is that when a *limited-edition plate* isn't listed any longer on the Bradford Exchange, it's finally acknowledged a loser. What that means is, yes there are losers. Nobody talks about them. As far as the B. & G. plates go, it is true they have all gone up in value every year, but no one points out that most take twenty years or so to go up enough to make much difference in an investor's pocket. In most cases, we're talking nickels and dimes. For instance, the B. & G. 1969 Christmas plate was issued at $14. Its current quote is $25. In ten years' time, it hasn't even doubled in value, but the 1960 plate issued at $10 has shown an impressive rise to $210. Going back to 1923 with an issue price of $2.00, we find a current quote of only $59. Through the years B & G plates show this uneven fluctuation. As in the antiques investment field, age isn't the criterion for value. Supply and demand, and the popularity of the subject, are more important.

To think that a multibillion dollar world market and a new industry was spawned by that first B. & G. issue! Today it encompasses not only B. & G. plates but items in glass, metals, porcelain, and pottery. There's probably something even in plastic.

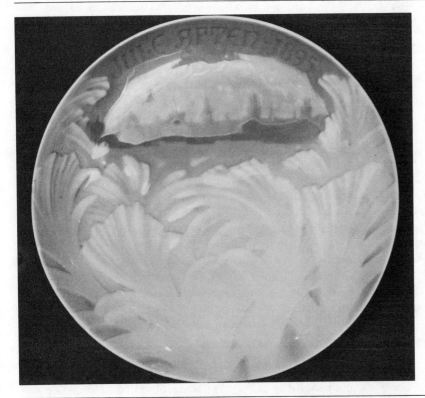

This plate, "Behind the Frozen Window," issued at Christmas 1895 by the Danish porcelain makers Bing & Grondahl, started the whole collector's plate concept. It was originally issued for approximately fifty cents. Its current value of over $3,000 makes it the most valuable collector's plate in the world.

Limited-edition collector's plates have created a spinoff: jewelry. This hand-crafted porcelain cameo is a replica of the famous collector plate made by Bing & Grondahl. As a framed wall plaque that can convert to a brooch, its issue price is $35.

CREDIT: Bing & Grondahl

There are bells, paperweights, figurines, liquor bottles, silver miniatures, spoons, jewelry, and dozens of other categories, all made in limited numbers after which the mold is broken.

Hardly a day goes by when there isn't a new limited-edition "something" added to the already bulging market. According to the dealers I spoke with, the end is nowhere in sight. It is "unlimited," and for the dealers that means unlimited money in the bank. To give an unnecessary boost to this giant market are several publications geared strictly to the limited-editions market as well as conventions, club meetings, exhibits, and whatever else can be used to promote the interest and sale of the limited editions market.

I haven't touched on the graphics market, since that would take an entire book all by itself. Out of all the limited-edition categories, the most flourishing appears to be the collector's plate market for which various factors can trigger an upswing. However, they are the same factors that also affect the art and antiques and collectibles market. One example is the *Wizard of Oz* plate issued as the *Over the Rainbow* series by Knowles China, the first series honoring motion picture classics. The first plate featured Judy Garland and was issued at $19. Despite plenty of publicity, including a letter from the president of the Bradford Exchange, not much is happening. Perhaps it's a matter of taste, but I feel the plates could have looked a little less like gaudy, cheap mass-produced efforts to make a quick buck on a fine old flick. Of course, what do you expect for $19? Apparently, thousands of people expect a quick return on their investment—say in two years or so.

Plate collectors follow the ups and downs of the Bradford Exchange current quotations as others follow the stock market. Briefly, Bradford Exchange is the world's largest trading center in limited-edition collector's plates. It is followed by dealers and more than one million collectors in the United States and fourteen other countries.

Every day the exchange may handle as many as 4,000 transactions. These include the posting and matching of buy-and-sell orders for any of the 1,000 major issues listed on the most recent Bradford Exchange current quotations sheet. In addition, there are numerous over-the-counter (non-listed plates traded between specialized dealers) issues and new issues made available to collectors. The exchange also keeps up to date the market performances in their Market Bradex. These are determined by quote-price/issues-price ratios of the twelve most significant plate series.

As quoted by Bradford, "Limited-edition collector's plates are all true collector's plates (since 1895) issued in limited editions." Editions are limited either by a function of quantity or time. At present, four limiting methods prevail:

1. Limited by announced quantity (plates numbered).
2. Limited by announced quantity (plates unnumbered).
3. Limited by announced firing period (plates may or may not be numbered).
4. Limited by year of issue (restricting the quantity to number produced during the year of issue; plates may or may not be numbered).

By definition, a collector's plate is any decorative plate made in a limited number specifically to be collected. In other words, your antique pewter plate was made to be used, not necessarily collected. The limited-edition pewter commemorative plate was made to be hung on the wall or put in the vault, but not to serve pretzels in.

For many, the confusion occurs over the word "limited" when manufacturers don't disclose the total number of an edition. These undisclosed editions can be as small as one thousand to hundreds of thousands. Technically, once the edition is "closed," the plate may never be manufactured again. It is up to the manufacturer to announce and decide how many. The public, therefore, must rely on the integrity of these thousands

One of a six-plate "National Parks of America" collection authorized by the U.S. Historical Society, this plate pictures the Shenandoah National Park. Each plate is limited to 5,000 copies worldwide.

CREDIT: Royal Copenhagen

This Spode collectors' plate had everything going for it, yet it is no longer listed in the Bradex market quotes. It was the first of a series on the popular issue of peace. Top-name designer Cecil Beaton created the art. Yet collectors did not find it appealing enough to put their money into it.

of manufacturers. Here again, a non-collector is forced to look objectively at this market and those involved in it. It's best to take the antiques market adage of "Buy only from a reputable dealer" and change it to "rely on a reputable manufacturer." In other words, how does the public ever really know how many editions of the Fuzzy Wuzzy spider plates were undisclosed editions not only in the United States, Europe, and Asia, but in Africa? The naiveté of the buyers in this new area of investing is astounding. It can be likened only to the beginning antique buyer who believes that because a dealer tells him a chair is a genuine Queen Anne, therefore it is. Because the market is new by comparison with the antiques market, buyers have a lot of learning to do. I am sure there are all kinds of shenanigans going on that probably won't be disclosed for decades. After all, it took that long before people like Wallace Nutting and Ruth Webb Lee exposed the back rooms of fancy New York shops where "antiques" were made to order as well as the practice of planting fake Stiegel glass in barns and shops around New England. Why should such a wide-open field as limited-edition plates and other items be an exception?

In a press release issued for the 1979 Plate Collectors Convention, the matter of investment was skirted nicely. "While no one can guarantee that a plate definitely will increase in value, collectors all over the country are finding that most of their plates are continuing to appreciate over the years." Taking that little paragraph apart, you see that "no one can guarantee" and that "most of their plates are continuing to appreciate over the years." Everything goes up somewhat in value every year, including last year's clothes and paperback books.

The market becomes a little more complicated when you learn about the *secondary* market. First you get a chance to buy through the manufacturer before the edition is closed. Stage two is buying, selling, and trading between dealers, owners, and collectors in the shops and through the Bradford Exchange. This is when money begins to change hands and prices normally go above the issue price as collectors vie for a closed issue. Hopefully there will be a demand for what you have just bought—and that is what every collector hopes will send prices sky high.

You can also buy through the mails, but collectors say this can be quite risky. Apparently, there are some fly-by-night plate operators who either take the money and run or deal in (would you believe?) fakes. There, the word has finally surfaced, even in the glowing limited-editions market. While I couldn't get one well-known dealer to tell me what some of the spurious plates are or how to tell what's not authentic, she at least admitted it happens. I guess you will have to do just as antique collectors do: become familiar with the characteristics of the genuine piece and be careful where you buy. The dealer's logic for secrecy is, "If the fakers know we are on to them, they'll change their tactics and techniques." That doesn't sound very clear to me either. I should think that the people in the limited-edition plate business would do everything they can to let the public know how to keep from being stiffed. Apparently, the public isn't supposed to know, just as it is in the antiques business.

Let's assume, though, that you are a serious investor or thinking of becoming one. Naturally, you will need the bi-monthly report, *The Market Bradex Current Quotations*. Every plate listed has a Bradex number and a country of origin, in alphabetical order; the plate maker within each country; the plate series of each maker in chronological order, beginning with the maker's first series; and the individual plate within the series, also in chronological order beginning with the first plate. To make it work, you request a buy or sell order form from the Bradford Exchange. Upon its return, the Exchange matches it with another buyer or seller. The price is determined by the current Exchange range. The Exchange is at 9333 Milwaukee Avenue, Niles, Chicago, Illinois 60648.

Assuming you have decided to sell a plate through the Exchange, a 20 percent broker's fee is deducted from the asking price. You didn't think it was all profit, did you? If you sell it through a dealer, you can expect her to take between 20 and 50 percent. It depends on how important the plate currently is and whether she can sell it for more than twice the amount she paid you. Again, this business is just like the antiques business. Don't expect to get $500 for a plate just because you see it listed at that in the Exchange. If, for instance, several thousand holders of the same plate decide to unload and pick up a fast $500, it will be a tiny bit difficult for you to sell instantly. And, even assuming you beat all of the others and find a buyer, remember that 20 percent fee. That leaves you with $400 and Uncle Sam waiting in the wings.

The Exchange has some interesting criteria to help give the investors a fighting chance. It begins with "Buy what you like." However, they do have a few rules that dealers and collectors have found helpful:

1. *Maker:*   Does the item show flawless craftsmanship of a quality beyond similar plates regardless of price? Is it handmade? Is it delicate or crude? Is the maker known for fine workmanship or mass production?

2. *Artistry:*   Is it original art created especially for this plate by a living artist of note? Is it unique or merely a copy? If a copy, was the copyist himself an artist? Or, is it merely a reproduction of something already published? Is the subject one of broad appeal but not trite?

3. *Rarity:*   Is it a first edition or a later one? Is it tightly limited, yet not too limited to create a market, or is it widely distributed in quantity? Even if the edition is closed, are dealers bidding in the secondary market, or do they still hold original stocks? Is it individually numbered on the plate itself and/or registered? Or neither?

4. *Collectibility:*   Is it one, preferably the first, of a collectible periodic series or merely a single issue? Is the series small enough for general completion yet large enough to become a true collection?

5. *Time of Acquisition:*   Can you acquire it at the right time? At issue, while the price is rising, or only after it has perhaps already peaked?

6. *Sponsorship:*   Is it issued by a government or an official nonprofit institution, or by the artist himself, or by a commercial factory without other sponsorship?

7. *Commemorative Importance:*   Does it commemorate a seasonal event or an historic event? If so, does it bring new insight to the event? Or, is it an event in the history of the artist or of the maker?

8. *Material:*   If made of metal, is it solid gold or merely pewter or bronze? If made of glass, is it genuine 24 percent lead crystal or common glass? If made of ceramic, is it true hard-paste (or hard-fire) porcelain, or is it bone china or fine china, or is it merely common china, stoneware, or earthenware?

Merely reading these investment criteria raises questions. For instance, not just any plate fits into the inner circle of plate collecting. It is most important that the plate be from one of the top manufacturers. There are, for instance, only twelve that make up the Market Bradex Index. Yet there are hundreds of so-called collector's plates

Some collectors believe that if you start out spending several hundred dollars for a single collector's plate, you have a good chance of doubling your money. This plate, a nine-inch exact reproduction of the famous "Adoration" by Andrea Della Robbia retails for $550. The manufacturer, River Shore Ltd., has fired only 5,000. It is an interpretation by artist Roger J. Brown.

CREDIT: River Shore Limited

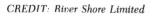

This metallic limited-edition plate issued in 1979 by the Goebel/Hummelwerk is an example of the increasing use of media other than porcelain. This plate uses 24K gold on brass. Titled "Star Breed," it is designed by the well-known artist Sasha Brastoff. The issue price was $125.

Goebel/Hummelwerk

Here is the 1976 "Alba Madonna," the first issue in Pickard China's annual series. It was named "Plate of the Year" because it rose faster in value than any other collector's plate in market history. Between September and December of 1976, it doubled its $60 issue price. The entire edition of 7,500 sold out immediately. Its June 1979 Bradex market quote was $320.

CREDIT: Pickard China Company

In just eight years' time, this W. Goebel Co. porcelain plate has risen from its issue price of $25 to nearly $1,000. Titled "Heavenly Angel," it was issued to celebrate the 100th anniversary of the porcelain factory. It also represents the first of a series of annual limited-edition plates with the M. I. Hummel designs. The growing scarcity of this plate will push prices upward for some time.

CREDIT: Hummel Art by John F. Hotchkiss

issued every year, from countries all over the world. If you are planning on spending several hundred dollars a month on plate investments, you will have to rely either on the taste of a dealer or your own. You also have to ask yourself this last question under criterion number 2, "Will this appeal to 99 percent of the collectors?" thus insuring its undying popularity.

There is obviously a major problem with number 4, collectibility. When you can't really be sure about undisclosed issues, how can you possibly know the size of the edition? Whatever you decide to do, read those eight points carefully, and then read between the lines.

Another problem, which isn't usually discussed, is seconds. Apparently, plates that for some reason didn't meet the quality standards of the manufacturer are sold by some dealers at less than usual retail prices. What is to keep some greedy collector or dealer from palming them off as being first rate, for the higher price? At this moment, nothing. Again, the burden of knowledge falls on the collector.

In one of the issues of *The Plate Collector,* it was noted that some dealers have held back items they knew were going to go up, hoarding and then dumping if the plates didn't go up as expected. Even worse is when a collector orders at issue price from a dealer and waits over a year for her plate. Finally, the dealer informs her that he can't get any because they were so popular at issue price. However, there are some on the secondary market for $100 or more. This true story was documented in a letter to the editor in *The Plate Collector* by someone who had ordered a plate originally priced at $65 and was told that it would be sold by dealers for $150. Further checking around the country by this collector showed that dealers had all upped the price. Obviously, this is a prime example of the hoarding and manipulating that faces the innocent plate collector who thought everything was just the way the ad read.

The same issue of the magazine also brought up the problem of two plates with the same design. According to the article, the collector who had invested in the first issue thought there would be a limited edition of that design. Imagine his surprise upon learning that there are double the number being issued. True, the back stamps are different, but isn't this confusing to the collector? Will issue number one be of as much value with issue number two following so close on its heels. Another allied problem is reissue with little variance in design. So you see, nothing is ever a sure thing, especially in the limited-edition plate market. The more you study it, the more complicated it becomes beneath the glossy surface of this multi-million-dollar promotional advertising market.

Since you now know that not every plate is loved and that prices may go way down as well as up, how do you sell a slow plate? In a few words, it ain't easy. Several dealers suggest running a private ad in one of the trades in the hope that there is either a collector missing that particular plate in a series or a dealer willing to buy cheap. As one dealer pointed out, if he has too large a supply of these slow movers on hand, all he can do is either use them as premiums to attract new customers or offer them in a grab bag package. If you have a large collection to sell that consists of both winners and losers, you are advised to contact a large wholesaler and offer the entire collection for half or 60 percent less than retail price at current issue price. Here again, just as in the antiques business, the collector has to know what his objects are worth before he can attempt to sell or trade.

After plates, probably the second most important limited-edition field is *Hummel art.* Last year, the collecting of Hummeliana had a listing of over 100,000 members in the Goebel Collectors Club, begun in 1977. This includes not only figurines but holy water fonts, bookends, candleholders, and many other items. Probably everything you ever wanted to know is contained in the book *Hummel Art* by John F. Hotchkiss. This art form, first produced from the drawings by Sister Maria Innocentia (born Berta Hummel) in 1935, has steadily increased in interest and value. Only in the last several years have prices for the earliest examples begun to sky rocket in value and collectors begun to consider their hobby as a serious investment. Like the plate market, prices are a matter of supply and demand, where you buy, and from whom. It is possible, from time to time, to buy the early Hummels from both specialized dealers and the antiques dealers. If you know a bargain when you see one, estate sales and garage sales can be treasure troves. Just keep in mind that not every seller is up on the latest Hummel prices, or even cares. To many, they are just charming little figurines worth maybe $5 to $25, depending on size. That is the way to build an investment.

In his book, Hotchkiss cites the action at auction that can temporarily hike a price. If two collectors battle over a single piece, the price can quadruple its actual market price. Like any items, the time alone will raise the value of a Hummel piece. Some much more than others. Figure on a percentage of breakage over the years, reducing the available number, and as a rarity, a piece could then be sold for many times more than issue price, if someone wanted to buy it. On the other hand, Hotchkiss pointed out what has happened to the 1972 Annual Plate. Issued at $38, it currently lists in price guides and at retail for $76. But if you sell that plate to a dealer today, it will pay you only $40, $2 above the original issue price. If you had put that same amount of money in a savings account, you would have made a profit of $15 or more.

On the upper strata of limited-edition collecting are names like *Boehm* (pronounced Beam) and *Cybis porcelains*. Both of these fine porcelain manufacturers always find ready buyers at auction. Prices of issues from ten to 100 show the biggest gains. These are truly limited editions, not usually exceeding an issue of 1,000. At issue prices of from several hundred to over four thousand dollars each, there are few buyers and fewer opportunities. Some of the most spectacular price gains in the Cybis porcelains have been prices jumping from an issue price of $250 to $2,500 in just one year. Unlike the limited-edition collector's plate market, this type of investor is buying status. She knows that a Baker display cabinet crammed wing tip to wing tip with Cybis or Boehm birds says, "I can afford to pay for only the best." This market is a more substantial one than the newer collector's plate market, for Cybis and Boehm porcelains have always been appreciated as a form of fine art. As such, they are a solid blue-chip item. Of the many makers of similar porcelains, they are top of the line, followed close behind by *Royal Worcester* and *Doris Lindner porcelains*.

There are probably 100 times as many *limited-edition whiskey decanter collectors* as Cybis or Boehm aficionados. They have their own buying, investing, and trading subculture, and for them it is quantity and names like *Michter, Lionstone,* and *Jim Beam* that count. They are just as convinced as the plate and Boehm collectors that they are investing in a collectible that is guaranteed to go up in price. Indeed, many of the Lionstone bisque-type figures have a look of quality and craftsmanship. While their bird and animal figures certainly aren't comparable to Boehm and Doughty or Cybis, they are at the least a mass-produced version and offer great variety to the collector. Prices for the more unusual sculptures such as the dioramas have more than doubled in the short time since issue, but highs for the majority fall in the $50 to $80 range.

Another giant in the limited-edition decanter field, *Jim Beam*, just keeps moving steadily along. However, one of their big blue-chip decanters, the *1957 Harold's Club Nevada*, seems to have leveled off at somewhere between $475 and $550, de-

This whiskey decanter in King Tutankhamen's likeness is a best-seller. A few notches up in the collector's ladder, you can buy a Tut mask in a limited edition of 1,000 for around $2,700, issued by the Boehm Porcelain Tutankhamen collection.

pending on who wants to buy and sell. Their limited edition of the National Bank of Chicago had a price range of between $2,500 and $2,700 a year ago, but so few of these ever appeared on the general market, they shouldn't be cited as a great example of what the Beam market is doing. Collectors should look instead at the medium prices for the majority of bottles that fall within the $30 to $50 range, with levels above and below.

America's oldest distillery, *Michter's,* hopped on the *King Tut* bandwagon in 1978 and put out three different sizes of the young king's image finished with liquefied 23-carat gold. The largest size was issued for $57.75. Collectors who are stashing away as many as they can afford feel this can't help but be a good investment. But when? In twenty-five years? "Yes, I'm putting them away for my grandson instead of buying stocks," said a grandmother. And she was quite serious. Like the other liquor companies, Michter's has a collectors' club, and scarcely a month goes by that a new coming edition isn't announced.

About ten years ago, when W. C. Fields movies were enjoying a revival, *Turtle Bay Distilling Company* put out a limited edition of *W. C. Fields decanters.* The price was around $9 as I recall. Within three years time, the price had reached $40. Two years later, a large Chicago liquor dealer was advertising the decanter for $100, a sure signal that prices would soon zoom up around the country. Yet today, you can still find that decanter in liquor stores for around $30 to $40. Does this mean it is a good solid buy at that price? Well, as time goes by and the number in existence disappear due to breakage, prices will go up again. But will you and I be around to cash in?

For one dollar, you can buy a copy of *Pictorial Bottle Review,* usually found in local liquor stores, to find out some of the ups and downs in value and generally what's happening. Prices for such bottles as Jim Beam, Ezra Brooks, and Grenadier are listed.

Another area of limited editions are the *silver miniatures* made by master miniaturist *Eugene Kupjack.* He signs and numbers his tiny replicas of such items as the Fabergé egg and Paul Revere silver. His rooms and individual miniatures are collected by museums, corporations, and anyone who loves miniature works of art. Talk about investments! One of his miniature rooms completed ten years ago for several thousand dollars was sold at an antiques show for $10,000. Others go for more. Yet, a beginning collector could buy several pieces of silver a year at a price of from $25 to $150 and know that the price of silver alone will keep it going up. This area is not as well known as the other limited-edition markets.

Let's see what a $50 investment in a limited-edition object would buy you. A plate, a Hummel figurine, a Lionstone whiskey decanter, or a Kupjack piece could all be purchased in that price range. In five years' time, one could be worth more than triple that amount. Which will it be? Or will it be all? One thing is certainly clear. An awful lot of people think they have the answer because they invest in thousands of types of limited-edition objects. Unfortunately, they can't all be right.

These sterling silver miniature reproductions of historic American pieces have been made in limited editions by Eugene Kupjack. Known as the master miniaturist, he follows every detail of the eighteenth- and nineteenth-century originals. An entire room by Kupjack costs thousands of dollars.

8.
Some Ups and Downs in Popular Antiques

Probably one of the best aspects of the antiques and the collectibles market is its mercurial nature. What's low in price may be worth a small fortune another year. A few months ago while browsing in an art and frame shop, I flipped through three *Walt Disney cels* from *Robin Hood*. The price on each was an unheard of $15. Out of curiosity, but without showing too much interest, I queried the salesgirl. It seems that a customer had brought them into the gallery three years ago and asked them to sell them for $50 apiece. Time passed and there was no interest, so naturally the gallery lowered the price. I took a closer look. Sure enough, they were authentic, complete with the official Disney studio stamp. Even though I didn't collect them, I knew somebody who did. After plunking down $45, I rushed home, made a phone call, and within minutes a collector had made off with them. As an investor in this type of art, he knew they were worth at least $150 each at that time. He later told me that he had sold them at that price and bought one rarity with the $450. He kept track of where they went next. During the 1979 Mickey Mouse birthday celebration, they were sold to yet another collector for $250 each; a perfect example of how yesterday's loser becomes a winner.

Not everyone is as lucky as the Disney collector. Another friend, a collector of primitive Americana, got carried away with the publication of a book on *tramp art*. This, if you aren't familiar with it, is chip carving done by traveling craftsmen from the early nineteenth century up to the 1940s. It was generally made into fancy boxes, mirror frames, and whatever struck the carver's eye. Materials used were wood cigar boxes and scraps, and decorations ranged from layered and inlaid wood trim to mirror fragments. Whatever appealed and was handy was used.

Figuring he could rush into tramp art before prices went too high, he bought anything and everything. The most he ever paid was $25 for a very ornate storage chest. He anticipated that the book would be followed by museum exhibits and lots of publicity, and that when prices began to double, he would be ready to unload.

These objects of tramp art (nineteenth- and early twentieth-century chip carving) are good examples of what can be done with wooden cigar boxes. At a current estimate, the total worth of the items in the picture is $1,000.

CREDIT: *Philip Trier collection*

Sure enough, before the year was out, there were exhibits and prices had doubled. Even so, twice $25 for a child's dresser in tramp art isn't exactly a fantastic sum. The collector waited, and whenever he found something unusual, he bought it. If all went well, there would be an important auction of a tramp art collection at someplace like Garth's Auction Barn or Sotheby Parke Bernet. While he fantasized, another year passed and interest in tramp art dwindled. Dealers for the most part were happy to give discounts on leftover pieces. If my friend were to sell now, he would still make a small profit, but hardly enough to pay for a newspaper ad. For the moment at least, tramp art is not a big seller. But what if there were an important auction, the type he's dreaming of? Would that do it?

Various dealers and collectors with whom I've discussed tramp art feel it's too early for it to be making profits for its owners. They do, however, point to folk art as a similar case. In order for something as specialized as folk art to catch on, there had to be large collections gathered over the years by serious collectors. Tramp art is still young, many of the items dating to the 1940s. Let it age for another twenty or so years, and it will become more appreciated. As the dealers pointed out, right now there is still plenty around, and, like drinking Scotch, it is an acquired taste. Now is the time to buy inexpensively, with the thought of future price rises in mind.

Twenty-five years ago, junk shops and salvage yards were filled with *brass beds*. Nobody wanted to have one of those clunky old things in their bedrooms. Suddenly, decorators began using them in New York apartments for a "country in the city" look, and presto! brass beds started climbing in price. They've been going up ever since, even reproductions of old styles. If you had bought one as recently as three years ago, it would have been yours for as little as from $500 to $600. Today $1,000 or more can buy you the same bed. From an investment standpoint, this may or may not be the time to buy. You have to ask yourself if brass beds have reached their peak. Have they been in the public favor too long? Or, will labor costs for new reproductions keep the prices on the same level and slowly rising over the years. Knowing how fickle the public taste is, I would say that they have peaked and will shortly be replaced by another fashion, but it will be several years before prices go down significantly.

Speaking of beds, the most expensive item these days is the massive, *Victorian high-back bed*. It's so popular, even at $1,500 or more, buyers don't even care if it engulfs their small bedrooms. The bigger the headboard, the more gingerbread the carving the better—and the higher the price. Looking back ten or fifteen years, it was a different story. "I can remember when those big beds were the dogs of the market," one dealer told me. "Now I just wish I had the ones I used to beg customers to buy for $200."

He's right. Anything Victorian finds buyers these days. The washstand with the marble top that once was a thrift shop or Salvation Army find for $50 is now $200 and up. Fortunately for collectors, plenty of it was made, and there's still a large amount around. Will prices keep going up? As long as the public likes dark woods and bulkiness, the prices will keep going higher, perhaps for another five years, or at least until another style replaces it. The question is, what will replace it? Some possibilities are the so-called mission pieces that are comparatively inexpensive and the Borax line of Grand Rapids furniture from the 1930s and 1940s. Just when you think everything from wicker to Art Nouveau has been rediscovered and nothing is left, something else comes along. Care to make any guesses?

Country furniture has always had a few dedicated collectors. What else goes with their collection of chalkware and pewter? There was a time when the old pine plank-bottom side chairs could be found for $8 a pair. About ten years ago, one-drawer night tables of pine were lucky to find buyers at $10 to $15. Generally, they were covered with layers of paint. These days, they sell for $150 each, with a new paint job that is supposed to be the original stencil scene. The way things are going, in a few years these chairs will have aged even more and nobody will even consider that their paint jobs are *circa* 1978. I don't see prices for country furniture going down for years to come, especially the chairs. Your best bet is to keep looking for some in need of restoration, and cheap.

Probably the Cinderella story of all time concerns *wooden iceboxes*. Heaven only knows how many of these languished in barns and junk shops ten years ago. Then in jumped the decorators! The old icebox was suddenly transformed into a *soigné* serving bar. The old brasses were polished and the oak finish rubbed to a gleaming surface. Prices went from $50 to $450, depending on the size. All at once, it seemed everybody had to have an oak icebox in their living room. Thus, a humble discard has been recycled into a high fashion antique furnishing. The oak icebox has found a niche in the antiques market and is here to stay. Who knows? It may find its way to an S.P.B. auction someday.

Quite the opposite is true of late eighteenth- and early nineteenth-century *English quality furniture*. As far back as almost anybody can remember, anything and everything English, from silver to porcelain, was the ultimate antique for Americans. While American Chippendale lowboys languished for want of a buyer in the early twentieth century (except for a few collectors such as Wallace Nutting), its English counterpart found high prices. Over the years, until recently, it was always a step ahead in price. It didn't seem to matter that 99 percent of the English antiques were actually fine reproductions of reproductions. It never really does for many of the collectors concerned with how a thing looks rather than what it actually is.

American country furniture has been popular since the 1930s. Many chairs have been restored, often with stenciling or hand-painted designs, then "aged." The price for these is around $150 each. The Bennington figurine on the table could sell for over $250.

CREDIT: Philip Trier Collection

In the 1920s and 1930s, bigger meant better in antique furniture. Now, because of smaller rooms with lower ceilings, the market for these magnificent pieces is lagging. This fine-quality English late–eighteenth-century Sheraton breakfront bookcase waited a long time for a buyer, at $12,500.

Perhaps it was the Bicentennial or the years leading to it that awakened American pride in craftsmanship. At any rate, American antiques began to go up in price, passing English pieces. This was especially true of massive break-front bookcases and desks. For the past few years, despite the flooding of the American market with English antiques, the old snob appeal has waned. Americans are buying American and breaking past price records. It is, for the most part, a new generation in their thirties and early forties who are doing the buying. At one S.P.B. Americana sale in 1978, a midwestern collector paid $57,500 for a large Chippendale carved mahogany block-front chest of drawers. The preauction estimate was $25,000 to $35,000. A comparable English piece would be lucky to get $14,000, these days. Not long ago, while browsing in a small suburban antiques shop specializing in English furniture, I spotted a handsome chest-on-chest (c. 1820). The dealer apologized for the low price of $900, saying, "There just doesn't seem to be much interest in English furniture in this area. Yet, when I opened my shop fifteen years ago, I couldn't keep it in stock."

There is a different opinion about English furniture in Washington, D.C., too. In 1978 at a Washington auction, results showed prices were up over the last five years. However, the buyers seemed to be dealers from London and New York. They were the ones who bought a Georgian walnut chest-on-chest for $7,750 and a set of sixteen Hepplewhite dining chairs for $5,000. Perhaps it depends where you live.

Once upon a time, you simply had to have *English porcelains* to go with your English antiques. Those little baubles ranging from Staffordshire to Royal Doulton figures could cost several hundred dollars each, and even the late nineteenth-century examples always seemed to keep within that price range. Even though Ruth Webb Lee, in her book *Fakes*, called attention to the many reproductions, people still bought them. They still do, but not often. Instead, they are putting money into Russian enamels or Bennington-type pottery figurines.

A pottery figure of a lion by a Pennsylvania potter, mid-nineteenth century, sold for $18,000.

Lustrewares have appealed to collectors for over 100 years. This bulbous milk jug is probably a reproduction, despite the obvious age cracking. The most desirable pieces are eighteenth-century. They were lustred inside and out. By the nineteenth century, many had a white lining.

In fact, if you had begun collecting the *yellow-ware pottery known as Rockingham,* made in the Bennington factory ten years ago, you would have seen prices rise. Not only the Rockingham from that Vermont factory has continued to escalate in price but so has similar pottery from other areas of the United States. For instance, a single small vase made in the nineteenth-century Galena, Illinois, pottery works wears a price tag of over $400. Yet, even several years ago, it was taken for granted and priced low. As interest and information about American pottery works grew, so did a sense of regional pride, and old pottery works in Wisconsin, Illinois, and Ohio were reevaluated. Prices began to rise as collectors realized that these pieces could be rare and desirable additions.

Since the Bicentennial, many books have come out discussing the decorative arts native to St. Louis and Illinois. Everything from the most utilitarian objects (soap dishes, spittoons) to elaborate pitchers and sculptures found buyers in the high hundreds of dollars. At exhibits around the country, it was no longer a "Bennington jar" but a "Peoria pitcher" or a "Galena jar" because it was no longer enough to lump everything under the label "Bennington-type." National pride had risen, along with prices. Collectors have become more sophisticated and interested in their roots. These rather simple pieces of pottery were treated as important decorative Americana, and it is doubtful that they will ever fall from grace. Even reproductions haven't affected them.

At the other end of the collecting field is a type of pottery known as *flow blue.* It was popular when it was first manufactured around the late 1820s and it was the bargain-basement crockery of its day. It has been sold and reproduced ever since. Some twenty years ago, it was easy to find a place setting or two for $15. Just as pewter was the everyday food server in the eighteenth century, flow blue was everyday for hundreds of folk around the world. Made in England, France, Scotland, Holland, and the United States, there are many potters and many marks. The important thing is that it has that rather hazy blue look to the patterns. Prices for the more interesting and scarce pieces really began to go up in earnest about seven years ago. Now you can pay as much as $250 for a large turkey platter. Yet there are still plates and cups and saucers to be had for as little as $20 or less. The problem is, there is still a lot of it around, and several years ago, reproductions showed up on the market. Despite what its most dedicated collectors say, it seems to have reached a standstill price-wise, and you would have paid more for it a couple of years ago than you would today.

There have been so many outright *fake pieces of Meissen sculpture* and *porcelains,* along with *reproductions,* that the United States market has been rather quiet for several years. A sign that the market might be changing appeared in a 1979 S.P.B. newsletter. Either the bidders were very informed and knew what they were buying, or they didn't mind dropping a few thousand to be able to show off a Meissen figure, for prices were exactly double those of the previous year for similar sales, according to Sotheby Parke Bernet. At the 1978 auction, a Utah buyer purchased a Nymphenburg figure of a Chinaman with a teacup for $11,500. The estimate was $4,000 to $6,000, still considerably less than prices for similar pieces in Europe six years before when an Augsburg-decorated Meissen teapot and cover went for $37,500 and a Meissen swan sold for $85,000. I guess the Utah buyer got a bargain. Meissen in the United States has nowhere to go but up. Clearly the American collector of this generation is striking out in new collecting areas. Like old master paintings and English furniture, Meissen has been over-collected and over-reproduced for years.

For the past several years, American collectors have found that early *Italian and Spanish majolica* (c. 1500 to the eighteenth century) goes with fine Americana. While it has always secured top dollar in the European auction houses, it hasn't been exactly a big seller here—that is, not until recently. As one American decorative arts collector told me, "There really wasn't much of the blue-and-white around until last year. Then, can you imagine, I started finding a piece here and there! Naturally, I bought it. Ninety dollars for a charger seemed quite reasonable."

Those words could have been said 100 years ago when Victorian collectors began to rediscover the beauty of these rather naive pieces of pottery. At that time there were revivals of the early techniques in Italy and Spain. Apothecary jars and chargers were favorite forms, usually with portraits of men and women. Then the public fancy turned to other types of pottery, and prices went down on the all but forgotten majolica. Once again, there is an interest, and there has to be a supply to meet the demand. Some of it comes from Mexico, other examples from Portugal. Doubtless many of the pieces are those Victorian reproductions, but buyers don't really seem disturbed about authenticity as they fork out several hundred to several thousand dollars. To date, none of them has come forward demanding their money back, and for the moment, at least, prices and interest are once again on an up-trend.

One of the most spectacular comebacks in the pottery and porcelain field has been *Japanese Imari patterns* with their bold combinations of iron red, blues, and golds. About seven years ago, one collector put together a sixty-piece plate collection in a year's time at about $5 a plate. Then she tired of it and sold the plates for $20 each. These days, shops will price the same plates at $50 and up. There are always buyers who think the price is reasonable. New Imari plates are being made to satisfy the current popularity, and again the question is when the public will turn to something else and, if so, whether Imari will hold its present price. As an interesting example of early Japanese pottery and porcelain, it stands a good chance of at least keeping its present price level.

Meanwhile, there are other types of porcelain waiting in the wings for their turn on the antiques market merry-go-around. One of these is *Haviland china,* made in Limoges, France, since the 1840s. Haviland was the wedding china of turn-of-the-century brides. There were dozens of patterns made and hundreds of pieces. As a result, it has remained reasonably priced for antique porcelain. The last few years have seen a big jump in prices that is only the beginning as it becomes harder to find. If you like it, there is no time like the present to buy, and chances are, it will continue to go up for the next ten years.

Five years ago, every dealer was scrounging around for *R. S. Prussia porcelain* made after 1869. Prices were whatever the traffic would bear until fakes and reproductions began to slow the market. There still are collectors, and prices are still several hundred dollars for large, unusual pieces. Chocolate pots can cost over $100. R. S. Prussia has obviously had its moment, at least a couple of decades. Start a collection for your grandchildren.

Jade was a big status symbol during the 1920s to about 1940, and jade carvings filled some of the fanciest curio shelves in the United States. Interest died down, until the last few years. Once again, whenever early pieces appear, they find a new generation of collectors willing to spend thousands. If you had begun buying just five years ago, you could sell today at a profit.

Many collectors are stashing away pieces of porcelain made in Occupied Japan. This decorative pitcher, about three inches high, costs around $6. Several years ago, $1 would have been the going rate. Occupied Japan pieces were produced during a short period from 1948 to 1952.

Oriental snuff bottles have had their ups and downs. After several years of a downtrend, a new record was set in 1979—$50,000 for this rare Ku Yueh Hsuan enameled milk glass bottle. Its preauction estimate had been $14,000 to $15,000.

Who wants an old car? Just about everybody these days, if it qualifies as an *antique car*. Yet, the old car craze didn't hit the general public until about fifteen years ago. Before that, last year's model was this year's junk, and few bothered to consider whether it might be a classic. To be sure, there always millionaires who collected old Excalibres and Rolls-Royces, but a 1950 Pontiac was strictly for salvage. Times change, and many a young collector has put that 1940s or 1950s car into shining working order. At a 1979 auction of automobiles and horse-drawn vehicles at Butterfield & Butterfield, San Francisco auctioneers, buyers bid on a 1901 Oldsmobile with estimates of $7,500 to $10,000. A 1925 Rolls-Royce was expected to go for between $30,000 and $35,000. This growing investment market hasn't begun to reach its peak.

For decades, if a piece of porcelain or lacquer said "made in Japan" nobody wanted it. Today they are the best investments around. *Japanese lacquer pieces* at a 1978 auction in San Francisco brought prices all the way to $2,500. *Japanese Arita* (blue-and-white porcelain, nineteenth century), long under-valued, is finding serious collectors. They find it a good substitute for the always popular Chinese Canton. "Too many reproductions and too high prices scared me away," observed one collector.

Perhaps there is hope, then, for collectors of *Occupied Japan products*. To date, the inexpensive figurines have found hundreds of serious collectors. The price is certainly right, only a few dollars or less apiece. Many of the figures copied not only eighteenth-century costumed pieces but Hummel figurines as well. Because of the shortness of the period (they were made with the O. J.—Occupied Japan—label from 1948 to 1952), eventually there will be a shortage. That and a new appreciation is what the collectors are hoping for, and they are on their way up now that there is a book and a price guide. Next thing you know, there will be a museum show. Whether you think they lack artistic merit or not, they are still of interest historically. Besides the figurines, there are ceramics, cloisonné, toys, carvings, and many different types of items that a collector could specialize. Among the most popular O. J. pieces are the salt and pepper shakers. One collector claims 100 sets.

Until the 1940s, every home and apartment had an *Oriental rug* on the floor of at least some form. Machine-made or hand-made, Orientals were one of the most popular home furnishings and had been used in American homes since George Washington's days until they were done in by wall-to-wall carpet. For at least twenty years, Oriental rugs kept sliding down in price. Now they are so expensive, some dealers are advocating that several collectors buy shares in a rug. A four-by-five-foot Tabriz silk prayer rug sold at auction for $24,200 in 1979, double the auction estimate. "The prices reflect a bullish market in the growing trend to acquire rare quality examples," said a Butterfield & Butterfield representative. "Escalating prices were being paid in March of 1979 for good to very fine and rare Oriental rug examples." How long will it last? Until another more interesting type of rug or floor covering comes along to take its place in the public's favor. Before you say it can't happen, remember wall-to-wall! Looking back, it is ridiculous to think that anything so commonplace could replace a work of art.

Another type, handmade *American Indian rugs*, have been going up in price for the past sixteen years. Before that, they were bought mostly by travelers as souvenirs or by parents for their son's bedrooms. Today, they are considered worthy of hanging on the wall as art. Prices seem to have leveled off after their quick rise. The best examples will continue to go up, but the most average ones will go down.

The most easily acquired antiques, those made of paper, are the hardest to come by. Except for old prints, valentines, and theatre bills, *paper items* were kept in drawers and between book pages. In fact, that is where many collectors still find them. A few years ago, collectors began framing their paper dolls and paper labels, and then paper items began to be treated with importance, along with other antiques of the same vintage. Covers from 1900s magazines and 1930s *Saturday Evening Posts* were put under glass and became part of a collection. The day of the paper collector had arrived. Several books and price guides came out, and dealers began going through their files and putting anything and everything made of paper under glass or glassine. This market is just really getting started. A carefully collected category of something as inexpensive as paper dolls can only rise in value. Post cards, advertising trade cards, and baseball cards are considered investments by their collectors, but whether or not they are or can be used as bank collateral is another matter. Only time will tell.

Sometimes a single collector or collection can set off a trend. One example was the Justin Schiller sale. Schiller, a collector of *Oziana* and also a children's book dealer, becan collecting anything and everything relating to the *Wizard of Oz* when he was a child. The Schiller collection included over $100,000 worth of first-edition books, games, piano rolls of the 1902 musical score, and just about anything ever created relating to the land of Oz. Even more important, Schiller founded the International Wizard of Oz Club. This made Oz items a genuine collectibles category with enough interested collectors to assure active buying, trading, and selling—the lifeblood to a new collecting category. This also assured Schiller of a built-in market for his sale, which grossed $94,000. Looking at it objectively, investors will see that a definite market with definite price records has been set by Schiller. Whether it is merely a fluke and an artificial market only time will tell. Certainly, $150 for a first edition of *The Magical Monarch of Mo* stands a chance of increasing over the years. As a first edition by a popular author, it has a built-in group of investors, the first-edition collectors. What will happen to other Oz items depends on rarity and general worth. For instance, as graphic art, a book or movie poster will always have a value to a like collector.

By comparison, take a look at what happened to *Raggedy Anne* and *Orphan Annie collectibles* with new productions of plays and cartoons. For at least a brief moment, Raggedy Anne dolls and books went up slightly in price, as did original comic art from the Orphan Annie strip. Now, both areas have quieted down. It may be at least another decade or two before there are revivals. From a collector's standpoint, it is a rather dead area for investing.

Until I wrote about my collection of old *German glass Christmas ornaments* five years ago, few people were aware of them as collectibles. Then Philip Snyder wrote *The Christmas Tree Book*, and the prices for every type of old Christmas ornament went up. The few collectors who had been able to build up impressive collections for nickels and dimes were forced out of the market by—would you believe—investors! A single blown-glass figural ornament of Charlie Chaplin with a piece out of his hat was sold to a collector for $75. Dime-store celluloid reindeer made in Japan before World War II suddenly became collectibles. Before this, they could be purchased by the handful for fifty cents at garage sales. Now even the mangiest reindeer can cost $2 to $3 apiece. The cloth and cardboard Santas glued to a cardboard airplane and stamped "Made in Japan" cost $10. Among the most expensive Christmas decorations are toy houses and churches with music boxes inside. They have light bulbs inside them that light up paper imitations of stained-glass windows. Made in the 1920s and

A few years ago, you could have bought these early twentieth-century hand-blown glass Christmas ornaments for a dime apiece. Prices have since sky-rocketed. The Indian bust now commands a price of $75. Other pieces shown range upward from $20.

the 1930s, they used to be found in shops for $5. Now they cost from $75 to $200. Any type of unusual figural ornament from the turn of the century wears a price tag of from $25 to $100. Originally, they came by the box for a few dollars. Probably one of the least appreciated lost arts, the old ornaments have a good future as investments. Their very fragility assures their scarcity. Often, just a change in humidity can shatter the thin glass.

In this same area of collecting are department-store *mechanical Christmas displays*, a spinoff of automatons. Among the most expensive are clock-work toys. When Marshall Field in Chicago sold its old displays last year, some choice moving Christmas display pieces became available. They dated from the 1930s up to a few years ago. With great interest, and even greater price increases in the field of automata during the past several years, this would seem a good opportunity for a future profit. In 1979, when a collection of nineteenth-century automata were sold at Sotheby Parke Bernet in Los Angeles, they exceeded their pre-estimates of $10,000. Quite a change from nine years ago when silent automatons usually went for from $200 to $300, even at the important auctions in both the United States and Europe.

A few steps removed from automatons are *dolls*. While the price range for the rare Jumeau dolls is in the low thousands, they keep rising. The last sixteen years has seen a phenomenal growth of interest in doll collecting. There are so many collectors of old and almost-new dolls that they can hold their own doll exhibits. As in other areas of collecting, there is always a fad doll that seems to have an outlandish price for the moment. Wise collectors have learned to study trends and buy cautiously. Reproduced heads, eyes, and general fakery of the most expensive dolls pose problems for even knowledgeable collectors. Just as a furniture collector doesn't want to buy a

Doll automata from the nineteenth century have found an increasingly good market. Several years ago, $1,000 for a French man-in-the-moon was considered quite a good price. Today $7,000 to $10,000 would be a reasonable figure. Musicians are the most common subjects for nineteenth-century automata.

Chippendale chair that has been built around one original leg, doll collectors do not want to buy an over-restored doll. And, just as some reproductions of antique furniture are becoming collectibles, so are some reproduced dolls. Only by keeping up with the current market through clubs and shows can an investor do well.

Nothing is as hazardous as the *Victorian glass market* from Bohemian to milk glass and just about all the types in between. The reason, of course, is the reproductions. Despite denials that Carnival glass prices are booming, there are rumors to the contrary among dealers. "Too many reproductions. We can't sell it," is one lament. "Nobody around here is collecting it," said one dealer in the Midwest. The same goes for those charming, covered animal and chicken dishes that were so popular twenty-five years ago. True, a dealer may have an unusual animal milk-glass piece in her shop priced at $150. It is also very dusty, and she isn't taking in any more, thanks!

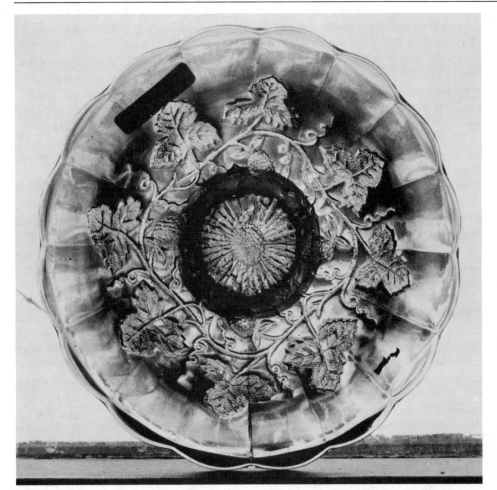

About seven years ago, prices for Carnival glass skyrocketed. Originally mass-produced in iridescent ornate patterns, it was collected by many Americans in the early part of this century. In certain areas of the country, prices are still high, but in others, dealers have a hard time getting rid of it at any price.

Another glass category that always had a few collectors willing to pay hundreds of dollars is *paperweights*. Due to recent exhibits of old weights, there is renewed interest in all types and ages, including those made in China in the 1930s and in America at the turn of the century. Reproductions aren't a problem for the well-versed collector. If the dealer tells you he has ground off the rough pontil on the bottom to make the piece more desirable, pay no attention. He has probably removed the telltale newness.

American weights that once went for around $25, now cost well over several hundred. However, since dealers are familiar with the look of weights from the New England and other American glass houses, they put much lower prices on them. Depending on where you buy them, prices can be under $20 for a really fine unrecognized American weight. Fine early French weights are, without exception, priced many times over $1,000. But there is always a chance for discovery: most areas for growth are in old American weights and in important new ones signed by some recognized masters of the craft. It is doubtful that this market will go down, as more pieces go into private collections and museums prices go higher.

It's a long way from the sauerkraut presser to a classification of stoneware crock on the elegant S.P.B. auction block. Who would have thought more than ten years ago that *stoneware* would be considered an antique investment, with a single crock valued at $1,500? Any lover of country antiques has probably bought at least one glazed stoneware jug or crock to set off other primitive pieces. Eleven years ago, an interesting early nineteenth-century double-handed glazed stoneware crock could have been purchased for $100 or less. That price would have been reasonable even for pieces attributed to the Bennington, Vermont, factory. You could have even found such unusual decorating as birds and flowers painted in cobalt-blue. Even those with a prized date or maker's name could be had for under $50.

About six years ago, collectors began to appreciate them as rare examples of American decorative art, and by the time the Bicentennial had arrived, prices for the same items had doubled. Currently, there is a shortage of the most elaborately decorated and early stonewear with resulting high prices. Collectors and investors will do battle for an important piece, to the tune of $500 and up. At those prices, nobody puts sauerkraut in them, only money. Their future looks bright. Even eleven-year-old reproductions are finding buyers for $50 and up.

Just when you think there isn't another category left for antique collectors, along comes *baskets* as an investment. Leading in prices are, of course, old Indian baskets followed by coiled rye straw made by the Pennsylvania Dutch. Equally sought after are baskets made by the Shakers as well as the Nantucket baskets. The major problem for beginning investors is paying for new Nantucket baskets thinking you're buying old, and buying new Mexican or South American baskets labeled Indian. Possibly because Nantucket baskets are still being made in the same old way, prices have gone down slightly in the last year. It's simply too hard to tell old from new, but when the price for the old is $800, it is nice to know which is which. Baskets, a fragile item in many cases and extremely durable in others, have a good future. They are just beginning to go up, and collectors should keep their eye out for the miniature baskets as well. Some cost as much as $50. Because of their size, many were thrown away or destroyed, creating a scarcity of nineteenth-century baskets.

Two collecting areas for eighteenth- and nineteenth-century items that are still underpriced are *copper and brass kitchen objects*. A severe problem faces collectors

American-made paper-weights from the New England Glass Company, Sandwich Glass Company, and even Steuben, can be found for $100. Pictured are two American weights, late nineteenth-century or early twentieth-century. The weight on the left is possibly from an Ohio glass house. The one on the right is not identified.

Though wall clocks like this were mass-produced in the nineteenth century, there aren't many around these days. Prices have quadrupled in several years. To be a good investment, the clock should be by a well-known maker, have the original paper label, and be in good working condition.

of copper: the United States has been flooded with fake items from the Near Eastern countries. Made from old copper pieces, they feature the same primitive dovetailing and handwork as old items. That's all right when the cost for a teakettle is $20, but it's a tragedy when the price is over $200. However, it is still possible to find trays, kettles, and dippers in both brass and copper that are authentic antiques. Prices depend on where you find them. Keep in mind that the American oldies are sold at auctions for $100 and up. For the last year, they have begun to show important upward spirals.

More than a decade ago, collectors began buying up *old clocks* of every description. The Victorian shelf clock that was mass produced in the late nineteenth century was rarely thought to be worth collecting, but nothing Victorian was doing much around ten years ago. The common schoolhouse clock that hung on the walls of nineteenth- and twentiety-century schools was certainly not considered an investment. Those that came up at country auctions were purchased for a few dollars, mostly by young couples who wanted a novel wall decoration they could afford and by decorators who liked the octagonal shape. Faster than you can say ding-dong, people began looking for schoolhouse clocks to go with their other antiques, especially their primitives. Hundreds were—and still are—made in Japan from old parts and then shipped to U.S. antique shops, where they they sell for up to $600. Obviously, the schoolhouse clock had arrived as an important antique, and along with it came shelf clocks and the popular wall-hanging Victorian clocks, among them the Vienna regulators. People were going cuckoo over clock collecting. Many thought nothing of having ten or more old clocks ticking away in their homes. Clock prices began to go up. Even the early O. G. clock with the painted face (c. 1835–45) began to rise from what had seemed a stationary price of $35 to $65 to the unheard of price of $150 to $175. Problems for collectors came with fake paper labels, new works, and the old trick of building a clock around one old piece (where have we heard that before?). Still, there were plenty of old shelf clocks available to keep their prices from going very high. In pressed oak or mahogany, they were still priced at under $100. That was yesterday. The growing interest in Victorian furnishings and their rising prices have carried the kitchen clock right along to the tune of $165 to $200. The problem for collectors is knowing a good clock repair shop and being able to afford the services.

Sometimes you and I wish that a book on a certain category had only come out sooner, not to raise prices but possibly to save an antique that was being forever ruined by those who didn't know it was supposed to have that peeling paint or that black design in the silver. One such antique category is *painted American furniture*. About four years ago, *American Painted Furniture* by Dean A. Fales, Jr., detailed the importance of American painted pieces, from finely detailed work by master cabinet-makers to simple country styles. Until that time, many rare examples of the eighteenth- and nineteenth-century work were destroyed by strip-happy dealers and antique buyers.

The American penchant for having every antique look brand new had made inroads on a lost art form. Sadly I recall an appearance I made on the Phil Donahue TV Show during which a woman in the audience told of removing the painted designs on an old family chest and "antiquing" it with a kit. She wondered about the value now that she had restored the chest. From her description of the chest, it must have been an early nineteenth-century Dower chest brought over by her German ancestors. As a painted piece, it has a value of perhaps several thousand dollars. After her "antiquing," it will be considered just a wooden chest worth probably $200. The loss was also historical.

Nonetheless, many painted pieces have come to light since *American Painted Furniture* was published. Prices can range from $800 for a painted simple chest to $2,000 for an interestingly painted chest-of-drawers. Consider the same pieces with ordinary wood finish: $200 for the chest and perhaps $300 for the chest-of-drawers. Collectors have gotten wise and don't hesitate to buy, even if the paint is peeling or faded and cracked. The smart ones know it's more apt to be original paint, and that's what makes for an investment. Sorry to say, many painters are making a living doing nineteenth-century–type paint jobs on old furniture. Beware when this much money is involved.

As recently as three years ago, almost any flea market had its share of *Civil War tintypes* and *daguerreotypes*. Millions were made during that period to send home. Prices ranged from $2 for the tintypes to $10 for the daguerreotypes, if the case was in good condition. These days, you don't very often see either category at flea markets. They moved up to the class antique shows, and so have prices. Somebody's great grandfather a la tintype can bring $25; prices for the daguerreotypes range from $50 and up, the more interesting the pose the more expensive.

Old *photographs* up to and sometimes including World War II, are rising in price. Collectors who want to get involved in what they see as an expanding market are buying in advance of it. In other words, there may not be a substantial market for what we call photo album pictures for several years. Taking the cue from other antiques and collectibles, they are buying up anything that looks even remotely collectible—by the bag. Yes, sometimes $1 will buy an entire grocery bag of old photos, like buying a bag of stamps in the hope of finding one good one. Depending on your preference, they seem to be doing all right. Old cars, demolished buildings that were once important, and sometimes rare pictures of famous people and events are what collectors hope for. One interesting photo turned up in a bag, the first Rose Bowl Parade float, complete with old cars. This type of photo is wisely considered for a future investment.

Mechanical iron banks from the late nineteenth century are one of the biggest investment success stories to be told. These banks, once made to teach American children thrift, are now out of the reach of children and the average adult purse. When they were made, they were sold for from seventy-five cents to $1.50 each. They are amazing mechanisms. Some have as many as fifteen to twenty separate bits of casting. Some fascinating subjects are a Punch and Judy Show, a frog eating a snake, and dozens of others. In 1940, when collectors were just getting interested, there seemed to be an unending supply, and dealers who bought them for fifty cents sold them for two dollars. It was not long before the finest examples had gone into collections. By 1948 prices had begun to go up even for lesser banks. Ten dollars was considered a high price to pay. Yet when the choice banks came back on the market, prices were from $40 to $75 each. Last year, prices ranged as high as $2,000 at auctions. Even ten-year-old reproductions have found a place on the market for more than double their original $25 price.

With high prices and scarcity, another generation has turned to the *lithographed tin mechanical banks* from the early twentieth century to the 1930s (pre–World War II). Six years ago, they were still found for around $5 at estate sales and for $10 to $20 in shops. A current 1979 listing shows that a Popeye knockout tin mechanical bank sold for $475; a monkey and parrot mechanical tin bank sold for $550. A quick run down of any and all old banks from an Apollo 8 iron to an A. & P. Coffee in tin shows price guide listings of several dollars. Just remember, at one time, those mechanical iron banks were sold for seventy five cents.

Authentic old iron mechanical banks like this jester are too expensive for the kids to play with. In the 1940s, before they had caught the eye of collectors, they could be bought for a few dollars. Now well-to-do adults fight for them on auction floors at prices from hundreds of dollars to $5,500.

It is always fun to read somebody's published opinion on what's going to be important in the antiques market, especially when it was written ten years ago. I keep returning to the 1970–71 Auction-Antiques Annual. A particularly fascinating quote about furniture deserves your consideration. "Last decade's craze for Victoriana seems to have faded, leaving behind only a slight overall rise in prices. Apparently the survivors have retired from the salesroom into the secondhand furniture shop." And, "Almost any piece of Sheraton, Hepplewhite, or Federal furniture can be bought for less than $5,000." I wonder what that writer thinks when she reads that a hand-carved Early Victorian walnut love seat was recently bought by a collector for $4,500. Even a utilitarian Victorian hall tree can easily find a buyer today at $500. As for Hepplewhite and Sheraton pieces, a fine American Sheraton sideboard can cost over $2,000; a Hepplewhite bow-front chest, also $2,000. The same early Federal gilded console with ovolo-frieze stenciling of lyres and fruit clusters sold for $1,200 in 1970 would have buyers fighting over it today for three times that price.

Because eighteenth-century English, French, and American furniture is usually out of the range of most collectors, many have been looking instead at *Dutch, Italian,* and *Scandinavian pieces.* Especially popular are the large cabinets and bookcase secretaries used as accent pieces. They still are available from time to time for under $2,000. Considering their fine craftsmanship, they are underpriced. In a 1970 auction catalog, a Swedish eighteenth-century Louis XV–style marquetry and parquetry *bombe* commode could have been bought for around $3,000 at a Christie's auction in London. When compared with other comparable pieces, this shows very little rise—in fact, perhaps a lowering—in price. If you bought it in Denmark, it would perhaps be four times that price. Antiques generally sell for more in their place of origin. The exceptions are, of course, fine French eighteenth century and American eighteenth and early nineteenth century. Even the Japanese have been buying American furniture for antiques investments.

In 1970 bronzes were so underpriced that it was considered an interesting field for a beginning collector with only a few hundred dollars to spend. Even then, collectors were cautioned that bronzes were a tricky area for collecting, because it was difficult to know whether a piece was a reduction of an original done many years later. At that time, Animalier bronzes by the Bonheurs and Barye were priced from $200 to $300. Those by established makers such as Giovanni da Bologna cost from $5,000 and up. The Dodge Auction changed the market completely, putting just about anything and every thing bronze out of the novice collector's class.

Again, in 1970 to 1971, *Scrimshaw carvings* were available at under $500 for fine examples. The major exception was a Scrimshaw mounted in South American silver, engraved with a ship and two boats attacking whales. This six-and-one-half-inch piece called "Susan's Tooth" sold for $11,000. In a February 1979 Americana sale at Sotheby Parke Bernet, a "Susan's Tooth" sold at a record for a Scrimshaw of $21,000. There were several known examples carved on the ship *Susan* and these are among the earliest known examples of American Scrimshaw. Yet another example of "Susan's Tooth" was discovered and sold at the June 1979 S.P.B. auction, this time for $29,011, to an antique dealer. And to think, that just a few years ago, Scrimshaw was considered underpriced!

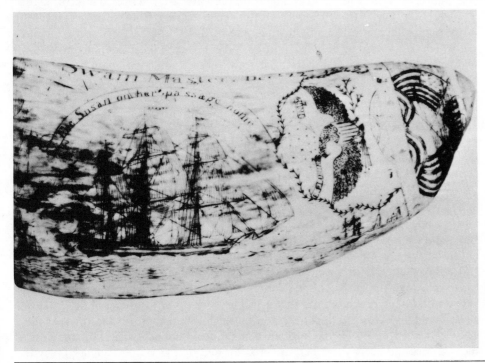

In 1971 this six-and-one-half-inch tooth carving, an excellent piece of scrimshaw known as "Susan's Tooth," was sold at auction for $11,000. It, or a similar piece known by the same name, was sold in 1979 at Sotheby Parke Bernet for $29,000.

Interest in mideastern antiques will probably continue to increase. This Iranian bowl from the eleventh or twelfth century would cost thousands if purchased at today's auctions. Less expensive mideastern antiques might be miniature Persian vases and silver Bedouin ornaments.

Observing the doubling and sometimes tripling of an object or a total area of objects makes careful study a must for investors. There is certainly a danger for would-be investors in getting overenthusiastic because of a dramatic price jump in, for instance, Scrimshaw or graphics. For example, a department breakdown of net sales totals for Sotheby Parke Bernet in North America from 1973 to 1979 shows literally no interest in Islamic art until the 1978–1979 season. Then the sales totals were $580,000. Should you interpret this to mean that a great future in Islamic art is on the way and you should invest now? Or, does it mean that because of world conditions or a recent exhibit, there is a temporary upswing and interest in Islamic art? During the same six-year period in yet another field, Chinese and Oriental art, sales peaked in 1973–1974 at $3,401,925. For 1978–1979, with all the experts saying Chinese art was a terrific investment, sales slipped slightly to under the 1973–1974 highs. By contrast, Japanese art, which had a total of $1,379,715 in 1973–1974, went up considerably in 1978–79 to a new high of $3,300,000. Now, that New York City auction house is only one of several in the United States. It is up to you as a potential investor to draw your own conclusions.

During that same time span, there was an amazing interest in American painting. Sales went from $4,325,923 in 1973–1974 to another plateau in 1977–1978 of $7,806,000. Then they shot to an all-time high of $8,520,000 in 1978–1979. This should tell you that the years to have made money in American painting were 1975 to 1977.

It would seem from studying the S.P.B. breakdowns that when there are two years in a row of good growth, the category isn't likely to go down, only up. Or you could follow a relatively new market, Art Nouveau/Art Deco, and see that sales have risen very slowly since 1973. By 1978 the yearly sales total had moved up to $1,519,000, but in 1979 there was a dramatic increase to $3,185,000.

Reading auction figures is much like reading the market board. The problem comes when your investment in antiques suffers a down-trend. Obviously, you will either have to find a buyer who thinks that it will go back up or just hang in there. This is all well and good for the upper-echelon buyer, but feel sorry for the small investor who has loaded up on 500 collectibles that suddenly nobody wants. In many cases, such an investment may not be recovered for decades. If you are going to play the antiques market, you must be prepared for its uncertainty.

9.
Sleepers That Seem to Be Waking Up

It is important to realize that not every well-publicized antique and collectible shows the complete market picture. For every Tiffany lamp and folk art carving that establishes a new auction record, there is an item that is silently creating a new market. Are you aware of the many collectors of printing memorabilia? Even as a remote a collecting possibility as orange crate art has its devoted collectors. Do these people know something you and others don't? Realistically, consider a collection made up of the color lithographs that used to be glued to the ends of wooden fruit crates. Are they nostalgia antiques or collectibles? Actually, perhaps they have a category all their own within the field of graphics. Certainly, they can't be classified as fine art. I can't recall seeing any that bear signatures of famous artists. Yet they are an art as surely as advertising and posters are, and they are collectible as an art form that is no longer being created. Therefore, as a "lost art form" they have a solid classification. They are also cheap. Most often they are found in abandoned warehouses or the basements of old houses where mold and tears are their worst enemies. They are the perfect example of a sleeper.

I recall finding a mother lode of early twentieth-century *orange crates* in the basement of an old Victorian house. There were hundreds. The elderly man who had stashed them away had used the wood to make quaint wooden weather vanes. He hadn't used the ends with the lithographed pictures, only the staves. A collector came upon the scene and, wildly waving her arms, exclaimed to the seller, "I want them all. How much?" The owner, in a state of shock, could only stammer, "Would five dollars be all right? Wood is expensive you know." Heavens knows how many were used as firewood.

Approaching this underdeveloped art market realistically, we have to admit that now is the time to get in on the ground floor. The time to buy, providing you like the item, is when nobody else wants it. Whether or not orange crate art will prove a viable investment remains to be seen. If old comic books can be worth hundreds, why not that old orange crate? Perhaps it's only a matter of time before Sotheby Parke Bernet

Now it may only cost $5, but wait a few years for fruit-crate art to mature. Examples are getting very scarce. At one time, such art could be found at flea markets for $1 or $2. Now, poster shops sell these pieces for $20.

Old typefaces are being collected as art. A single old wooden initial can cost $50. The most sought-after pieces are woodcuts with ornamental designs used for nineteenth- and early twentieth-century advertising. 1920s and 1930s copper examples are cheaper.

offers the "rare orange crate art collection of Oskar Rockadollar." When that happens, it's too late for you.

As for *printing memorabilia*, not only is it finding serious collectors, but there are shops that specialize in type faces and old type. Early aficionados were advertising agency executives who used oversized letters to decorate their offices. About six years ago a shop specializing in old advertising artifacts began buying up typesetting equipment, drawers, and type faces. All of a sudden it caught on, and a new collectible was born. Prices began to rise. Wood and metal type, especially turn-of-the-century pieces, can now cost from ten to hundreds of dollars. Most expensive are turn-of-the-century transportation or fashion display type. A large beautifully carved type letter of cherry or boxwood can set you back at least $50.

There is even a spinoff industry from printing items. Cleverly arranged into decorative designs, letters, numbers, and display faces are mounted inside wooden frames to become novel coffee table tops. Other times they are categorized for use in one specific room. A bathroom, for example, may display shaving items and different styles of type letters forming the word "bath." Thus, a collectible has taken on a new form of decorative art, a combination of the old and the new usage. Therefore, it has value as printing memorabilia and possibly as tomorrow's folk art as well. Collectors advise making the cutoff date the Art Deco period. Even these, when highly stylized, cost upwards of $10 for a small copper or metal display type. If you have the space, you can join print memorabilia collectors who buy printing presses. The oldest presses, which are the rarest as well, are early hand-and-foot operated. They have a collector value of over $7,500 for floor-mounted models and of $50 to $500 for bench-mounted types.

Camera collecting has been gaining momentum during the last four years, along with photographs. Like anything else, you have to know the history before you can decide what to specialize in. Perhaps you decide on the 1920s, which are still in abundance, or harder-to-find 1900s types. Early on, a decision must be made as to whether you plan to use the cameras or just display them. A rare, nonworking camera may or may not belong in your collection. Some of the old cameras use obsolete film sizes.

There are still many 1930s box cameras around, and flea markets are a good place to start looking. They were usually made by Argus, Kodak, or Agfa. Real leather covered the oldest types. If you buy in a shop, expect to pay the going price-guide rate. Sorry you couldn't have begun a few years ago as now there is always a "picker" at estate and garage sales looking for old cameras. Those turn-of-the-century Kodaks can cost from $60 to $100.

Condition is considered all important for early cameras such as the Soho reflex, which looks much like a Graflex. With a nonworking shutter, damaged bellow or woodwork, their value would be only $100. It costs a bundle to restore this rarity. In top condition, it would be worth $200. The most valuable cameras are the early nineteenth-century daguerreotypes and wet plates. During the past several years, record prices were established on the London market, but only recently have cameras been doing as well at American auction houses. Daguerreotypes keep climbing as do the lesser-known detective cameras, which were designed to be hidden under clothing or in a woman's purse. The very first Kodak, made in 1888, is investment potential. It was the first to utilize rolled films. Here again, firsts can make a difference worth hundreds of dollars in investing.

Several years ago, a serious collector, Mickey Pallas, tried to bring cameras as collectibles to the attention of Chicagoans with the opening of his Center for Photographic Arts. He hoped to offer the public not only a photographic historical society and gallery but to stimulate their interest. At that time, there wasn't enough general interest to keep it going, and the gallery closed. Like many collectors, Pallas was ahead of the market. At the time he opened his gallery, his collection of over 200 historical cameras was valued at $50,000. Today, that figure would be tripled. The most valuable camera in his collection dates from the middle 1830s and was used to make daguerreotypes in France. A camera doesn't have to be that old to be valuable. The 1890s Kodak No. 1 is worth over $2,000. "It looks like that old box Kodak your mother gave to the church rummage sale last week," Pallas observed wryly.

Right on the heels of camera collecting is *photography*. Actor Dustin Hoffman called attention to photography as an important new investment when he paid a record price of $750 for a *carte de visite* portrait of Abraham Lincoln attributed to the famous Civil War photographer, Mathew Brady. This took place at a Sotheby Parke Bernet photography auction in October 1978. Hoffman also bought a 1950s silver print by photographer Philippe Halsman entitled "Nixon Jumping." Another monied bidder at the same auction was the National Portrait Gallery of Washington, D.C. It paid $3,000 for what is believed to be a self-portrait upon which Mrs. Thomas Eakins based her posthumous oil portrait of Eakins that is now in the Philadelphia Museum of Art. Other photographs by lesser-known photographers of the nineteenth century sold for as little as $75. The auction of approximately 405 lots totaled $142,545.

According to one observer, many potential buyers "sat on their hands waiting to see which way the photographic winds were blowing." As a result, there were many lows among the presale estimates. For the beginning collector with not a lot of cash, this was the perfect auction.

What suddenly made photography so important to private collectors? Some say the book *Roots* made Americans more conscious not only of their own family histories but also of American history. What better way to latch on to a piece of American history than through photographs depicting its progress? Another stimulus to collecting was the acceptance in 1977 of photographic images by the National Portrait Gallery and the opening of a photograph department. Its curator began assembling fine examples from around the country, and the collection was then put on display. It covered American portrait photography from the 1830s to the 1940s. This would serve new collectors as beginning and cutoff dates for their own collections. Other important museums around the country have since formed their own photographic collections.

How do dealers and collectors decide which is a valuable photograph and which is not? Just like they do most other areas of collecting: how good was the photographer, how well known then and now, quality of work. Unlike the field of art, which photographs fit into, photos are not signed. The collector has to learn to recognize the photographer's technique, just as he would a painter's. The nineteenth-century names most collectors look for are Brady, Southworth, and Hawes. Generally portraits aren't as important to collectors as historical street scenes and objects or transportation vehicles. The exception would be a portrait of a famous person by an equally famous photographer.

You may decide to collect calotypes, tintypes, daguerreotypes, or ambrotypes. They are just a few of the possibilities in a market that is off and running. If a big bank puts its money into photography, something must be right for you as well. More than ten years ago, the Exchange National Bank of Chicago began purchasing photographs by important modern masters as well as pioneers. Today, that collection contains over 2,000 prints and has its own curator. If it serves as a helpful hint, their core collection includes the work of Ansel Adams, Edward Steichen, Walker Evans, Lewis Hine, Man Ray, Alfred Steiglitz, Edward Weston, Paul Strand, Henri Cartier-Bresson, and Yousuf-Karsh. One nineteenth-century American landscape photographer, William Henry Jackson, is being avidly collected. Almost twenty years ago, large Jackson prints sold from $15 to $35. Today, those prices are up to $1,000.

In the porcelain market, there are several sleepers, among them is *Victorian majolica*. Once given away as premiums with the purchase of baking powder, these sometimes quaint, sometimes ugly pieces are emerging sleepers. One collector, Ron Kropke, began buying majolica eleven years ago. As he recalled, he had been antique hunting in New Orleans. "Quite accidently I came across a figure of a slave woman with a basket made up in a type of pottery I wasn't familiar with." The glaze was different from anything Kropke had seen before—a brightly colored, leaded glaze over a heavy pottery base. Later research proved it English. The price at the time was $65. Today, the price would be double. "And I'd have a hard time finding such a fine example," Kropke noted. "There is majolica, and there is majolica. American majolica isn't really majolica. True majolica was originally made in Spain and then shipped to Italy from the island of Majolica (Majorca), 500 years ago. At that time, it was glazed in white tin enamel, then covered in any one of several vibrant colors: dark blue, orange-yellow, and green." He then explained that "in Holland, cobalt blue was used with a similar art technique. This is known as delft, but it's majolica. See what I mean? Apparently every country since has produced a form of majolica, but the Victorians added their own touch of overkill. Granted, it's not for everybody, but now it has its serious collectors." Prices are on the rise.

Prices for hand-painted China have remained stagnant for five years. This charming Limoges powder box with its Art Nouveau motif has a good future. Similar signed examples can currently be bought for from $40 to $60. In a few years, the prices could be over $100.

The crackle glaze and the tulip motif are similar to pieces done by Dedham Pottery around the turn of the century, but this piece lacks the Dedham mark. It may be one of the many types of pottery done as part of the Arts and Crafts movement.

Look for distinctive Victorian pieces that are molded to form and have raised decorations. Flowers, leaves, birds, and shells were the most popular raised subjects. Sometimes, pieces were also flat, with similar designs. The pieces you are most likely to find in shops and garage sales were made from 1880 to 1899 by the thousands. The shell and seaweed designs with soft blues, pinks, and grays are considered the finest examples of this period. There are complete sets of dinnerware as well as unusual individual pieces. "If you know what to look for, you can find it, even under coats of paint," Kropke said. He remembered a pair of mid–nineteenth-century English compotes he found in a New Orleans dealer's shop. Even though they were painted with gold paint, he paid their rip-off price of $20. After the paint was removed, they emerged as a $130-a-pair investment.

With authentic eighteenth-century and early nineteenth-century American furniture being super expensive and generally out of the average collector's reach, *Victorian* is coming into its own. Not long ago a chest-of-drawers in the cottage style could be purchased for $75, even in an antiques shop. Not so today: $150 is the going rate. Keep in mind that cottage furniture was generally pine or walnut, painted in a standardized design. Later versions were sold mail-order style by Sears Roebuck.

Growing interest in the furniture of Gustav Stickley and other Arts and Crafts designers is pushing prices up. This Stickley writing desk and chair are of oak with a dark finish. The popularity of such pieces may well cause prices to double in the next few years.

Something old that is a "something new" sleeper is *movie memorabilia*. As in every other type of collecting, discrimination is of the essence. Not just any Marx Brothers poster will necessarily become a valued investment. After all, not every piece of Victorian furniture has doubled or may ever go up in price. Here is one example of what has happened to an original one—a sheet poster of Humphrey Bogard in *Treasure of Sierra Madre*. If you had bought it in 1970, you would have paid from $75 to $100, depending on where you bought it. The black-and-white movie lobby cards were often available for $1 to $2. By 1979 the poster had gone up to $2,000, and the lobby cards had found buyers for from $10 to $50. Another example of this growth cycle is the two-sheet poster of the Marx Brothers in *Horsefeathers*. In 1970 kids were buying them for $7 or less and hanging them up with thumbtacks in their bedrooms. By 1975 their fathers had had them framed and insured for $12,000. Granted, that is a bit of a freaky price jump. By 1980 the poster may have leveled off at $500. In this still highly speculative market, it is wise not to be carried away by news stories of super high auction records.

Unless you can afford to drop a few thousand casually or love to live with a possible loser, it is dangerous to speculate on such a new collecting market. In the first place, many of the collectors bought their pieces years ago, when the price was at rock bottom, and they are now waiting to find a heavy cash customer to unload on at a profit. Generally their market isn't the same as, for instance, the market for American Impressionist paintings or folk art. It is like comparing the Excaliber buyer to the Cadillac buyer and in turn to the Pinto buyer. The movie memorabilia market isn't where the heavy pocket collector is putting serious money.

This is still a growing market and a good time to begin building a broad movie memorabilia collection. It is still something a teenager can afford. There are many shops that now specialize in movie posters, lobby cards, and fan magazines. The golden age for collecting posters is considered to be from 1930 to 1940. During that decade, the big name stars such as Garbo, Gable, and Davis were publicized to the hilt. Money was no object when it came time to promote one of their flicks. As a result, colorful and dramatic posters were produced. The novice collector should know that many of the best posters have been rereleased. When legitimately sold, they are a fraction of the originals. They can be recognized by the letter "R" followed by two digits (the year) followed by three digits (order of release).

What should you include in your collection? There are toys, tableware, figurines, and postcards, along with paper items like magazines, Big Little books, and paper dolls. Another related category would be recordings of sound tracks from movies and tapes taken from television specials such as "That's Entertainment" and "That's Entertainment II."

Let's say you want to collect anything and everything relating to a particular star. Included in the collection could be movie posters, films the star appeared in, sound tracks, sheet music, and even personal objects. The auction of the effects of Judy Garland and Joan Crawford would be examples. The red slippers Garland wore in the *Wizard of Oz* and a copy of the original script would be prizes for any specialist in Garland movie memorabilia. How do you go about collecting movie memorabilia? Carefully and cheaply.

Consider one person who collects only *Gone with the Wind* mementos. His collection has gone beyond posters, the original first edition of the book, and record albums of the film score; he has every edition of the book published in the United States not only in hardback but also in paperback, book club, film as well as foreign language editions. The collection contains thousands of objects. Is it an investment?

Such a highly specialized collection is more than a financial investment. It is a

Among the most important sleepers in the collectibles field are movie posters and memorabilia. You can pay hundreds of dollars for a rare popular 1930s movie poster or as little as $10. Smart collectors are buying new posters with growth potential.

historical investment. Therefore, it could eventually be given to a museum, or per-haps become a museum in its own right. What it is worth, therefore, becomes a murky point. Certainly it is irreplaceable. Also, if an antique or collectible is to be considered an investment, it must have someone waiting to buy it. Doubtless there are many *Gone with the Wind* collectors. They will, however, have to set price evaluations among themselves. The items will have to come to some sort of auction and even-tually set a price. Where they go from there, up or down, is still speculative. If they go up, the question is how high will they go up, and will they remain at that particular level or double from there. Logic shows that they will go up as time goes by and more items go into private collections and off the market. Assume that in the near future there will be both movie and TV memorabilia museums, or at least segments of museums devoted to collections of movie memorabilia. Already there are galleries in several historical societies in major cities containing permanent exhibits of the early beginnings of the movie industry. One such exhibit can be found in the Chicago Historical Society, where the Essanay and Selig studios once flourished.

In many instances, categories overlap. In the case of movie memorabilia, the overlaps go into specialties such as *sheet music* nostalgia and collectibles. Another overlap not as familiar to collectors is *original artwork*, the drawings, paintings, and sketches made before the poster or sheet music cover was printed. These are extreme-ly scarce and expensive. About two years ago, I ran into some original movie poster art from the old Selig studios predating World War I in a shop in Dania, Florida. The asking price was from $500 and up. If they are still on the market, that price has doubtless doubled or even tripled.

Another spinoff would be *Mickey Mouse* and other cartoon *memorabilia.* "Mickey," who has always had his share of aficionados, became a really hot item and a serious investment with the advent of his 50th anniversary on November 18, 1978. Lucky is the collector who began collecting during the Golden Age of Mickey Mouse, considered to be the 1930s. At that time, the first Mickey Mouse Club was formed. During the 1930s some eighty-seven cartoons were produced. Mickey's official birthdate was November 18, 1928, when he appeared on the screen in *Steamboat Willie*. Another generation of youngsters were introduced to Mickey via television in 1955. This in turn spawned another category of Mickey Mouse items and membership in the Mickey Mouse Club. Lucky are the kids of the 1950s whose mothers mailed away for the "Mouseketeers T-shirts, Mouseguitar and caps with king-size mouse ears. As part of a Mickey Mouse collection they become investments bound to rise in price. Think of them in comparison to such early radio premiums as Jack Armstrong and Buck Rogers giveaways. You're talking hundreds of dollars. If the past is any gauge, you might say, "Well, anything from a radio, TV, movie, or cartoon is an investment, even the shows the kids watch today." Eventually most everything rises in value. But not everything rises enough to put it into the investment category.

At a big Disneyana auction held at the S.P.B. auction galleries, there were many surprises. One collector, Gene London of Philadelphia, had collected Mickey toys, and a high bid from his collection went to a Mickey and Minnie Mouse painted metal Lionel handcar for $350. An early Walt Disney Mickey and Minnie Mouse painted, celluloid swing toy went for $475. Even a stuffed Stieff Mickey doll found a bidder for $425. Other high bids went to a Mickey Mouse tin Ferris wheel for $525 and a Mickey Mouse painted cardboard and tin drum for $525. Assuming that the original owner had either owned the items as a child or had bought them for under $100 each several years ago, he made a killing in the marketplace.

There has been quite a growth in the Mickey market since it was first auctioned at

Sotheby Parke Bernet in Los Angeles in 1972. At the P.B. Eighty-four auction on June 21, 1978, Disneyana, comics, and toys brought a total of $50,485. The Gene London collection brought in $22,000. Original comic strip art, auctioned for the first time as a collection, brought $7,655. Perhaps even more interesting is who did the buying. Much was purchased by two private collectors who plan to open a gallery. The other major buyer was a Washington, D.C., hotel proprietor who plans to use the Disneyana items as hotel window displays.

Let's analyze what actually happened to the Disneyana market. First, a price record was set in several fields: toys, cels, comic art, and memorabilia. That means if the two gallery owners hold on to most of the items for several years, they expect to at least double their money. Meanwhile, when similar items come to market, they will be offered at the record setting prices. Let's assume the worst, that nobody buys at the record price. Then, obviously, the investment will not be doing very well. Many people may panic and sell low, hoping to at least regain their original investment. Sounds just like the stock market, doesn't it? Those who don't sell will watch trends country- and worldwide, and many will find this the ideal time to add to their collections cheaply. After all, they have other funds to rely on and can afford to wait, but how well can the average investor do in this untried market?

Often, a once-popular comic category such as Superman will take a downturn. It takes something pretty spectacular to put it back on top of the market. That something was the 1978 movie *Superman*. One collector, Danny Fuchs, was delighted when *Superman* became box office "boffo." His Superman collection includes 1,500 comic books and over 700 related objects of toys, puzzles, and radio premiums as well as novelties, phonograph records, and books. According to an interview that appeared in the *American Collector*, the rarest Superman item he owns is a 1940 Marx windup toy that matches Superman's speed against an airplane. Quoting from the article, "It is believed to be the first three-dimensional figure of the character ever produced and is worth about $500 in good condition." Fuchs acquired his toy at two different times, in two parts. The first half he purchased was the airplane for $10. Five weeks later, a friend bought the missing Superman figure for him for $5. Another valuable investment is a point-of-purchase display poster issued in 1947 by the W. K. Kellogg Co., Battle Creek, Michigan, sponsor of the early Superman radio shows. He has refused offers of $300 for it.

Taking a close look at what makes this collection an investment we see: (1) continued and increased interest by the collecting public in Superman; (2) new growth due to a reintroduction of Superman to the public via motion pictures; (3) many items that represent a first in their field, that is, the airplane windup toy; and (4) rarities, either because only a limited number was made or because they were destroyed when they became out of fashion. The point-of-purchase poster is an example. It should come as no surprise to collectors in almost any field, from antiques to Superman items, that the greatest potential value often lies in paper and cloth items that were meant for short-term use and then destroyed.

Television has indeed brought about a new source for collectors. Most notable are the *Star Trek* items. However, if the Smithsonian Institution display of the original Archie and Edith Bunker chairs is any indication, "Anything goes." Shortly before his death, Edgar Bergen sent his entire cast of wooden dummies to a permanent home at the Smithsonian.

Architectural antiques and memorabilia is finally coming into its own. Currently, the most important material is that relating to Frank Lloyd Wright. A complete portfolio of a set of his architectural drawings made in 1910 would find buyers at

$10,000, according to one collector. The prolific, long-lived Wright designed everything from books to furniture. Collectors will find a bibliography of items designed by Wright an invaluable source for their collections. While most Wright decorative arts have remained in the original homes they were designed for, others crop up periodically. Other important architects such as Louis Sullivan left their imprint on many wrought-iron building ornaments. Collectors watch for the demolition of a building designed by a renowned architect and scramble for the pieces. One museum curator discovered a magnificent iron gate designed by Louis Sullivan in a Chicago antiques shop. It is worth about fifty times as much as he paid for it. He knew what he was looking for, and when he stumbled on the piece, he immediately recognized its value. He considers it an investment.

In most major cities across the United States, there are antiques shops that specialize in nothing but architectural antiques, including mantlepieces, leaded-glass windows, built-in cupboards, and countless metal items from ventilator covers to exterior trim. If they are refinished, you'll pay more. If a famous landmark building or architect can be tied in with the items, prices will be higher. A stair baluster or even a newel post can be an historic antique. Among the first to collect architectural antiques were quite naturally, architects. They had the advantage of knowing when and where buildings were going to be demolished and whether or not the work was that of an important architect. As you can imagine, with the interest in saving American landmark buildings only a recent movement, many fine examples went directly to salvage yards.

Early collectors, not architects, found other uses for the stone carvings and iron grillwork that decorated turn-of-the-century buildings. Favorite items with decorators have been bank tellers' cages from demolished banks and fancy ironwork elevator doors. While the pickings aren't as good at salvage yards as they once were, you never know when novel items will turn up. The possibilities are limitless no matter where you live. There is always an old building being torn down. The only problem with this type of collecting is that it requires lots of space, unless you incorporate your discoveries into your own room interiors.

Another sleeper that has just started to rouse itself is *record collecting*. Not long ago the last items to sell at the neighborhood garage sale were the old 78's. Two dollars for a big box of albums was the usual price. Now, with the help of the A.L.S. Mammoth Music Mart and other specialist dealers, old records are rapidly becoming investments. Price guides and trade publications are available, but because the field is so new, it is hard to get an accurate fix on prices. In this area, age doesn't necessarily make a record more valuable, as evidenced by the skyrocketing prices of Elvis records shortly after his death. Condition is all important, and the original jacket should be intact.

Included in this category are the nostalgia tapes of old radio shows, movie soundtracks, as well as early cassette players and stereo components. Because the field is so broad, my advice would be to specialize in the records cut by only one or two performers or in a particular style of music.

If you can't afford a carousel horse for several thousand dollars, how about a nineteenth-century *hobbyhorse?* If it is hand-carved from wood, it can classify as folk art. The earliest ones were simply a stick attached to a carved horse head. By the late eighteenth century, they were made in America with rockers. Those considered choice were made by toymaker Benjamin Potter Crandall, whose hobby horses have tails and forelocks of horsehair and colorfully hand-painted noses and eyes.

It's almost too late to get into the field of early (up to 1900) *poster collecting* (not to be classified with the old movie posters). Reproductions have been adding confusion to the market. These days, such fine reproductions as the 1950s Toulouse-Lautrec "Moulin Rouge" posters go for several hundred dollars. In the 1950s, you could buy an original for those prices. Collectors today should be looking into 1920s or 1930s posters, and there are also World War I and II recruiting posters still available. To avoid buying a reproduction, expect the paper of originals to be brittle and at least yellowed with the years. If you are spending hundreds of dollars for a rarity, get a letter of authentication with a money-back guarantee. Some possibilities that aren't cheap are old circus posters and broadsides. If you buy from one of the old poster specialty shops, you'll pay top prices. Otherwise, take your chances on lucky finds.

One of the first things a beginning collector of *Steuben glass* should realize is the vast variety of styles and techniques pioneered by Frederick Carder, one of Steuben's founders. You can specialize in a single technique or a design. You'll find that in every style, from Art Nouveau to contemporary, the emphasis is on the prismatic qualities of the crystal itself. It is important to know that Carder designed so many pieces for so many years that he often signed those he thought he had made. They were signed "F. Carder" with a dentist's drill. There are also table services designed by Carder for individuals. Some combined family crest, personal monograms, and coat of arms with a specially designed pattern. By 1933 Scandinavian influence prevailed, and clear crystal was used in a variety of forms.

For years, there have been many collectors of *Christmas tree ornaments and decorations*. However, much to their unhappiness, two books recently came out on the subject. One, *The Christmas Tree Book* by Philip Snyder, alerted the public that a potentially serious investment field had been born. The second book, a price guide, *The Glass Christmas Ornament Old and New* by Maggie Rogers put prices on many items that had been formerly thrown away. Instantly, prices began to rise and dealers used their best as permanent window display pieces. Ads reading "Wanted: Christmas ornaments" began to appear in papers and trades around the country. One collector who used to balk at paying a dollar for a hand-blown figural ornament has almost given up finding those ornaments at any price. A hand-blown Santa "top" was sold by a dealer for $65. Still, there are other areas that haven't been touched on. Paper ornaments and chalk figures as well as carved wooden chains and cardboard ornaments are still unappreciated by the mass of collectors in this field. Yet, a complete investment type collection would do well to have representations of all types. In the same area of holiday collecting, don't overlook *Easter decorations*. Old hand-blown eggs, hens, and chickens as well as cardboard eggs that were made during the 1930s to the present are possibilities.

Attention was called to *handmade knives* with a 1978 Los Angeles S.P.B. auction. At that time, a collection of over 250 handmade knives from a private collection came to the block. Contemporaries sold from $100 to the high hundreds. Most of the knives in this collection were made during the last fifteen years. Currently, there are over 400 contemporary craftsmen creating these antiques of tomorrow, and the finest examples come from the South and Southwest. Names to look for are *Jimmy Lile* of Russellville, Arkansas and *Leonard Liebowitz* of New Cumberland, West Virginia. Collectors can specialize in any of several types. Certain to keep appreciating are the mass-produced versions of the famed Bowie knife made in Sheffield, England. They have patriotic mottos and subjects etched on their blades and can still be bought for $100 up. The same versions in miniatures are also good additions.

This Steuben Bicentennial bowl cost hundreds of dollars but has already increased in value. It was designed by James Houston and engraved by Paul Schulze in a classic shape used by Paul Revere.

These limited-edition, signed, numbered knives were done by one of the top craftsmen in the field, Leonard Liebowitz of New Cumberland, West Virginia. They were part of a collection auctioned at Sotheby Parke Bernet in Los Angeles last year, where they sold for hundreds of dollars.

CREDIT: Sotheby Parke Bernet, Los Angeles

Regional pottery from New England has long been collected and has become a serious, established investment. Now, pottery from regions such as Galena, Illinois, Sheboygan, Wisconsin, or Cincinnati, Ohio are becoming recognized as important historical examples of an old craft. They may date as early as some New England pieces (early nineteenth century). Some pieces will have their own regional characteristics or be a combination of other areas.

American brass candlesticks, pots, and other utilitarian objects haven't done much financially during the past few years. One of the problems for beginning collectors is turning up honest-to-goodness made-in-America pieces of nineteenth- or early twentieth-century brass. Never mind if those andirons look like they are early nineteenth-century American. Chances are, if you unscrew all the parts, you'll find a mark that says "made in Japan." Oh yes, even those Early American andirons were and probably still are being made in other places. Since few American brass pieces were signed, try the process of elimination when looking for them. If they aren't stamped "China" or "India," keep going. If they don't ring, that means they are new and brass-washed iron, not solid brass. If they emit a beautiful bell-like tone, it is possible they are made of bell metal and may be American.

Learn the style of the different historical periods. Early eighteenth-century candlesticks often had square, low-domed bases with canted corners. Near the end of the eighteenth century, candlesticks matched the classical styling of andirons. Round bases and vase-shaped shafts combined with urn-shaped wide-rimmed candle cups. By the nineteenth century, many had dish-type bases and small wax catchers under the candle cup. By the 1840s, spring candlesticks were popular. Many of these types are still found in shops for $30 or more each. The trick is to buy where the shop isn't that familiar with old brass. It happens every day!

You know that *children's furniture* has to be on its way up when a child's ladderback painted chair has a S.P.B. pre-estimate of $300 and a child's small brass bed goes for the same price. Every style of furniture had its counterpart for small-fry use. If you are collecting adult-size Windsor or wicker, look for complimentary small-size pieces. Even a 1927 Sears catalog offers possibilities. The wicker rocker advertised therein can cost $50 in a shop. When bought from somebody's garage sale, $4 still holds.

Several years ago, a traveling exhibit, "Remember the Ladies" displayed items made by pre-Suffragette women. This was a clue that a new collecting field had opened. It might include photographs taken in the nineteenth century by Julia Margaret Cameron, a book of poetry, or stories by eighteenth- or nineteenth-century women, prints, paintings, or needlework. Here is a wide-open area that could include recent women's liberation movement items as well. *Items of sociological change* are a long-term investment with plenty of growth potential.

Transportation is another collectibles category that could include anything from cars to ships, trains and planes. Early auto items offer a world of possibilities. If you can't afford to collect old autos, how about old auto accessories or parts? There are early lighting devices and mechanics manuals. Sheet music and post cards with auto themes could make up a specialized automotive portfolio.

Old clothing, not just any old rag, mind you, is a field that offers good potential, and is one that is currently not overcrowded. Comb the thrift and rummage shops for nothing but the finest. Prime examples by name designers of the twenties and thirties are acceptable; Schiaparelli and Chanel will do nicely. Or, go earlier and find nov-

This unusual brown earthenware basin was purchased for $24 in Galina, Illinois. The herringbone pattern resembles a type of tool decoration used in Massachusetts in the eighteenth century. If the basin can be properly identified, it may be worth many hundreds of dollars.

You could pay as much as $3,000 for a rare duck decoy made in the 1920s. Many other decoys, however, are comparatively low-priced in today's Americana market. This crow decoy (c. 1930) carved by Fred J. Ellis of Canton, Illinois, is a museum piece.

elties such as the proper bathing suit or tennis outfit for ladies at the turn of the century. The problem with such a collection, however, is how to store it and display it, unless you are a museum.

Until the last few years *Japanese blue-and-white porcelain* was looked upon by dealers with distain. Never mind. Unlike the Chinese, the Japanese exported their best porcelain to Europe and the United States. The blues are a different blue than the Chinese blue-and-white version. Sometimes it's a pale, almost washed-out shade. Other times, a cobalt blue underglaze decoration was used. Most of the older pieces available were made after 1860, and much was brought to the United States in 1876 for the Philadelphia Centennial Exhibition. Prices are half of the ersatz Chinese Canton flooding the antiques shops.

With the scarcity of good, authentic pieces, a secondary market has developed for *fine reproductions of eighteenth-century American furniture* by Wallace Nutting. Nutting, famed for his books on American decorative arts and furniture, was equally known for his fine cabinetry work in the 1920s and 1930s. A stickler for detail, his pieces often looked better than the originals. His name is branded into his pieces. After all, if reproductions of reproductions of Louis XV furniture get top prices, why shouldn't American?

Theater memorabilia, such as old theater bills and posters, offer an interesting category to collectors. The more interesting the covers or famous the stars, the more they are worth.

Call them sporting collectibles or Americana, *duck decoys* are high-priced enough to be called investments. Even recently made decoys by contemporary craftsmen keep rising in value. Combine old with new. There are still plenty around at prices from $20 up.

Early nineteenth-century American square pianos are one of the most underpriced items of all time. One reason is that would-be buyers are discouraged from buying by piano tuners. Beautiful examples in rosewood, some with mother-of-pearl decorations, are still available at $250 at estate sales. You don't have to fill your house with pianos to secure an investment in this area. If you have the space, two would constitute a "sleeper" with good potential. Names to look for are Chickering, Stewart, and Steinway. Like any other antique, the square piano can be restored.

There are still good buys to be made far from the sea in *nautical antiques.* The farther the objects get from water, the lower their prices. For the same reason folk art is more expensive in the East, nautical items are more costly at their source. It is very hard to get a good price for a nineteenth-century bottle with a tiny ship inside in the Midwest. The same bottle would go for over $100 elsewhere. Small items of scrimshaw (carved objects made from whalebone) include everything fron snuff boxes to dominoes. Ships models dating as late as the 1930s can be considered sleepers. Most expensive would be those made by professional woodcarvers and ship designers as models. Well-done amateur efforts can be found for as low as $25 to $50. These go at auction on both coasts for as high as $1,200. It depends on how fine the workmanship is. Carvings from old ships, from mast boards to rudderheads are among the most expensive nautical items. They just keep going up in price.

For years, nothing was deader on the antiques market than old Victorian pianos and melodeons. At estate sales, they went for as little as $250. Now the market has picked up. This melodeon was made by George A. Prince and Co., Buffalo, New York, around 1853.

Ship models, whether in glass cases or bottles, are getting more costly. A nineteenth-century miniature in a glass case was recently sold at auction for $2,000. The pictured example was made around the turn of the century and found in a shop for $85. It would probably find a buyer at an eastern auction for around $400.

This toy tin ship found a bidder at a record $21,000 in a 1980 P. B. Eighty-four auction. It has generated a new interest in turn-of-the-century toys.

CREDIT: P. B. Eighty-four

Slot machines have become a popular collector's item, especially since a P. B. Eighty-four auction that saw prices of from $1,000 to $12,000. This five-cent Illinois Tool Company machine with music box went for $12,000 in 1980.

CREDIT: P. B. Eighty-four

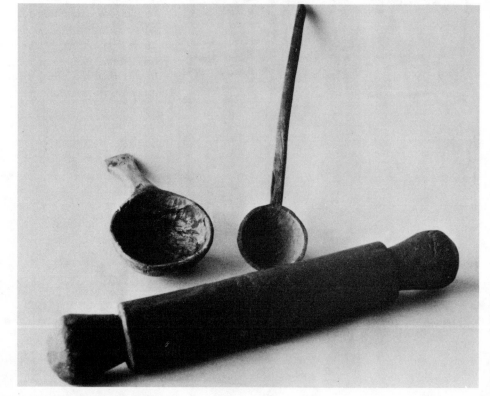

Eighteenth- and nineteenth-century woodenware is still priced low by comparison with other hand-made objects of Americana. The average hand-carved rolling pin or spoon may cost as little as $20. The most expensive item in this photo is the dated burl scoop at $65.

Coin-silver pieces made by some of America's early silversmiths such as Samuel Kirk are presently underpriced. Those dating from the early nineteenth century are what you're likely to find. Finely made tablespoons by Kirk & Ives can still cost as little as $50 each. Those items were not actually made from coins. The term is more apt to mean that the piece was equal in pure silver content to a U.S. coin, or 900 parts out of 1,000. Look particularly for regional examples. Most of the large towns and cities in the United States had their own silversmiths. Many are now waiting to be rediscovered.

Collectors already know about *hat boxes* made in the mid-nineteenth century by American Hannah Davis and others. Prices are over $200. Collector-investors are now turning their attention to interesting hat boxes and *paper shopping bags* with Art Deco designs from 1900 to the 1930s. Their perishable nature as throw-aways practically secures them a place among tomorrow's antique rarities.

Another long underpriced area for collectors are *wooden handmade games* and mass-produced children's games. Smart collectors find them in attics and garages for nickels and dimes. After all, who would consider a wooden cone with a wood ball attached to it on a long string as an investment? Hopefully you.

Kitchen helpers from the mid–nineteenth century to the mid–twentieth century have a good investment future. Look what happened to early woodenware and tinware prices. Included are tin dippers, corkscrews, and pie crimpers to name a few of tomorrow's antiques. Of course, the earlier and more unique the better.

The early versions of small plaster-of-Paris figures *(chalkware)* have been going up in price for years. There are still discoveries to be made, from banks to baskets of fruit and animals. Again, when found away from their sources (the East), they may be unrecognized and cheap.

About ten years ago, a choice chalkware bird or dog went for around $200. Since then, interest has died down. This duck, for instance, cost $8 in an antique shop. It is a very nice example of late nineteenth-century American chalkware.

I have yet to see an important *perfume bottle collection* hit the fancy auction houses, or any auction houses for that matter. The field is wide open, from interesting Victorian scent bottles to those made by Gallé, Mount Washington Glass Works, or Lalique. Maybe your collection will be first to set an auction record.

Rustic furniture is starting up in price. Like tramp art, it is pretty roughly made and dates from the 1870s to the 1940s for use in vacation homes in the Adirondacks of upstate New York. Featured are towering cupboards and chairs in naturalistic forms. Early examples of mass-produced pieces by the Old Hickory Furniture Company rate a second look.

Riverboat and hotel glassware is still underpriced for the period 1835–1870. Colors may be sapphire, cobalt blue or ruby as well as clear. All the riverboat pieces are distinguishable by their thick heavy bases.

Prices for heavy pressed glass made in the nineteenth century for hotels and riverboats are still reasonable— $40 for a compote such as this one. There are still enough pieces around for a novice to start an inexpensive collection.

Japanese cloisonné is slowly going up but still a bargain compared to prices for Chinese counterparts.

Early American pressed glass has done nothing much in years, so it's about time it started going up.

Prices have already begun to climb for *hand-carved early fishing lures and rods.* Fly fishing rods can be works of art when they bear the names of H. L. Leonard or Thomas H. Chubb Company.

From candlesticks to old stoves, collectors are slowly appreciating *iron antiques,* hand-wrought or cast.

Prices for early American lighting fix-tures range from $15 to over $100, and a rare pewter oil lamp may cost $300. These three objects—an early brass Betty lamp, a nineteenth-century iron candlestick, and a brass sparking lamp —were found for under $15 each. All are worth many times that.

There already are clubs for collectors of carousel animals and late nineteenth-century amusement park/carnival display pieces. Wooden horses dating from the early 1900s are now well over $500 for the best examples. Even those of plaster-composition are considered collectible. Most desirable are early wood-carved figures.

Just as American Indian artifacts have risen out of the average price range, we can expect early *Alaskan artifacts*—carvings, baskets, and textiles—to go up in price. Strangely enough, contemporary stone carvings may cost more than ivory from the nineteenth century. To date there hasn't been enough publicity or shows to call this area to the attention of dealers. That's in your favor.

The most popular hobby of this decade has spawned thousands of *miniature items* and miniaturists. The secret is to buy the handmade, one-of-a-kind items by the top artists. Another area, miniature books, probably represents the best investment going. There are few publishers of one-of-a-kind, hand-tooled books, which makes them an even better "sleeper."

Prices for large Victorian garden ornaments are relatively low, from $10 to $50 for a concrete plant container. This figure of a seated child costs around $70.

Is it a salesman's sample, an apprentice piece or simply a miniature? Does it really matter when it's early nineteenth-century English and worth several hundred dollars? Fine attention to details from the inlaid burl to good brass hardware make it an important investment on its way up.

10.
Buy Low, Sell High

So you're ready to sell those treasured pieces of flow blue and art glass. Some fortunate collectors may unload to museums, or even to the White House or the period rooms of the State Department. Perhaps you have considered lending or donating the pieces and taking a *tax deduction*. Currently, if you are thinking of making a gift of your collection, keep in mind that the Internal Revenue Service allows deductions up to 50 percent of income. Sometimes these can be spread over the years.

What if you buy low, which hopefully you have, and sell high? There is a *taxable capital gain* of course. Even the weekend antiques seller or flea marketeer knows that there is an I.R.S. man lurking among the potential customers. If you are selling free lance, be prepared to show your talley to the I.R.S. However, it's going to take a lot of government snoopers to keep up with the nationwide army of garage sale sellers and their profits. In other words, the collector still has a fighting chance to keep a little of the gravy, but if you sell in the upper echelons, such as Sotheby Parke Bernet, for a profit of hundreds or thousands of dollars, you have to share it with Uncle Sam as well as the auction gallery.

With every new purchase, many collectors make a dash to the nearest appraiser and then make arrangements to up their *insurance coverage*. God forbid a hurricane should sweep through your oceanfront condo and wash away your collection of famous autographs or first editions. Granted, you probably can't replace those rare documents or your fire-damaged Chippendale side chairs, but the insurance money can dry your tears, give you a chance to bid on something similar when it comes up at auction, and possibly pay for repairs. Before you spend money on an appraiser, check with your insurance company as to how much they will insure your items for and if they will accept the word of any appraiser you select. For the average collection, valued from a few hundred to around $20,000, a simple *floater* added to your home or renter insurance policy will do. Renter policies can offer adequate coverage when carried along with household items also insured.

Prices for European and American art glass have risen phenomenally. A few years ago, these pieces would have brought several hundred dollars each at auction. Now they can go for up to $25,000 for a fine signed Gallé or Tiffany piece.

CREDIT: Chase Gillmore Galleries

Dolls are among the most widely collected items. Even dolls from the 1940s are being put away by collectors for future appreciation. Rare eighteenth- and nineteenth-century dolls go for prices as high as $5,000.

For really important collections whose appraised value runs over $100,000, a *fine arts policy* is a good idea. Since costs vary from city to city and state to state, check with your local agent. Collections are not insured at their top appraisal value but at a point between high and low.

When it comes to buying, who are you going to listen to—the experts or your intuition? Two years ago, one expert, Guy Hannen, observed, "Buying art for capital gains is risky and not necessarily profitable." But did Hannen include American nineteenth-century art and folk art in his thinking? Perhaps he was thinking of the then saturated eighteenth- and early nineteenth-century English paintings market. At that particular time, a Romney or a Gainsborough oil could have been picked up for a fraction of its cost a decade ago. The reason was the many estate sales from the Great Houses of England, whose owners were feeling the bite of high taxation. They apparently came to the conclusion that you can't munch on a Romney painting. Many American art dealers took advantage of this unloading to bring back many fine oils by famous names. "We'll just wait a few years and the market will be better than ever," said Lynn St. Albus, a midwestern dealer in quality art.

On the other hand, give Hannen two points for noting the unpredictability of paintings. Take 1975, a very bad year for the works of old masters, French Impressionists, post-Impressionists, and younger French and American paintings. Yet, by 1976 French Impressionist paintings topped the list of items making an impressive comeback. According to *Barron's* weekly financial magazine, they were up 230 percent. A Paul Gauguin canvas, "Nina Maruru," sold for $950,000 in 1974, but in 1965 it had found a buyer for only $275,000. Apparently, one secret is to buy low and hold on until you see signs of interest for your particular artist or type of painting.

If you had been one of the early collectors of *vintage cars*, you would have noticed the growing trend spiraling up and up in 1974. Bonnie and Clyde's old Ford sedan fetched $175,000, about 300 times what it cost new. Ah, but it had a little help from some friends, Warren Beatty and Faye Dunaway in their popular flick, *Bonnie and Clyde*. In 1975 a top seller was a 1933 Hispano-Suiza J12. At a French auction, it sold for $70,900.

Among the lists of best investments in 1974, with a 215 percent gain, was *antique American furniture*. It was a good year to sell, but if you had noted the coming of the Bicentennial celebration, it was also a good time to buy for future investment. Those who thought they were paying a stiff price for American pieces have been rewarded. For example, a country-style Hepplewhite chest-of-drawers that would have cost $500 in 1974 was up to several thousand dollars by 1979. If the piece were unusual, its value would be even more today.

Collectors who have seen their investments in American furniture pay handsomely advise looking for the most individualistic pieces for the least money. "The unseasoned furniture collector feels safer buying the more commonplace chair or chest. He's seen reproductions and copies, so there is no doubt in his mind what he's buying," observed one collector. "That's where he makes his mistake. The savvy furniture investor looks for the rarity. He has learned to spot the more valuable one-of-a-kind piece and has the confidence to snap it up when the price is low. He also knows that while the average piece will continue to go up in value, his unique object may double or even quadruple."

It all sounds so easy. Just buy low and sell high. There's only one little problem: *who do you sell to?* Are there vast hoards of interested buyers waiting to fight each

Even without a date or signature, a nineteenth-century amateur painting may still be a good investment. They may be found in shops for from $25 to $75. The pictured oil might find a buyer at an eastern auction for several hundred dollars.

other to the death over your Windsor chair or your early American primitive painting? Just for fun, let's go back in time two years. The place, my home in a midwestern suburb. Tulips were just coming out after a long Chicago winter, and spring sunshine was peeking through the air pollution. It seemed the perfect time to unload all those antique overbuys I had researched and written about, and an ideal time for bored antique hunters to charge out in search of new finds. Keep in mind that I am a fifteen-year veteran of house sales antiques buying. I'm supposed to know what I'm doing.

Thinking I was terribly clever, I selected Mrs. X. to hold a conducted house sale on the premises. According to my observations, not only did she always have customers lined up for her sales as far as the eye could see, she also always had high price tags on the items. For her services, she charged 25 percent of the take, placed ads and mailed notices to the hundreds of happy antique-buying customers on her list. It was the mailing potential that made a quick windfall seem obvious. In addition, she furnished workers and watchers. The former put price tags on, took in the money and organized the odds and ends. The latter followed the light-fingered around and were known to cut thefts by 20 percent. (We were all aware of one weekend flea marketeer who worked in tandem with her teenage son. His specialty was spoons and small pieces of silver that he slipped into his back pockets. Hers was removing the brass pendulums from clocks or distracting one of the watchers while she pocketed a small bauble.)

It sounds as though I couldn't lose, doesn't it? To make the sale even more successful, I personally put price tags on the better pieces, such as an eighteenth-century Windsor chair, a Victorian bird's-eye maple chest, and a fine early nineteenth-century Canton bowl. Because I wanted to get rid of the tagged items, I priced everything half of both the retail and the current price guide, in some instances even lower. I rationalized that after all I had originally purchased the pieces for a *soupcon* of the retail value. I could afford to be munificent. There was, for instance, a charming ship's model in a glass case that I had purchased for $80. Similar ones had gone at recent S.P.B. auctions for $1,500. Knowing that the Midwestern market wasn't as high paying as New York, I put a price of $250 on it. That gave dealers and collectors a fighting chance and me a profit, I thought.

I also put a price of $200 on the bird's-eye maple chest-of-drawers. After all, it was missing a drawer pull and the other pulls weren't right for the period. Besides, I had paid $15 for it at a house sale five years ago. A large late–nineteenth-century American landscape with a locomotive going through the mountains had recently been given a preauction estimate by Sotheby Parke Bernet of between $1,500 and $2,000. Reasoning it would cost me probably $50 or more to have it crated and sent to New York and that the auction house would also be taking its cut, I decided to put it in the house sale. I marked it at $800. Again, I could afford to be generous, as I had only paid $25 for it, plus a restoration of $150. Happily, I figured that even after Mrs. X had taken out her 25 percent, I would still have a total profit of around $10,000. I was moving out of state and wanted literally to clean house. Old pots and pans, clothing, dishes, and the dog's dish along with antiques and collectibles—all were priced to sell.

Licking my chops in anticipation, I turned loose the house sale workers and Mrs. X to complete pricing. It wasn't a matter of minutes before Mrs. X was changing my price tags. "Why did you mark that bird's-eye maple chest $50?" I screamed. "And that primitive $100? Are you out of your tree?" I hadn't reckoned on the Jekyll-and-Hyde personalities of house sale conductors. Curling her lips back in disdain at my lack of knowledge, she said, "That isn't a Victorian chest and it isn't bird's-eye maple. It is simply a piece that needs refinishing. Look at those dark brown stripes on the sides."

Keeping my cool, I began again, "Those stripes are the graining of the original tiger maple finish. The drawer fronts are bird's-eye." Pulling out a drawer, I pointed out the construction. "See, these are double dove-tailed, front and back. The piece is handmade." Would you believe she still didn't believe me? Did it matter that I had written four books on antiques and had a nationally syndicated column? Did it matter that hundreds of people have written, asking me to identify their own antiques? Of course not. She did house sales, therefore she was the expert. Needless to say, we were locked in mortal combat. She was determined to sell at any price for profit and, doubtless to mark down prices earmarked for friends.

Three days before sale day, it dawned on me I hadn't heard anything about her mailing piece. Guess what? She had decided the year before that mailings were too expensive. Unfortunately for me, she was the only house sale conductor who had made that decision. Any of the others I might have chosen would have done a mailing. However, she did run two large ads, one in the metropolitan paper and one in the suburban chain papers, but for some odd reason, she had decided in her infinite wisdom to have the sale on a Friday night and a Sunday afternoon. Why not Saturday? Another argument ensued. In a state of exhaustion and trepidation, my family and I sat amidst our price-tagged *objets d'art* waiting for the opening of the starting gate.

What starting gate? Where was the lineup of cars and people that Friday night? One thing for sure, they weren't waiting for the "Friday Midnight Madness Sale." All of Mrs. X's close friends and old customers turned up on Friday. What did they buy? Not the antiques or the collectibles. The dog's dish went first, followed by my ratty bathtowels, and old clothes. A Queen Anne-style dining table found a buyer for $150. After some haggling on my part with one of the customers, I said goodbye to a secretary bookcase desk (c. 1830) for $175. It was in lousy condition. The total take for that night was around $1,500. Finally, Sunday arrived and several hundred people as well. I began to take heart. Mrs. X hissed in my ear that we had better start reducing prices if we expected to get rid of the things. "Reduce? They're already ridiculous," I gasped. At this point I believe I should mention that Mrs. X had forgotten the friendly smile and manner that she had shown when I had invited her to do the sale.

"Well," Mrs. X whispered, "things aren't going that well. I thought you said you wanted to sell all of these things, not take them with you."

"Sell, not give away," I countered.

By the time the Sunday receipts were added to the Friday total, I came out with the less-than-grand total of $3,500 after 25 percent was deducted for Mrs. X and her helpers. What was left? All of the good antiques. What had been sold were the run-of-the-mill prints, pieces of Oriental art, Victorian glass, and a turn-of-the-century handmade maple bed with mattress, as well as battered pots and pans, and junk. Buyers had passed up two early nineteenth-century rope beds, in original finish with side rails, priced at an absurd $150 each.

"Tell you what," Mrs. X offered, "I can bring some people in who will buy the rest at a lot price, minus my 25 percent. Or you can give it all to charity." I blew my already incendiary top, declining her generous offer.

My next step was to run my own ad for a house sale. One week later I had unloaded quite a few things and had come out $900 richer. However, I still had the fine antiques, paintings, and rope beds. My last sales pitch was to a dealer who ran a huge antique barn in one of the outlying country towns frequented by tourists looking for bargains.

By that time, I had cleared off twelve long book shelves of odds-and-ends, and what was left filled two. This was the showdown, horse trader time. The dealer, a tough old broad whom I shall call Betty, "cut a very fine deal" as they say in the trade. She had eyes that could cover every item in the room at one glance and come out with a grand total: low. We played the usual game. "How much do you want for everything in this room," she asked?

"Sweep the shelves and include that French poudreuse and the Sheraton-style game table and the rope beds for $2,000," I said.

She gave a practiced laugh of scorn. "I have to make some profit, Anne."

"O.K., so include what's in the garage and the big maple chest upstairs," I said.

"Not unless you reduce that poudreuse," was her response. The tag on it was $350. It was a rare inlaid Victorian dressing table that would sell in any shop for $750. Back and forth we went. I ended up with another $900. She got the junk, rope beds, and one Victorian oil that I had been trying to unload for years. I still had, and still have, all the fine antiques. I simply couldn't find buyers in that short a time who were willing to give me a fair price. I plan to hold on to them until I find a collector for each of the categories. Or I may take them to New York, where there never seems to be a shortage of buyers for any kind of antique.

The moral of my little tale is: "Sell in haste and repent at leisure."

To make a profit you must first *find a market*. It may be in your own area or it may be in California, New York, or Nebraska. It depends on what type of object you are selling. First, you should make a list of the items you think you can live without. Take a good glossy photo or a color slide. Write a brief description of the item; type of wood, date, provenance, etc., just as you have done for your appraisal and insurance files. Now, buy copies of the publications that generally run ads on your types of antiques or collectibles. They will also list coming antiques shows that specialize in your collecting areas. Let's say you have political items to sell. It would be very worthwhile to go to any meetings or exhibits where such collectors are apt to appear. It may not be quite cricket, but not much really is in the antiques business. Hang around the display booths. When you see a likely collector, ask if he knows of anyone who might be interested in your items. Chances are, you'll get a lead into a collectors' club. With even more luck, it will have a publication you can advertise in.

At the World Antiques Market Conference in New York in May of 1979, collectors were told *how to save tax dollars*. I'm sorry to report that according to William Lehrfeld, a Washington tax attorney specializing in the Federal and state tax problems of nonprofit organizations and philanthropists, it is the collector's problem to prove that a collection is actually an investment. "To show that one's collection is for investment purposes, collectors should maintain good business records, have periodic appraisals, and keep the collectibles clean, properly maintained, and temperature-controlled. They should also attend antique-related seminars and have the collections exhibited regularly by a museum or some organization."

There are many timely pamphlets and booklets on how to deal with the I.R.S. The problem is that almost before they are in print, they become outdated. Since you have to start somewhere, try *Financial Management of our Coin/Stamp Estate*, c/o Information Services, Box 9027, College Station, TX 77840. Cost is $16 and the book, despite the title, is applicable to all types of collections. *What Every Artist and Collector Should Know about the Law* was published by lawyer Scott Hodes in 1974, but still has plenty of good tips. However, Hodes told me, "For the most recent changes, get in touch with a legal firm specializing in this field."

The chapter in the Hodes' book dealing with contributions in installments remains quite pertinent. It is possible to get *charitable deductions* for the full value of art works (antiques) by giving them to the museums and other institutions in install-

This magnificent Amberina glass decanter has been a steady winner for the last five years. While other types of colored Victorian pressed glass haven't found buyers at any price, Amberina has doubled in value.

Ten years ago, you could have bought anything in this photograph for less than $400. The most expensive item would have been the painted chest in the foreground. The corner cupboard in the background would have been about the same price. Today the folk art carvings alone would be worth thousands of dollars. The painted chest and cupboard would probably sell for from $1,500 to $5,000 each.

ments. "The problem arises when the donor wants to give an art object whose value exceeds his limitation in any one year. "If the gift were in the form of cash, the donor need only to arrange to make the contribution in installments in different tax years. But, where the contribution is in the form of property, the taxpayer may give fractional ownership interests in the work," Hodes said. "Under this plan, the donor could work out a system that would call for regular fractional contributions each year up to the amount of the maximum charitable deduction allowable."

In order to avoid leaving your collections to Uncle Sam instead of your family, an appraiser who spoke at the World Antiques Market Conference suggested making use of the annual $3,000 *gift exemption tax* to heirs and charitable trusts. Having an antiques or collectibles investment takes a bit more time and forethought than any other form of investment.

Another interesting idea has been offered: setting up your collection as part of a *Keogh retirement plan.* Instead of selling, you put some of the antiques or collectibles that are in your permanent collection into a bank storage (vault). Not every bank is equipped either for storage or for setting up such a plan. Generally, this plan is being successfully tried in larger cities. It also involves the bank in making additions to your collection, working with the collector-investor, and presumably another qualified person. This method is a bit like having your cake and eating it too.

To implement this plan, you begin by presenting the bank with a portfolio of your current investments of antiques and collectibles. This should be no problem, since you supposedly assembled a portfolio when you first became a serious investor, listing the items, their provenance, and current values. (See Chapter 2 for details.) The whole idea, of course, is to sell the bank on the idea that, like stocks and bonds, your collection is financially sound. Since the Keogh funds must not have more than 10 percent paintings or graphics (or some established art medium) and 10 percent high-priced antiques or collectibles, the balance will have to be divided between eight or ten mutual funds. The burden of proof is on you to show that your antiques and art have been sound investments that can only continue to go up.

As of this writing, a self-employed person can take 15 percent of annual income, or $5,500 per year, and set it aside in a program carried out by an approved organization. You aren't taxed until the actual withdrawal begins. If you withdraw earlier, you are subject to penalties. Of course, you have to plan how long it will be before you plan to retire. A long-range plan or more than ten years would mean you would have to select price ranges accordingly for your permanent collections. For instance, with time allowed for good growth, you might put aside such novel items as tin windup toys of the 1930s and 1940s, or small pieces of Art Deco silver or Georgian silver. Also included might be some good examples of contemporary American Indian art and original book or magazine illustrations prior to 1940. All of these items show good potential. They are also small enough to be stored easily in a bank.

If, on the other hand you see yourself retiring within the next ten years, you'll have to make up for those extra years by putting more expensive items into your fund. Some people say that putting only items with a value of $10,000 or over into a short-term fund limits the number of buyers. I disagree. As this book has pointed out, there are always collectors waiting to buy really good, expensive art and antique items. It is only when you deal with the more speculative middle-range item and buyer that it becomes harder to sell. Logically, money is no object to the millionaire collector but an obstacle to the average collector. This is a matter to discuss with your banker, however.

How do you figure whether it's *the right time to sell?* Easier than you think. Select a category from your collections and follow its activities for several months or even years. Let's take one of the most popular antiques, the Chinese snuff bottle. In 1974 the market was down due to the sale of a major collection. The following year, it was even lower. An interior-painted rock crystal snuff bottle by Ma Shao-Hsuan, signed and dated late nineteenth century, couldn't even find a buyer in the Midwest for $400. Five years later, at a March 1979 S.P.B. auction of snuff bottles, a similar bottle had a preauction estimate of $800 to $1,200. It was sold for $1,300. As this book goes to press, it's too soon to know whether waiting another year for a special auction of snuff bottles will bring even more, but there's a good chance the prices will start at those of the previous year. It might go for even more. This particular bottle is most desired by collectors. Only about two inches in length, the opening in the neck one-quarter inch in diameter, it contains a delicately detailed painting on the interior. While it will always have value, it will pay to wait for the right moment to sell. Whether it is better to sell it on the West Coast or the East Coast doesn't matter, but it will do better if it is part of a large collection or from the collection of a famous name collector. The National Snuff Bottle Collectors Society will alert its members to any such sale, and you better believe snuff bottle collectors don't care how far they have to travel if they can find something rare and new for their collections.

Sotheby Parke Bernet has six Oriental auctions every year. In its April 1979 news-letter, James Lally, an Oriental expert with S.P.B., noted, "During the six Chinese auctions already held this season, one has seen a great broadening of interest in the collecting of Chinese works of art. We've set new records for areas which have long been undervalued, such as a snuff bottle ($17,000) in February. During the early 1960s, one could buy ten snuff bottles in a lot for $100." If this is a clue that the snuff-bottle market is definitely on the upswing, now could be both the time to buy and the time to sell.

Another clue as to an important influence would be the *announcement of an auc-*

In the not-too-distant future even this contemporary American Indian coiled basket will be a rarity. Basketry is rapidly becoming a lost art among American Indian artisans. This example might cost as much as $500. For collectors of American Indian artifacts, it represents a long-range investment.

CREDIT: *Towne Collection*

tion first. For instance, in March 1978 P.B. Eighty-four held its first specialized smoking pipe auction, a private collection of everything from carved meerschaum to a Chinese jade opium pipe. The prices recorded from this auction were the basis for future prices of fine pipes. Where they go from here is anybody's guess.

In 1973 the first major New York auction of *Shaker furniture* didn't even rate the posh S.P.B. Madison Avenue gallery. It went instead to S.P.B.'s subsidiary, P.B. Eighty-four, where second-class citizens of the antiques and collectibles world find new homes—and many a savvy collector finds a bargain. This auction was the first time any large quantity of Shaker furniture came to market as an important collection. Until 1973 interest had grown slowly. First indications of a newcomer was an auction held the previous summer with highest recorded prices to date, at which point the serious investor should have taken notice and at least have kept track of prices at the October P.B. Eighty-four gallery. If he was truly observant, he would have previously been alerted to the Shaker Exhibition scheduled for November of that year at the Renwick Gallery in Washington, D.C.

By the time of the Renwick exhibit it was high time for investors to begin collecting Shaker pieces. The exhibit, of course, would have educated them as to what to look for. The Shakers never originated any forms of furniture but took the model from the outside world and simplified it to produce the most functional, sturdy item. In 1973, when Shaker furniture first hit the big-time galleries, the would-be collector should have had a museum catalog and an auction catalog to chart the beginning prices of his investment and keep track of their rise and fall. In 1975 market values for Shaker began to go up. Supply and demand were the reason, and there was little around because museums had been buying it up.

According to Robert Bishop in a September, 1975 article for *Antiques Monthly*, "A simple four-slat rocking chair from Mt. Lebanon could be purchased for between $65 and $85 in 1970. A survey of antique shops in Maine indicated that this same piece is now being offered for prices ranging between $285 and $350." At the same time, there was a benefit exhibition of Shaker drafts in Hartford, Connecticut. Another opinion came from Mary Black of the New York Historical Society. "The revival of interest really comes about because of the perfection of the handwork they did, especially in cabinetmaking and small crafts, but also because of the direct relation to modern design." At that time, some prices had tripled. A tape back rocker that sold for $200 five years prior to 1975 was selling for $500 by 1975. Not all Shaker is rising in price. Pieces made during the late Victorian period reflect the Victorian style and are harder to sell. Only if they are rare will they command the same high prices. As with so many antiques, the problem is the passing off of items as Shaker. Baskets are hard to identify as definitely Shaker except by an expert collector or dealer, and many fakes are also on the market.

In 1974 Sotheby Parke Bernet announced another first for their auction house: five pieces of *Art Nouveau furniture* by Carlo Bugatti, father of auto designer Ettore Bugatti, who designed chairs in Milan in the early twentieth century. Another first was the introduction of an Art Deco writing desk, signed Ruhlmann. Jacques-Emile Ruhlmann was the most famous of the Art Deco period furniture makers. His pieces were designed to be the most expensive furniture in the world. Even though the Bugatti and Ruhlmann pieces were priced out of the range of the novice furniture collector, they offered another look into the future: a market that had been quietly developing for the past several years was coming into prominence. Shortly, even lesser-quality Art Nouveau and Art Deco furniture would find speculative buyers. In fact, by 1974 there was no doubt that the Art Nouveau market was of investment quality, with Art Deco coming up fast.

By 1976 major museums were turning attention to the *Arts and Crafts period* between 1876 and 1916 and on into the Art Deco period. Furniture designed by Gustave Stickley and Elbert Hubbard, considered among the American masters of the Arts and Crafts movement, suddenly rated positions in exhibitions. Prices began to rise, but they were still comparatively low and had yet to make it to Sotheby Parke Bernet.

Only this past year have major trade magazines paid much attention to collections of items from the Arts and Crafts period, and scant space is given to them in the price guides. This is the time for savvy investors to read as much as they can on the subject and to begin quietly collecting. I say "quietly" because once the mass of dealers get wind of a coming attraction, prices for the worst as well as the best examples will be on the brink of absurdity. It is only after the rush subsides that prices level off and reason returns. Consequently, you either begin to collect now or wait it out. All you have to do is study the development of the art pottery market to see what will happen to the Arts and Crafts objects.

Shaker designs were adapted from existing furniture styles and simplified to suit the functional Shaker style. Seven or eight years ago, this table might have cost as little as $100. It could easily fetch five times that today.

The collector who puts his money into museum-quality Art Nouveau furniture can't go wrong. This bench was made between 1880 and 1910 in France or Belgium. Periodically, good pieces come to auction from private collections.

CREDIT: The Art Institute of Chicago

A couple of years ago, this charming wash set could have been bought for from $80 to $125. As a rare example of a fine Art Nouveau pattern, its value has gone up to around $250.

CREDIT: Allen Baker collection

This may or may not be the time to sell any *art pottery* you bought cheaply. It depends on how cheaply you bought it and whether you feel it has reached a peak and will now level off in price. This holds true for any type of object you plan to sell. Ask yourself: did you buy for pleasure or serious investment? As one very successful investor told me, "Rule number one in this business is never to become too attached to anything you collect. If you love it too much, you may be holding on to it past its prime selling time."

Let's say that you have a super collection of various examples of *folk art*, not of the stature of the Gregory collection, but some nice pieces. You have grown to love the hand-carved small wooden figures, the two small primitive oils, and the chalkware figure of a duck you acquired over the past five years for a total of about $300. A current appraisal shows they have a retail value of around $2,000. Ignoring the retail value, you believe they can go for far more at the proper auction in the East—but you really don't want to sell them.

Serious investor-collectors would be very objective about such a small collection. They would take into consideration the fact that folk art of all kinds is presently getting some ridiculous prices. Even the least exciting pieces seem to find buyers. A study of the folk art market, based on a survey of auction figures and price guides over the last five years of so, would reveal that the market for fine items has nearly peaked. Two important collections came to market, the Garbisch collection in 1974 and the Gregory collection in 1979. It isn't likely that such opportunities will come up in quantity for at least another year. Still, interest is quite high for anything and everything that is folk art, and this would be the time to unload some mediocre pieces at inflationary prices. If you wait another six months, the collectors' market and those fat auction prices may wither away. By unloading now, you can come away with the cash to put into some better pieces. Even if you don't sell at auction, you can probably even do well selling to a dealer. If you want to set your own price, the best thing to do is run an ad in trade publications that seem to reach folk art collectors. Choose those whose articles frequently deal with the subject. Even if your prices seem absurd to you, keep in mind that this is the current value. Soft-hearted investors are soft-headed sellers who get soft prices.

Many investors have found that running a continuing ad in a local or neighborhood paper for what they collect turns up bargains. One specialist in Steuben has built up a valuable collection this way. He tries two different approaches:

Wanted: Collector looking for your old glassware from 1900 to 1940. Goblets, plates or what have you. Top prices paid.

The other ad reads:

Wanted: any glassware marked Carder or Steuben. Any color glass dinner services unmarked.

Of course, much of the glassware he has turned up is Depression glass. If it is cheap, he buys it as well and sells it to Depression glass collectors. Some choice pieces of Carder glass without their paper labels have been purchased this way for just dollars. A choice find was a six-place setting of Rosaline for $50. The owner had never liked the "icky pink color" but had held on to it because it had been a wedding present. I don't have to tell you that Rosaline is currently one of the most expensive early Steuben glasswares, and that six-piece setting was worth several hundred dollars.

By the same token, you will know that this doesn't seem to be the time to sell

Stretch glass. In fact, it is doubtful that you could find a buyer. The problem is the age-old one of reproductions, in this case from West Germany. It is even difficult for collectors of much turn-of-the-century colored glass to decide what is old and what is new. As a result, not only Stretch glass but other types and patterns are now a glut on the market. For the serious glass collector it is almost more important to know what is new than what is authentic, for the process of elimination will tell him that perhaps a particular shape of bowl or vase does not exist among original pieces.

Being realistic about the quality of your collection is one of the first steps toward both buying and selling. Let's assume your collection of *American pewter* has been padded with late Victorian and early twentieth century pieces for display purposes. Now comes the day to sell and put things in their proper perspective. To be sure, there is a right buyer for each example. Deciding who gets what depends on quality, age, and current popularity. You are pretty sure of being able to get a good auction or collector price for the early nineteenth-century pieces. Some of the interesting Victorian and Art Deco-styled examples should be separated and sold as Victorian decorative objects (Art Deco) rather than just pewter. Collectors that might not otherwise be interested may buy because the items are in the period they collect, while pewter collectors may probably pass them up, since they generally look only for early nineteenth- and late eighteenth-century examples. An often overlooked pewter category is Chinese. While your pewter collector wouldn't be interested, an Oriental collector would be. Do you have a novelty piece that could be considered a collectible? This would be an addition to yet another category buyer. The problem is how to save time and money running several ads or running around to dealers. One way to solve the problem is to place in a magazine like *Hobbies.* Try an ad like:

200 years of pewter from unique collection. Includes six 18th-century American chargers, two Victorian candelabra: assorted pieces, one Art Deco cigarette box and match holder, four Chinese boxes with enamel trim, several novelty Disney figurines. Many museum quality. Priced to sell.

In other words, the ad includes something for everyone. Two important phrases are "museum quality" and "priced to sell." The pewter specialists will be intrigued by the opportunity to buy museum quality items at bargain prices. Well in advance, establish your figures: high, medium, and last resort. Despite what you may have read about generally selling at less-than-retail, this refers to everything *but* those museum-quality pieces. If you have a rarity in mint condition, you should hold out for whatever the latest going auction figure has been, and in some instances ask a little more. Don't forget, dealers buy at auctions and what they pay will then be raised, often double auction price. You'll have to show proof of your reasoning on prices to most buyers. Even then, you are bound to get the reply, "But that's in the East and everybody knows prices are higher there. This is Antioch, Illinois." Your reply (if the item is priceless) should be: "Dealers from Antioch buy in New York too. Their prices reflect mine at any antiques show. This is a one-of-a-kind item." If you feel the objects are worth a trip to New York and the fancy auction houses, with a tidy profit on top of expenses, take off.

Another approach, if your collection is large enough, is to show your collection at the local library or art center. Type up a nice publicity release for the papers announcing the historical significance of the collection, and say "Several of the items are for sale." It's pretty hard to use the library for a retail store to sell everything, but once you make your contacts, you can sell after the show.

If you have some interesting *graphics*, you might consider selling them through a direct mail. Work out a percentage arrangement. Whatever you do, don't sell them outright to the dealer, for you then put yourself into the old wholesale-versus-retail price setup.

The most difficult item to sell is *antique jewelry*, not only because of the problems of inviting a thief into your home, but lack of knowledge of gems and metals and the ins and outs of their pricing. For instance, did you know that a one carat *mine-cut* diamond in its old setting will sell for a fraction of what it would if it were recut into the brilliant cut? Are you also aware that most jewelry dealers who advertise that they will buy your old diamonds mean they will buy your old diamonds only if they are *brilliant cut and* larger than a carat. Another problem with antique jewelry is that the stones are often glass topazes, aquamarines, or turquoises. On the other hand, they could be the real thing and you might not know it. Before you sell antique jewelry, you have to first spend some money for authentification and appraisal.

If you can categorize your jewelry as an Art Deco bracelet or an Art Nouveau Pin, it will be easier for you to sell at a better price. This is one instance where it can be more profitable to sell to a dealer, once you're sure of its value. However, the roughest, toughest of all the dealers I have encountered are those who buy and sell jewelry. If you have a really spectacular period piece, it might be wise to hand carry it to one of the big-name, reputable auction houses where it will get bigger money.

Whatever the item, one of the worst places to try to sell any kind of antique or collectible is the antiques mall. I find it very depressing. It works something like this: you bring the Satin glass vase you inherited to the front desk at the mall. The dealer behind the desk informs you that four out of the fifty dealers who buy this type of thing are at the mall. You are instructed to sit at a table and the four dealers, one at a time, take a look to see if any are interested. Because they see so much merchandise in quantity all the time, their interest is next to nil—and so are their offers. "It really isn't the best example of Satin glass. We're lucky if we can get $40 for that," is a typical comment, and a shock to you, since you have seen lesser examples for $350. If you're smart, you'll run out and never look back. Head, instead, to the expensive dealer in your town who pays high rent. If he buys Satin glass, you may have a quick sale for $225.

While I've been telling you some ways to sell and buy, I have almost omitted the most important part: *keeping records* of what you bought and sold and the expenses involved. It is a pain in the neck, but not only are such details important for your taxes, but they also determine whether your collection is really worth it all. Perhaps you will find that by the time you have paid for replacements and repairs, ads to sell it, and gasoline to call on potential buyers, you are actually losing money. Perhaps you'd better hold on to it for a few more years until prices go up again.

One of the *best times to buy from dealers* is *when they are going out of business*. The causes are numerous, ranging from too many bad buys to having a bad business location. The ideal situation is when a dealer has more taste than knowledge. A dealer might love anything with a Victorian look, but unfortunately hasn't been able to resist anything in that category regardless of price, rationalizing it can always be used for window display. One day the dealer finds he has acquired mostly show pieces, and because he paid too much for them, he can't find a buyer at anywhere near his prices. In his rush to clear out, he underprices many of the items that he always meant to do research on, like that little wooden carving or the strange basket. His mistakes will be

Collecting little ivory baubles like this can cost thousands of dollars. It takes an expert to know if a piece is antique, let alone real ivory. Many so-called old ivory pieces were made in Italy, then finished in Taiwan or Hong Kong.

your gain. The ten-dollar carving may be worth $500 as a rare example of folk art; the basket may be an old Shaker basket worth hundreds instead of the $20 price tag he put on it. You never know, but that's what makes the odds better for collectors.

The other time to buy from dealers is *when you spot an interesting American painting*, for example, in a shop that specializes in collectibles. Because it is a painting, the dealer has put what he thinks is a high price on it: $200 for a small oil. But he has only priced it as an oil, not as an early nineteenth-century oil by a little-known but top American artist. Thus, a painting overpriced as an oil becomes underpriced as an early American oil painting by several thousand dollars. This isn't to imply that all dealers are stupid dolts. To the contrary, most are very well-read, informed folk— in the areas that interest them. It is up to collector-investors to discover which dealers aren't well informed in their particular areas of expertise.

In the opposite instance, it is sometimes wise to *cultivate a specialist dealer* who knows and looks only for items in your area of collecting. This may seem to cost you more initially, but not when you consider the rewards. For instance, a knowledgeable dealer may purchase a rare antique doll for $400 and sell it to you for $800. In another two years, that rarity goes up considerably in price. Perhaps there is a special doll show and this doll maker is given great publicity. Interest grows in your doll, and again prices go up. If you hadn't spent more money to begin with, you might not have acquired the doll.

The business of buying and selling antiques and collectibles for profit and pleasure is quite complicated. Only by years of experimenting and making your share of mistakes will you be able to decide which method works best for you. It is a very personal matter. Right or wrong, only *you* can decide the best way to invest in the antiques and collectibles market.

Index